Claude Lévi-S

The Formative Y

Lévi-Strauss is one of the major intellectual figures of the twentieth century. His theory of structuralism has been influential not only in anthropology, but across the entire field of the humanities and social sciences. This book looks at the formative period of his career, from the 1940s to the early 1960s, where he attempts to define both his own place in anthropology and the place of anthropology in the wider context of the human sciences in France. Through a close reading of key texts, Christopher Johnson provides an introduction to important aspects of Lévi-Strauss's thought, at the same time posing more general questions concerning the construction of theory and the different modes of conceptualization that inform theory. Johnson looks at the ideological and autobiographical dimensions of Lévi-Strauss's work, and demonstrates how the impact of structuralism as an intellectual movement has clearly been greater than the sum of its theoretical parts.

CHRISTOPHER JOHNSON is Professor of French at the University of Nottingham and a member of the editorial board of *Paragraph: A Journal of Modern Critical Theory*. His previous publications include *System and Writing in the Philosophy of Jacques Derrida* (Cambridge University Press, 1993), and *Derrida: The Scene of Writing* (London: Phoenix, 1997).

Claude Lévi-Strauss

The Formative Years

Christopher Johnson

University of Nottingham

CAMBRIDGE
UNIVERSITY PRESS

PUBLISHED BY THE PRESS SYNDICATE OF THE UNIVERSITY OF CAMBRIDGE
The Pitt Building, Trumpington Street, Cambridge CB2 1RP, United Kingdom

CAMBRIDGE UNIVERSITY PRESS
The Edinburgh Building, Cambridge, CB2 2RU, UK
40 West 20th Street, New York, NY 10011-4211, USA
477 Williamstown Road, Port Melbourne, VIC 3207, Australia
Ruiz de Alarcón 13, 28014 Madrid, Spain
Dock House, The Waterfront, Cape Town 8001, South Africa

http://www.cambridge.org

First published 2003

Printed in the United Kingdom at the University Press, Cambridge

Typeface Times 10/12 pt   *System* LATEX 2$_\varepsilon$ [TB]

A catalogue record for this book is available from the British Library

ISBN 0 521 81641 6 hardback
ISBN 0 521 01667 3 paperback

1 0 0 3 3 2 4 8 6 X

La génération à laquelle j'appartiens fut essentiellement préoccupée d'introduire un peu plus de rigueur dans nos disciplines; elle s'est donc efforcée, chaque fois qu'elle étudiait des phénomènes, de limiter le nombre des variables qu'il fallait considérer.

(Lévi-Strauss, 'Anthropologie, histoire, idéologie', 184–5)

(My generation was essentially concerned with introducing a little more rigour into our disciplines. So each time that we studied a particular set of phenomena, we tried as much as possible to limit the number of variables under consideration.)

For my sisters, my elementary structure of kinship

Contents

Acknowledgements

Earlier versions of parts of chapters have appeared in the following publications: 'Lévi-Strauss and the Place of Anthropology', *Paragraph* 13.3 (November 1990), 229–50; 'Elective Affinities, Other Cultures', *Paragraph* 16.1 (March 1993), 67–77; 'Cinna's Apotheosis: *Tristes tropiques* and the Structure of Redemption', *French Studies* 48.3 (July 1994), 299–309; 'Authority', *Paragraph* 17.3 (November 1994), 200–6; 'Lévi-Strauss et la logique du sacré', in Christopher Thompson (ed.), *L'Autre et le sacré: surréalisme, cinéma, ethnologie* (Paris: L'Harmattan, 1995), pp. 249–59; 'La Leçon de philosophie: de Derrida à Lévi-Strauss', in Michel Lisse (ed.), *Passions de la littérature – Avec Jacques Derrida* (Paris: Galilée, 1996), pp. 125–39; 'The Writing Lesson Revisited', *Modern Language Review* 92.3 (July 1997), 599–612; 'The Voice of Lévi-Strauss: Anthropology and the *Sciences humaines*', in Seán Hand and Irving Velody (eds.), *Who Speaks? The Voice in the Human Sciences*, *History of the Human Sciences* 10.3 (August 1997), 122–33; 'Introduction', 'From Mauss to Lévi-Strauss' in Christopher Johnson (ed.), *Sociology and Anthropology*, *Modern and Contemporary France* 5.4 (November 1997), 405–8; 421–32; *Derrida. The Scene of Writing* (London: Phoenix, 1997); 'Structuralism, Biology and the Linguistic Model', in J. Wolfreys, J. Brannigan and R. Robbins (eds.), *The French Connections of Jacques Derrida* (Albany: State University of New York Press, 1999), pp. 135–48; 'Ambient Technologies, Uncanny Signs', in *Technologies of the Sign*, *Oxford Literary Review* 21 (November 1999), 117–34. I would like to thank the editors and publishers for permission to reproduce the relevant sections of these publications.

I wish also to express my gratitude to the different institutions which, at the various stages of this project, have provided me with the freedom, facilities and stimulating environments necessary to its completion: Trinity College, Cambridge; the Humanities Research Centre at Irvine, California; the universities of Keele and Nottingham. I wish to thank the many individuals, friends and colleagues, who in their different ways have given me encouragement, inspiration and support, in particular Malcolm Bowie, Marian Hobson, Diana Holmes, Peggy Kamuf, Diana Knight, Judith Still and Michael Worton. I thank Jessica Kuper and the editorial team at Cambridge University Press for their sympathetic and expert guidance through the publication of this book. I thank the three anonymous readers whose informed comments and criticisms were so essential in the final stages of the project. Finally, I wish to pay tribute to the intellectual inspiration of a thinker whose work has always helped, and continues to help me to think, Jacques Derrida.

Abbreviations

Works by Lévi-Strauss in French

*AS*1	*Anthropologie structurale*
*AS*2	*Anthropologie structurale deux*
CC	*Le Cru et le cuit*
ELS	*Entretiens avec Claude Lévi-Strauss*
HN	*L'Homme nu*
*IM*1	*Introduction à l'œuvre de Marcel Mauss*
MC	*Du Miel aux cendres*
OMT	*L'Origine des manières de table*
PD	*Paroles données*
PL	*De près et de loin*
PS	*La Pensée sauvage*
RE	*Le regard éloigné*
SEP	*Les Structures élémentaires de la parenté*
TA	*Le totémisme aujourd'hui*
*TT*1	*Tristes tropiques*

Translations and texts in English

AM	*Anthropology and Myth: Lectures 1951–1982*
*CLS*1	*Conversations with Claude Lévi-Strauss* (Charbonnier)
*CLS*2	*Conversations with Claude Lévi-Strauss* (Eribon)
ESK	*The Elementary Structures of Kinship*
HA	*From Honey to Ashes*
*IM*2	*Introduction to the Work of Marcel Mauss*
MM	*Myth and Meaning*
NM	*The Naked Man*
OTM	*The Origin of Table Manners*
RC	*The Raw and the Cooked*
*SA*1	*Structural Anthropology*

SA2   *Structural Anthropology 2*
SM   *The Savage Mind*
T   *Totemism*
TT2   *Tristes tropiques*
VA   *The View from Afar*

Introduction   Before and after structuralism

Claude Lévi-Strauss can be regarded as one of the major intellectual figures of the twentieth century. An anthropologist by profession, author of works whose technical complexity would seem to exclude all but a small group of initiates, everything about Lévi-Strauss would seem to confine him to the more esoteric spheres of academic exchange. And yet his reputation extends far beyond his original area of specialization. In France, by the end of the twentieth century, he had assumed the status of the elder of the tribe, a respected sage, a 'living national treasure'.[1] Repeatedly, surveys of the French intellectual scene have designated him as France's leading thinker, and he has been the subject of countless interviews.[2]

Born in Brussels in 1908, Lévi-Strauss's original training was in philosophy, but like a number of his contemporaries he quickly became disillusioned with the subject and decided to concentrate on ethnology. After a year in secondary education he was offered a teaching post in sociology at the University of São Paulo, which enabled him to undertake a series of fieldwork expeditions into the Brazilian interior. His contacts with the indigenous inhabitants were vividly described in *Tristes tropiques* (1955), an autobiography which has since become a best-seller and ensured his wider celebrity. The crucial experience, however, was the period spent teaching in New York during the war, when he met most of the leading American anthropologists of the day, and began what was to be a lifelong friendship and collaboration with the Russian phonologist Roman Jakobson. Decisively, Jakobson introduced him to the methods of structural linguistics, which he would go on to apply in his pioneering work on kinship structures and mythology. After the war Lévi-Strauss remained in the United States as the French cultural attaché in New York, returning to France at the end

---

[1] Cathérine Clément, in *Magazine Littéraire* 311 (June 1993), 22.

[2] See, for example, the poll of students, intellectuals and politicians published in the journal *Lire* in April 1981, cited in David Pace, *Claude Lévi-Strauss: The Bearer of Ashes* (London: Routledge and Kegan Paul, 1986), p. 1; Pierre Bourdieu, *Homo academicus* (Paris: Editions de Minuit, 1984), p. 281; *Homo academicus*, trans. Peter Collier (Cambridge: Polity Press, 1988), pp. 261–3. More recently, a survey of contemporary French intellectuals in *Le Nouvel Observateur* places Lévi-Strauss at the head of the different thinkers reviewed, before both Gilles Deleuze and Jacques Derrida (*Le Nouvel Observateur* 1508 (30 September – 6 October 1993), 4).

of the 1940s. In 1950 he was appointed to the chair in comparative religions at the Ecole Pratique des Hautes Etudes, and in 1960 took up the chair in social anthropology at the prestigious Collège de France. In 1973 he was elected to the Académie française.[3]

For many, the most important contribution Lévi-Strauss has made to contemporary thought has been his theory of *structuralism*. Lévi-Strauss believed that linguistics, following the ground-breaking work of Ferdinand de Saussure earlier in the century, had been the only discipline within the so-called human sciences to have achieved a level of analytical consistency comparable to that of the natural sciences. His ambition was to introduce a similar degree of rigour into his own discipline, anthropology. Taking inspiration from Saussure's anticipation of a *semiology*, or science of signs, of which language would be only one particular instantiation, he argued for the *symbolic* nature of social institutions. The collective constructs that mediate relationships between the different members of a community are symbolic to the extent that their construction is a matter of arbitrary convention and that they together form a system in many ways independent of the lower levels of social infrastructure. If one accepts this definition of society, then it follows that the same methods of analysis developed in structural linguistics are applicable to different aspects of social life.

Lévi-Strauss's version of structuralism has been immensely influential, not only in anthropology, but in a range of other disciplines, from history and psychoanalysis to philosophy and literary studies. The phenomenon of structuralism, as it developed in France in the 1960s in particular, captured the attention of the Parisian intelligentsia and set the terms of intellectual debate for the entire decade. With its combination of science and humanism, structuralism was seen as the logical successor to existentialism, the philosophical movement which, under the charismatic leadership of Jean-Paul Sartre, had dominated French intellectual life since the war. What is often ignored is the extent to which Lévi-Strauss's original formulation of structuralism was embedded in problems specific to anthropology, not simply problems of anthropological theory, but more generally problems of definition – definition of the nature and scope of anthropology and its relationship with the other human sciences. By comparison with Britain or the USA, the emergence of anthropology as a separate and autonomous discipline was a relatively late occurrence in France. Systematic fieldwork was begun only in the 1930s, and for a long time the discipline lacked a strong theoretical framework. On the institutional plane, anthropology was normally viewed as a subdiscipline of sociology, itself a relative newcomer and far from being firmly established in the traditional university curriculum. Various reasons are given for the late development of anthropology in France. The first

---

[3] For a more detailed account of Lévi-Strauss's biography, see Marcel Hénaff's chronology in *Magazine Littéraire* 311 (June 1993), 16–21. To date, there has been no standard biography of Lévi-Strauss.

and perhaps most significant is the continuing influence of Durkheimian sociology, with its highly developed programme of research and well-defined rules of methodology. Though the initial impetus given to French ethnology owed much to the efforts of Durkheim and especially his nephew and collaborator, Marcel Mauss, the reverse side of such distinguished origins was subordination to the theoretical programme of the school, allowing little scope for independent development. As for fieldwork, one of the crucial defining features of the discipline, its late appearance in France is frequently attributed to the disappearance of many of its most promising candidates during the First World War.[4]

Whatever the different reasons for the late emergence of anthropology in France, Lévi-Strauss was clearly an instrumental figure, both in facilitating and completing that emergence. Viewed in chronological sequence, his career follows almost symmetrically the different phases of professionalization and institutionalization of the discipline. In the 1930s he was part of the first generation of French ethnologists to undertake fieldwork. In the 1950s and 1960s the academic positions he occupied, first at the Ecole Pratique des Hautes Etudes, later at the Collège de France, reflected the growing importance of anthropology as a key discipline within the new human sciences. While it would be wrong to discount the important contributions of other prominent ethnologists of the same generation – Bastide, Dumont, Griaule or Leiris are the names that spring most immediately to mind – it is Lévi-Strauss who provides the most consistent and comprehensive programme for French anthropology in the years following the war. Through Lévi-Strauss, what in France had been termed *ethnologie* became *anthropologie*, not simply another of the human sciences, but *the* human science *par excellence*. Thanks to Lévi-Strauss, and despite the qualified and at times hostile reception of structuralism, a discipline that had suffered from a distinct lack of theorization became arguably the most theoretical of the human sciences.

The purpose of this book is not to reopen one or another chapter of the structuralist debate in France, which has for the most part been discussed, documented and finally assimilated into standard accounts of contemporary French thought.[5] Nor is it concerned with the more circumscribed and specialized

[4] See Paul Mercier, *Histoire de l'anthropologie* (Paris: Presses Universitaires de France, 1966); Victor Karady, 'Prehistory of French Sociology' in Charles C. Lemert (ed.), *French Sociology. Rupture and Renewal since 1968* (New York: Columbia University Press, 1981), pp. 33–47 and 'Le Problème de la légitimité dans l'organisation historique de l'ethnologie française', *Revue française de sociologie* 23.1 (January–March 1982), 17–35; Jean Jamin, 'L'Anthropologie française' in Pierre Bonte and Michel Izard (eds.) *Dictionnaire de l'ethnologie et de l'anthropologie* (Paris: Presses Universitaires de France, 1991), pp. 289–95.
[5] In particular, see Vincent Descombes, *Le Même et l'autre. Quarante-cinq ans de philosophie française (1933–1978)* (Paris: Editions de Minuit, 1979); *Modern French Philosophy*, trans. L. Scott-Fox and J.M. Harding (Cambridge University Press, 1980); see also François Dosse, *Histoire du structuralisme, I: Le Champ du signe, 1945–1966; II: Le Chant du cygne, 1967 à nos jours* (Paris: La Découverte, 1991 and 1992); *History of Structuralism*, 2 vols., trans. Deborah Glassman (Minneapolis: University of Minnesota Press, 1997).

question of structural theory in anthropology and the social sciences.[6] Instead, its intention is to focus on the formative period of Lévi-Strauss's career, a period of approximately twenty years, from the mid-1940s to the early 1960s, when he is establishing the foundations of his theoretical work, but at the same time, and often inseparably, articulating a more general programme for French anthropology. The approach of the following chapters will be to concentrate on what the author considers to be some of the defining texts of this 'first' period of Lévi-Strauss's career, from the early fieldwork monographs to *Totemism* and *The Savage Mind*.[7] By the time of publication of these last two works, in 1962, the main outline of Lévi-Strauss's programme for anthropology has been delineated; following the appearance of the *Mythologiques* cycle in 1964, it could be said that he is practising a form of 'normal science' within the parameters of that programme.[8] From this perspective, the texts of the pre-1964 period are qualitatively more diverse, and arguably more interesting, than those of the second period, in that they represent an extended work of construction, the construction of what to all intents and purposes one could term a *paradigm*, a set of premises and practices, concepts and values adequate to the new anthropology. The following study will be looking at five areas of paradigm construction in Lévi-Strauss's work:

- The institutional and interdisciplinary context. In his earlier work, Lévi-Strauss's declarations on the place of anthropology in the human sciences are not pronounced in a disciplinary or institutional vacuum: the terrain is, to say the least, an overdetermined one, requiring a systematic definition of the nature, methods and objectives of anthropology in order to establish its specificity within the present configuration of disciplines in the university. This extended work of definition, and Lévi-Strauss's various attempts to situate anthropology in relation to adjacent disciplines in the human sciences,

[6] See, for example, Alan Jenkins, *The Social Theory of Claude Lévi-Strauss* (London: Macmillan, 1979); Simon Clarke, *The Foundations of Structuralism. A Critique of Lévi-Strauss and the Structuralist Movement* (Sussex: Harvester Press, 1981); Marcel Hénaff, *Claude Lévi-Strauss* (Paris: Belfond, 1991); *Claude Lévi-Strauss and the Making of Structural Anthropology*, trans. Mary Baker (Minneapolis/London: University of Minnesota Press, 1998).

[7] This approach will not exclude reference to later texts that might give retrospective insight on this or that aspect of Lévi-Strauss's thought. Most important in this respect are the different interviews Lévi-Strauss has given since the late 1950s, notably the conversations with Didier Eribon (1988), which are an invaluable source of information on the background to his intellectual development.

[8] As Gary Roth remarks, 'Commentators and critics of Lévi-Strauss alike have agreed that his ideas exhibit a remarkable consistency from beginning to end. This, no doubt, is due (at least in part) to the fact that he had already completed his intellectual evolution by the time his ideas were exposed to widespread and close scrutiny. Certainly by 1964 and the publication of his first volume on myths, this was true.' ('Claude Lévi-Strauss in Retrospect', *Dialectical Anthropology* 18 (1993), 52).

is the subject of chapter 1. It emerges that there is a systematic exclusion on Lévi-Strauss's part of anthropology's closest disciplinary neighbour, sociology, the effect of which is to place anthropology at the centre of the human and social sciences. As a general theory of culture, it becomes the indispensable reference point for all discourse on human society. However, Lévi-Strauss's strategic promotion of anthropology is not without its ambiguities, as it appears that there is a certain tension in his text between the claims to scientific interest of his discipline and the desire to preserve its force as a radical form of cultural critique.

- As has been noted, the development of French anthropology owes much to the activities of the Durkheimian school earlier in the century. An important aspect of Lévi-Strauss's early work is how he comes to terms with the past of his discipline, in short, how he is able to assimilate but also transform the Durkheimian tradition. Chapter 2 looks at his mediation of the work of Marcel Mauss, whose model of exchange is the starting point of his theory of kinship. We examine how Lévi-Strauss's theory of reciprocity attempts to give a philosophical foundation to the sociological model provided by Mauss, and how, more generally, there is an attempt to unify the different modes of social interaction, including exchange, under the category of communication. Finally, there is an analysis of one of Lévi-Strauss's rare excursions into political anthropology, where he uses the model of exchange to examine relations of power and authority in so-called primitive societies.

- While Lévi-Strauss's early work was concerned principally with problems of social organization, culminating in 1949 in the monumental *Elementary Structures of Kinship*, his election to the Ecole Pratique des Hautes Etudes in 1950 carried with it a change of specialization, from kinship studies to the anthropology of religions. Chapter 3 looks at the detail of this transition, how Lévi-Strauss's negotiation of his new area of research involves both the strategic delimitation of a domain susceptible to objective analysis and the development of a method adequate to such analysis. In the seminal *Introduction to the Work of Marcel Mauss*, published in 1950, we see that the ambivalent homage paid to the father of French anthropology is the pretext for a more personal exploration of the field of structural anthropology, the different statements on the symbolic nature of social institutions preparing the ground for the programmatic texts of the 1950s. We also look at the early texts on magic and shamanism, which articulate some of the central premises of Lévi-Strauss's anthropology: the effectiveness of symbolic representation; the essential rationalism of native thought. In our commentary on

'The Structural Study of Myth', taken as a working example of structural analysis, it is argued that Lévi-Strauss's interpretation of the nature and function of myth cannot be understood with reference to the linguistic model alone, and needs to be read in the context of the ambient science and technology of the period, as exemplified in disciplines such as information theory and cybernetics.

- For Lévi-Strauss, the first goal of anthropology, as a human science, is objectivity, the discovery of structural constants that would be independent of the contingent observer and his or her particular categories, values or beliefs. He is resistant to the idea of a possible *application* of anthropological knowledge, the subordination of its research mission to narrowly utilitarian ends, as can be the case in other branches of the social sciences. At the same time, the influence of structuralism in France cannot be reduced simply to the effect of its theoretical content. An integral part of Lévi-Strauss's programme for anthropology is his concern with its *missions*, how anthropology as a human science speaks to the moral consciousness of modern humanity. This articulation of a new humanism, as it was called, does not necessarily mean a separation of the scientific and the ideological, as some commentators have suggested.[9] In chapter 4 we look at the different components of the new humanism, and show how the values Lévi-Strauss advances in his work are in each case continuous and consistent with his theory. In particular, we examine how the humanist claims of social or structural anthropology effectively challenge the position of philosophy as the traditional source of humanistic discourse in France. Lévi-Strauss's construction of a specific genealogy for his discipline, and his designation of Jean-Jacques Rousseau as its founding father, would be part of this strategic decentering of philosophy.

- A common distinction made between the natural sciences and the human and social sciences is that in the first it is normally possible to dissociate items of objective knowledge from the individuals or groups responsible for their construction. A particular advance in scientific knowledge might attach the name of an individual or group of individuals to a law, theorem or model of interpretation, but once absorbed into the current paradigm of the discipline in question, these constructs will take on a quasi-autonomous existence in relation to their creator or creators. In the human and social sciences, by

---

[9] David Pace argues that there is a division or 'split' in Lévi-Strauss's thought and personality between 'the narrow and austere scientist' and 'the speculative and passionate philosopher' (*Claude Lévi-Strauss*, p. 17). This is, in my opinion, too dualistic an evaluation of both his 'character' and his work.

contrast, such dissociation is more problematic, there being much more of a tendency to retain and emphasize the link between a 'thinker' and a 'corpus' of thought, even where certain concepts or models derived from that corpus might have become more or less integrated into the deep structure of a discipline. This tendency towards the biographical, that is, the maintenance of an *articulation* between 'life' and 'thought', is perhaps even more marked in the case of individuals recognized as the founders of particular disciplines or movements. In this case, there is the additional complication of discipleship, the interpersonal field which forms around an individual and a doctrine and which works to ensure their continuation. The same problem of association is clearly present in the case of Lévi-Strauss. Though in his attempt to construct a coherent paradigm for his discipline, Lévi-Strauss's manifest desire was that structuralist method should become in a sense detached from his person, that it should, by analogy with the natural sciences, acquire a truth and self-evidence independent of its instance of enunciation, the reality is that it has become inseparable from the name and persona of Lévi-Strauss. This has partly to do with the ideological component of structuralism, noted above, but the picture is further complicated by the fact that at a critical stage in his career, Lévi-Strauss published what is essentially an autobiographical text, *Tristes tropiques*. It will be seen in chapter 5 – and this may be the paradox of a certain kind of autobiography – that in the case of Lévi-Strauss, the incidence of the 'personal' on the development of a discipline can be both slight and considerable, that the definition of a discipline can in some senses be inseparable from a process of self-definition. This essential implication of the theoretical, the ideological and the biographical is examined through the example of a number of curious statements or confessions, made in *Tristes tropiques* and in subsequent interviews: the author's description of his 'neolithic' mind, comparable to the semi-nomadic existence of his ethnographic subjects; his composition of a play, 'The Apotheosis of Augustus', at a critical point in his fieldwork experience; his confessed distaste for fieldwork; his comments on his deficient memory; and his professed lack of a normal sense of personal identity.

One of the most significant points to emerge from the following study will be the high degree of *continuity* between the different areas of analysis detailed above, their overall coherence. This is not the projected coherence of the commentator anxious to impose a degree of order on his or her subject of study; rather, it is internal to Lévi-Strauss's work itself, the result of a *willed* coherence that permeates every part of his thought and his writing. As we shall be seeing,

Lévi-Strauss is a systematic thinker. The example of his earlier texts is that of a constructor, establishing in sequence, step by step, the different conceptual cells or building blocks that will make up the edifice of structuralist theory. At the same time, we will discover that this is not a purely epistemological enterprise. The close articulation of the epistemological and the ethical in Lévi-Strauss's work, the manner in which he articulates his life and his work, means that this work – this *life-work* – possesses an aesthetic unity that transcends the narrowly scientific programme of structuralism. Indeed, in the course of our analysis it will become apparent that the paradigm of structuralism cannot simply be equated with the field of structuralist theory, and that it amounts to something altogether more complex.[10]

Before we begin, however, a word on language.

There is an episode in Lévi-Strauss's professional biography which is perhaps not always given the attention it deserves. This is the period he spent in North America during the Second World War, and for a few years following the war, a period that covers the larger part of the 1940s.[11] On the one hand, his initial departure to the United States in 1941 was a necessary one – given his Jewish background, to have remained in France at this point would almost certainly have meant deportation and death. On the other hand, this enforced exile is presented as a particularly fortunate twist of fate, as the teaching position Lévi-Strauss was given at the New School for Social Research in New York was the occasion of the decisive meeting with Jakobson in 1942. One may speculate on what the history of structuralism might have been had this meeting not taken place, indeed, whether structuralism itself would have taken place at all. From the point of view of the history of French anthropology, the picture is a little more nuanced. The introduction to Jakobson was certainly a key moment, but no less important, perhaps, was Lévi-Strauss's personal contact, during his stay in the United States, with many of the prominent figures of American anthropology: Boas, Benedict, Kroeber, Linton, Lowie.[12] Added to this were the countless hours spent in the New York Public Library, quietly sifting and assimilating

---

[10] It is not my intention in this book to deal with the question of Lévi-Strauss's aesthetics. This represents a whole area of study in itself, and has already been the object of an important monograph by José G. Merquior (*L'Esthétique de Lévi-Strauss* (Paris: Presses Universitaires de France, 1975)).

[11] On the importance of Lévi-Strauss's North American experience, see Anne Cohen-Solal, 'Claude Lévi-Strauss aux Etats-Unis', in *Claude Lévi-Strauss*, special issue of *Critique* 50.620–1 (January–February 1999), 13–25.

[12] *Conversations with Claude Lévi-Strauss*, trans. Paula Wissing (University of Chicago Press, 1991), pp. 35–9; *De Près et de loin* (Paris: Plon, 1988), pp. 54–60. Page references for Lévi-Strauss's major works will henceforth be given in the main text, with titles abbreviated in accordance with the list of abbreviations provided on pages ix–x. In each case the reference for the original French text follows that of the English translation. I have provided my own translations for texts for which there is no available English translation.

the mass of ethnographic documentation deposited there. On Lévi-Strauss's own admission, what he knows of anthropology, he learnt during this period (*CLS*2, 43; *PL*, 65).

It is one of the ironies of the history of the reception of Lévi-Strauss's work in anthropology that he has sometimes been reproached by his French colleagues for his undue attachment to the 'Anglo-Saxon' tradition, while his English-speaking colleagues have criticized his 'French' penchant for speculation, abstraction and generalization, a rationalism that can be economical in its treatment of observed fact. Leaving aside these conventional and mutually constraining stereotypes of the 'French' and the 'Anglo-Saxon', what is interesting about the North American episode is that it is not simply a professional apprenticeship, but also and inseparably a cultural and linguistic experience. While the fieldwork expeditions of the 1930s may have provided Lévi-Strauss with his first experience of radical displacement, it could be said that the North American experience represents a second stage of defamiliarization, a form of participant observation of much longer duration and much deeper implication. This second initiation, as it were, required a linguistic competence that had been singularly lacking in his fieldwork experience – this very French academic suddenly found himself having to speak, teach, read and write in English. It is the last of these activities, writing, that particularly concerns us here, as it is a fact not frequently commented upon that a number of Lévi-Strauss's important early texts were originally written in English. The monograph on the Nambikwara Indians was first written in English in 1941, several years before its appearance in French, as part of Lévi-Strauss's doctoral thesis, in 1948.[13] Even more importantly, perhaps, several chapters of *Structural Anthropology*, including the seminal essays on linguistics and anthropology and the structural analysis of myth, also made their first appearance in English.[14] This is not an idle point of bibliographical detail, of interest only to scholars of Lévi-Strauss. In a world where French theory has become an exportable commodity, a powerful contributor to the international circulation of ideas, the question of translation, of the quality and depth of translation, is a crucial one. When, as is the case with Lévi-Strauss, there is the additional complication of a *bilingual* formulation of theory, then one is entitled to take a moment to reflect on the matter. Lévi-Strauss himself is in fact sensitive to the possible problems of his intellectual transactions between English and French. In the preface to the French edition

[13] See *Magazine Littéraire* 311 (June 1993), 18. In his 1972 interviews with Jean José Marchand, Lévi-Strauss says that he wrote the monograph in English in order to teach himself the language, as his post at the New School For Social Research required him to teach in English (*Archives du XXe siècle*, part 3).

[14] 'Language and the Analysis of Social Laws' (1951), 'Social Structure' (1952), 'Linguistics and Anthropology' (1953), 'The Structural Study of Myth' (1955). 'The Place of Anthropology in the Social Sciences' (1954) was first published both in English and French.

of *Structural Anthropology* published in 1958, he apologizes to the reader for what he considers to be the unevenness of the essays, from the point of view of their composition. This part of the preface, which takes up over half of the French text, is left out of the 1963 English translation, but it is worth quoting the passage to get an idea of Lévi-Strauss's own linguistic experience, and the difficulties he encounters when working between two languages, English and French. He writes:

When putting together this collection of essays, I came up against a difficulty of which I feel I must inform the reader. Several of my articles were written directly in English, so I had to translate them. As I worked through these texts, I was struck by the difference of tone and composition between those written in one or the other language. The result is a certain heterogeneity which, I fear, is detrimental to the overall balance and unity of the book.

This difference can doubtless be explained, in part, by sociological factors: one doesn't think and doesn't present a paper in the same way, when one is addressing a French- or English-speaking audience. But there are also personal factors. However accustomed I am to the English language, a language I've taught in for several years, my use of it is inaccurate and my range limited. I think in English what I write in this language, but without always being aware of it, I say what I can with the linguistic means at my disposal, not what I want. This explains the feeling of strangeness I get reading my own texts, when I have to transcribe them into French. Since the reader will most likely share my feeling of dissatisfaction, I thought it was necessary to give the reason for it. (*AS*1, i–ii, my translation)

It is easy to see why the translators left this passage out of the English translation. In a sense, it does not directly concern the English-speaking reader, who is interested only in the content of the translated text and not in questions of linguistic priority or provenance. It is, however, of particular interest to us here. Because although, in fact, only four or five out of the seventeen chapters of *Structural Anthropology* were first written in English, those chapters are among the most theoretically demanding and complex texts in the book. Lévi-Strauss's solution to the problem, as he sees it, is to make a very free translation of the English, paraphrasing some passages and extending and developing others. The result in the final English translation of *Structural Anthropology* is a strange hybrid of the original English text and the translation of Lévi-Strauss's French modifications. Inevitably, there are omissions, compressions, ellipses.

The problems Lévi-Strauss encounters when working in the foreign medium of English, and the problems he has in retranslating that intellectual experience into his native tongue, are a useful reminder of the somewhat analogous position of those of us involved in the mediation of his work. If, as he confesses above, Lévi-Strauss experiences a kind of defamiliarization when reading himself in English, then the present author has frequently felt a similar sense of strangeness when reading the different English translations of Lévi-Strauss's work. While this book has been written for an English-speaking readership, with all quoted material provided in English, my practice has been to read all of Lévi-Strauss's texts in their French version, and it is on this primary reading that the analysis of the following chapters is based. As mentioned above, an important aspect of this analysis is the tracking of continuities in Lévi-Strauss's work, the various conceptual and thematic constants that appear from text to text. By essence, these constants are linguistically embedded; their primary mode of expression is first the national language of French, and second, Lévi-Strauss's own peculiar handling of that language, his own particular idiom. While the available translations of Lévi-Strauss are generally of a good standard, inevitably the linguistic resonances of his original text, the networks of verbal associations that link together the different parts of his thought, are frequently lost in the transition to English. Part of the process of commentary that follows, when quoting what are often central passages in Lévi-Strauss's work, will be to reconstitute, when necessary, the meaning and register of the original French. This is done with the intention not so much of faulting the many translators of Lévi-Strauss as of indicating something of the complexity of working – thinking, reading, writing – between languages, something we are inclined to forget when faced with the simple but false transparency of the translation. For the reader interested in consulting the French text, I have for each quotation or reference to Lévi-Strauss given the page numbers of the French as well as the English editions of his work. Finally, for the epigraphs that figure at the start of each chapter, I have adopted the practice of quoting first in French, with the English translation following in brackets. This statement and reminder of linguistic provenance is, I believe, a necessary, if limited, gesture in what unfortunately, and to our collective detriment, is an increasingly monolingual world.

1   The place of anthropology

> On entrevoit ainsi le bizarre carrefour de disciplines où se trouve aujourd'hui placée l'anthropologie.
> (We perceive the singular crossroads of disciplines at which anthropology stands.)[1]

The publication of *Anthropologie structurale* in 1958 can be viewed as a defining moment in the history of French anthropology. The title of the work is itself a provocative statement of intention. The epithet '*structurale*' signals the resolutely theoretical approach Lévi-Strauss was proposing for his discipline, but no less bold perhaps is the very designation of this discipline as *anthropologie*. The more common term in France was *ethnologie*, and his preference for *anthropologie* therefore marks a conscious decision to widen the normal definition of the discipline.[2] The distinction he makes in the book between three moments or stages of anthropological enquiry is clear enough: ethnography, the empirical instance of observation in the field, is followed by ethnology, the preliminary synthesis of data provided by ethnography, both of which are subsumed in the global perspective on humankind offered by anthropology (*SA*1, 355; *AS*1, 388). By itself this proposed extension of the scope of French ethnology, by analogy with its British and American counterparts, seems a relatively innocent gesture, but it is far from so if one considers the interdisciplinary context in which it takes place. Not only do Lévi-Strauss's definitions of anthropology, of its object, methods and scope, serve to ensure the internal consistency of the discipline; equally and inseparably they help to determine the *place* of anthropology in relation to a number of neighbouring disciplines, and inevitably this place is a problematic one. On the one hand, there was in France the historical subordination of ethnology to sociology – in this context the new designation of 'anthropology' reads as a kind of declaration

---

[1] *SA*1, 368; *AS*1, 403.

[2] It is significant that the entries relating to anthropology in the *Grand Robert* dictionary quote directly from *Anthropologie structurale* for the main substance of their definitions (Alain Rey (ed.), *Le Grand Robert. Dictionnaire alphabétique et analogique de la langue française*, 2nd edition (Paris: Robert, 1985)).

12

of independence. On the other hand, the widened scope of the new anthropology also affects the status of other, less proximate disciplines such as history and philosophy. The situation is complicated by the institutional demarcation between *sciences sociales* and *sciences humaines*, a distinction which, it will be seen, is used by Lévi-Strauss to accentuate the differences between sociology and anthropology.

If one takes into account the interdisciplinary implications of Lévi-Strauss's different descriptions and definitions of anthropology in his earlier work, then his decision to open *Structural Anthropology* with a chapter on history and ethnology is perhaps less surprising than would seem at first glance. In actual fact a good part of the chapter entitled 'History and Anthropology', originally published in 1949,[3] deals with the more circumscribed problem of historical reconstruction in anthropology, considering and criticizing in their turn evolutionist, diffusionist and functionalist approaches to the problem. Moreover, when Lévi-Strauss does come to define the relationship between history and ethnology, it seems that an implicit concern of this definition is the exclusion of a third discipline, sociology.

The chapter begins with an evocation of the situation earlier in the century, when Hauser and Simiand defined the respective methods of their disciplines, history and sociology. However, since that period, and in contrast with the 'modest' and 'lucid' progress of history, sociology has, according to Lévi-Strauss, failed to realize the ambitious programme it had set for itself: 'In this discussion we shall not use the term *sociology*, which has never come to stand, as Durkheim and Simiand hoped it would, for a general science of human behaviour' (*SA*1, 2; *AS*1, 4). In fact, the only notable development in French sociology has come through the remarkable progress of two of its tributaries, ethnology and ethnography (1–2; 3). If the study of so-called 'primitive' societies can one day be integrated with the sociological analysis of 'complex' societies, only then will sociology merit a place at the centre of the social sciences. That point not having yet been reached, sociology in France and elsewhere remains little more than a 'social philosophy', best viewed as a special case of ethnography, which is considerably more advanced in both its results and its methodology (2–3; 4).

From the very first pages of *Structural Anthropology*, therefore, Lévi-Strauss excludes sociology – more precisely in France, post-Durkheimian sociology – from his discussion of the relation between the synchronic and diachronic study of society. History and anthropology remain in the arena, and he goes on to determine their relationship. Contrary to appearances, they are not as different as might be supposed:

[3] *SA*1, 1–27; *AS*1, 3–33.

The fundamental difference between the two disciplines is not one of subject, of goal, or of method. They share the same subject, which is social life; the same goal, which is a better understanding of man; and, in fact, the same method, in which only the proportion of research techniques varies. They differ, principally, in their choice of complementary perspectives: history organizes its data in relation to conscious expressions of social life, while anthropology proceeds by examining its unconscious foundations. (*SA*1, 18; *AS*1, 24–5)

This complementarity is expressed later in the chapter by the figure of Janus: history and anthropology are both going in the same direction, but with different orientations, history looking backwards, anthropology looking forwards (24; 32). The kinship between the two is further emphasized when Lévi-Strauss qualifies that their complementary relationship is not exclusive: there are 'dosages' of each perspective (the conscious and the unconscious) in the two disciplines (23; 30–1).

It is evident that the history Lévi-Strauss associates so closely with anthropology in 'History and Anthropology' is a specific type of history. When at the start of the chapter he refers to history's 'modest' and 'lucid' progress, he seems to be thinking of *la nouvelle histoire* (new history) rather than the more traditional history of events and individuals, focused on the political rather than the social and the cultural spheres (23; 31). What we are in fact presented with then is a 'new' discipline, ethnology, and a 'new' history, as pioneered by the *Annales* school. However, it would be limiting to see in the alliance Lévi-Strauss proposes between history and anthropology simply the expression of a project for future research, a peaceful collaboration in the pursuit of truth. This is because such an alliance is also in a sense a pact of non-aggression, the object of which is the exclusion of a third party, sociology. Lévi-Strauss's pact with history, or rather, a specific kind of history, lays to rest the perennial conflict between history and sociology, but at the same time removes sociology from the centre of the stage. This exclusion becomes definitive in the concluding paragraph of 'History and Anthropology': 'If anthropology and history once begin to collaborate in the study of contemporary societies, it will become apparent that here, as elsewhere, the one science can achieve nothing without the help of the other' (25; 33). Whereas earlier in his argument, Lévi-Strauss was prepared to envisage a future reinstatement of sociology at the centre of the social sciences, here the projected study of contemporary society falls to the coalition of ethnology and history, with no mention of their excluded cousin.

Lévi-Strauss's effective dismissal of sociology in 'History and Anthropology' is symptomatic of the uneasy cohabitation of the two disciplines in France from the late 1940s onwards. Despite what Lévi-Strauss considers to be the relatively undistinguished profile of French sociology since Durkheim, it is clear that institutionally sociology continues to enjoy a certain pre-eminence due precisely to the earlier success of the Durkheimian school, and that it therefore occupies part of the terrain Lévi-Strauss sees as belonging to his new discipline, anthropology. In a later chapter of *Structural Anthropology* he notes, rather euphemistically, that the relationship between sociology and anthropology is an 'equivocal' one (361–2; 395). On a more concrete level this ambivalence can be seen in his relations with the Russian-born sociologist Georges Gurvitch. After the war Gurvitch had emerged as the leading figure in French sociology, occupying the chair at the Sorbonne until his death in 1965. In 1945 he had asked Lévi-Strauss to write the chapter on French sociology for the volume he was to edit on twentieth-century sociology.[4] In the wide-ranging survey he produced, Lévi-Strauss's summary of Gurvitch's contribution to the discipline was a qualified and not particularly enthusiastic one.[5] A few years later, Gurvitch asked Lévi-Strauss to write the introduction to the first published collection of Mauss's works, but in Gurvitch's short preface to the book he carefully dissociated himself from the 'very personal' perspective of the author.[6] In the ensuing years, relations between the two men were to deteriorate rapidly; Gurvitch's criticisms of the concept of structure, for example, provoked a particularly acerbic response from Lévi-Strauss.[7] Finally, in 1959, Gurvitch attempted to exclude Lévi-Strauss from the official celebration of the centenary of Durkheim's birth.[8] The conflict between sociology and anthropology, or at least between two of their principal representatives, Lévi-Strauss and Gurvitch, was therefore a very real one. Lévi-Strauss's meagre estimation of the progress of sociology in 'History and Anthropology' can only have irritated a Gurvitch intent on preserving the place of his discipline at the centre of the social sciences.[9]

---

[4] 'French Sociology', in Georges Gurvitch and Wilbert E. Moore (eds.) *Sociology in the Twentieth Century* (New York: The Philosophical Library, 1945), pp. 503–37; French translation *La Sociologie au XXe siècle* (Paris: Presses Universitaires de France, 1947), pp. 513–45.

[5] *Sociology in the Twentieth Century*, pp. 532–3; *La Sociologie au XXe siècle*, pp. 540–1.

[6] The detail of the context surrounding the publication of *Sociologie et anthropologie* in 1950 is inevitably lost in the presentation of the English translations of Mauss's essays. The translations of Lévi-Strauss's Introduction and three of Mauss's essays (*The Gift, Seasonal Variations, A General Theory of Magic*) have all been published separately, while translations of the remaining essays are regrouped under another title (*Sociology and Psychology*). Gurvitch's short preface disappears altogether. The effect of this reorganization of the text is to lose the ambivalence of the original title, the dissonance between preface and introduction, and the context of incipient rivalry between Gurvitch and Lévi-Strauss.

[7] Chapter 16 of *Structural Anthropology*.

[8] See the opening footnote to 'What Ethnology Owes to Durkheim' in *Structural Anthropology 2* (*SA2*, 44n; *AS2*, 57 n.1). See also *CLS2*, 69–70; *PL*, 102–3.

[9] Already, in 1950, Gurvitch is asserting this centrality: 'For all of these reasons, sociology should take a central place in the system of knowledge in the second half of the twentieth century, without necessarily returning to the "imperialist" claims that marked its beginnings, nor with the wish of assimilating this or that branch of the social sciences or philosophy. It seems equally certain that sociology will prefer to concentrate its efforts not on society's past history, nor even on already crystallized social situations and structures, but on present society in the very process of its self-creation, with all its struggles and turmoil' (Georges Gurvitch (ed.), *La Vocation actuelle de la sociologie* (Paris: Presses Universitaires de France, 1950), p. 4. My translation).

Before going on to consider in more detail Lévi-Strauss's attempted marginalization of sociology, it could be asked what the implications of the pact or collaboration he proposes in 'History and Anthropology' are for history itself. While the relationship he describes appears to be an equal and reciprocal one, the perspective inevitably remains that of an anthropologist and not a historian. It would be useful therefore to consider briefly the case of Lévi-Strauss's opposite number in history, Fernand Braudel. In the same way that Gurvitch provides a counterpoint to Lévi-Strauss in sociology, very quickly Braudel assumes the role of spokesperson for history. The texts he publishes in the late 1950s on history and the human sciences are visibly written in the wake of *Structural Anthropology*, and could be seen at least in part as a response to its challenge.[10] By contrast with Gurvitch, however, the response is generally a positive and constructive one. Braudel welcomes Lévi-Strauss's attempts to give some theoretical coherence to the social sciences, which he (Braudel) considers to be in dire need of a common language, and even goes so far as to call his own approach to history, focused on *la longue durée* (long duration), a 'structural' history.[11] More generally, Braudel and Lévi-Strauss could be seen as fellow travellers to the extent that both share a mistrust of a traditional (political) history that privileges the event and neglects other levels of social reality. At the same time, however, Braudel questions the applicability within historical research of the kind of formalization Lévi-Strauss is proposing for anthropology, and reminds us that Lévi-Strauss's structural models are only properly understood when placed in the enveloping context of *longue durée*.[12]

These last two restrictions are sufficient reminder that while open to the interdisciplinary challenge of Lévi-Strauss's programme for anthropology, Braudel is also concerned to ensure the integrity and centrality of his own discipline. In fact, Braudel's view of what he terms *les sciences de l'homme* – the sciences of man – is notably more inclusive than Lévi-Strauss's. If he is willing to view Lévi-Strauss's structural anthropology in a favourable light, he does not share the latter's dismissive attitude towards post-Durkheimian French sociology, and even manages to reconcile the two in his 1958 text on history and sociology, where he refers to Gurvitch and Lévi-Strauss as representatives of the different theoretical tendencies in sociology with which history might profitably collaborate. It is with a degree of impatience, it seems, that he summarizes the contrasting approaches of the two rivals:

---

[10] These articles are gathered together under the heading 'History and the Other Human Sciences', in the first section of *On History*, trans. Sarah Matthews (London: Weidenfeld and Nicolson, 1980); 'L'Histoire et les autres sciences de l'homme' in *Ecrits sur l'histoire* (Paris: Champs Flammarion, 1969).

[11] Ibid., p. 74; p. 112.

[12] Ibid., pp. 75–6; p. 114. In his interview with Lévi-Strauss, Didier Eribon questions him on the suggestion made by some that Braudel's article on *la longue durée* was written to counter Lévi-Strauss's influence on historians (*CLS2*, 123; *PL*, 172).

Georges Gurvitch is almost excessive and overscrupulous in his desire for a complex, hyperempirical sociology, in the image of what he not unreasonably sees as an abundant reality. Claude Lévi-Strauss cuts through this abundance and destroys it in order to bring to light the deep-seated, slender line of human continuity. Does one really absolutely have to choose and decide which one of them is *the* sociologist?[13]

What emerges from this discussion and Braudel's other writings on history and the social sciences is a history wishing to avoid the imperialistic ambitions of its past but which nevertheless sees itself as the natural point of intersection of a number of different disciplines. Whereas the centrality Lévi-Strauss is claiming for anthropology is in large part justified by its strong theoretical bias, the centrality Braudel envisages for history seems to be for the opposite reason: as the least 'structured' of the humanistic sciences, it is able to learn from and reflect the progress of its neighbours.[14] At the same time, he argues that awareness of the temporal dimension, more precisely of the *plurality* of time – his own concept and history's contribution – is essential to the creation of a common methodology for the human and social sciences.[15]

Braudel's picture of the human and social sciences is inevitably a more ecumenical one than either Gurvitch or Lévi-Strauss's. He is obviously attempting to think beyond the border conflicts that seem to characterize relations between these disciplines at this point, as is evident in his conclusion to 'History and Sociology':

On the practical level . . . I would hope that the social sciences, at least provisionally, would suspend their constant border disputes over what is or is not a social science, what is or is not structure. Rather let them try to trace those lines across our research which if they exist would serve to orient some kind of collective research, and make possible the first stages of some sort of coming together.[16]

Like Lévi-Strauss, then, Braudel wishes for a certain convergence of the social sciences. Unlike Lévi-Strauss, he does not wish this to be at the price of the virtual exclusion of one of its members. Though the 'structural' history of Braudel's *longue durée* seems both theoretically and temperamentally closer to Lévi-Strauss than to Gurvitch, it is significant that Lévi-Strauss's proposal for an exclusive collaboration between anthropology and the new history finds no direct echo in Braudel's text.

That all three disciplines – history, sociology, anthropology – should in their different ways be claiming a place at the centre of the human or social sciences, is a reflection of how contested this terrain had become in postwar France.

---

[13] *On History*, p. 73; *Ecrits sur l'histoire*, p. 111. First published in Gurvitch's *Traité de sociologie*, vol. I (Paris: Presses Universitaires de France, 1962), pp. 83–98.
[14] *On History*, pp. 26, 70; *Ecrits sur l'histoire*, pp. 42, 106–7.
[15] Ibid., p. 26; p. 43.   [16] Ibid., p. 52; pp. 82–3.

The spirit of rivalry and of jealously guarded borders has doubtless always been a feature of relations between cognate disciplines, but the situation at this particular time seems an unusually volatile one. A significant factor here was clearly the arrival of this 'new' discipline, anthropology, especially in the form Lévi-Strauss was proposing for it.[17] He himself was fully aware of the difficult and ambivalent position of anthropology. In the final chapter of *Structural Anthropology*, 'The Place of Anthropology in the Social Sciences' (1954),[18] he uses a cosmological metaphor to describe its equivocal arrival:

It is as though social and cultural anthropology, far from appearing on the scene of scientific development as an independent subject claiming a place among the other disciplines, had taken shape somewhat in the manner of a nebula, gradually incorporating a substance previously diffused or distributed in another way and, by this concentration, bringing about a general redistribution of research subjects among the humanistic and social sciences. (*SA*1, 347; *AS*1, 378)

This metaphor describes what is basically a double-bind situation: anthropology is unable simply to impose itself as an autonomous discipline – it must negotiate the context of adjacent disciplines and the history of its emergence in relation to those disciplines. At the same time, as the nebular metaphor implies, the rightful place of anthropology is at the centre of these disciplines: it incorporates diffusely distributed matter and achieves a certain critical mass, in the process redrawing the map of the social and human sciences. Though the metaphor is suitably vague, it is not difficult to see that the realignment described would concern those disciplines seen as being closest to anthropology: history and, especially, sociology.

It is important to remember here that the social and cultural anthropology Lévi-Strauss is describing is distinct from ethnology as traditionally practised in France. If anthropology occupies or ought to occupy a central position within the human and social sciences, then this means that it cannot simply be equated with ethnology, the study of exotic societies, even if historically this is its provenance. The general anthropology which Lévi-Strauss is projecting here, and in other similarly programmatic texts of the same period, would be applicable to *all* societies. The object of anthropology, he stresses, is not simply the 'primitive': 'It is important to realize, from the outset, that anthropology is not distinguished from other humanistic and social sciences by any subject of study peculiar to

---

[17] One would have to return to the beginning of the century to find an analogous situation in France, where Durkheim's construction of sociology posed similar problems of demarcation from cognate disciplines such as history, philosophy, ethnography and law. See Victor Karady, 'Durkheim, les sciences sociales et l'Université: bilan d'un semi-échec', *Revue française de sociologie* 17.2 (April–June 1976), 278–9 n.33; 'Stratégies de réussite et modes de faire-valoir de la sociologie chez les durkheimiens', *Revue française de sociologie* 20.1 (January–March 1979), 53.

[18] (*SA*1, 346–81; *AS*1, 377–418). First published in 'The University Teaching of the Social Sciences' (Paris: UNESCO, 1954).

it alone. At first, indeed, it was concerned with so-called savage or primitive societies' (347; 378). He goes on to argue that

- the interest in exotic cultures is in any case shared by an increasing number of disciplines;
- the societies traditionally studied by ethnologists are rapidly disappearing;
- as a consequence of this, anthropologists are now turning to 'civilized' societies as objects of study;[19]
- and finally, that rather than arising from its object of study (the 'primitive') the specificity of anthropology resides in 'a particular conception of the world or... an original way of approaching problems', acquired in the study of qualitatively different societies (*SA*1, 347; *AS*1, 378–9).

The final point, emphasizing the originality of anthropology's research methods, is essential to understanding how Lévi-Strauss effectively contests the place of sociology at the centre of the social sciences. It will become apparent that while, as is clear in this instance, anthropology and sociology might potentially share the same object (society in general), for Lévi-Strauss they are distinct in their aims and methods, and that it is this distinction which enables him to establish an implicit hierarchy of disciplines, premised on the values of *objectivity* and *authenticity*.

However, the ideal position or evolution of anthropology, expressed in this passage, is in sharp contrast with both its history and its actual predicament: 'Anthropology is too young a science for its teaching not to reflect the local and historical circumstances that are at the root of each particular development' (348; 379). The institutional reality of the teaching of anthropology is that it is grouped with various of the other social sciences, and most frequently with sociology (ibid.). In this passage, therefore, Lévi-Strauss oscillates between what anthropology is and what it ought to or will be, between the ideal and the actual. Inevitably, what appears to interest him most is the future of anthropology, what it promises, rather than the reality of its present entrenchment within the social sciences.

This brings us to the question of the relationship between the so-called 'social' and 'human' sciences, and the exact location of anthropology within them. Braudel, as has been seen, normally brings the two together under the more general and more inclusive description, *les sciences de l'homme*, the sciences of man. For anthropology, Lévi-Strauss appears to modulate between the two

---

[19] 'As anthropology deepens its reflections on its subject and improves its methods, it feels more and more that it is "going back home"' (376; 413). According to Gérard Althabe, however, the effect of Lévi-Strauss's formulation of anthropology as a science of cultural distanciation was to downgrade the ethnological study of French society, as it had traditionally been practised, in favour of an ethnology of the exotic ('Vers une ethnologie du présent', in Gérard Althabe, Daniel Fabre and Gérard Lenclud (eds.), *Vers une ethnologie du présent* (Paris: Editions de la Maison des sciences de l'homme, 1992), p. 249).

terms, with, it seems, an increasing bias towards 'human' as opposed to 'social' science.[20] The most coherent articulation of the distinction between the two is to be found in a later text, 'Scientific Criteria in the Social and Human Disciplines' (1964), subsequently published in *Structural Anthropology 2*. While, as its title suggests, this text is not concerned exclusively with the example of anthropology, the series of divisions, subdivisions and oppositions Lévi-Strauss posits both within and between the social and human sciences on the one hand, and the 'exact' sciences on the other, are very instructive as to how he views anthropology and sociology as, respectively, 'human' and 'social' sciences.

The text itself was originally a response to a survey initiated by UNESCO on the principal trends of research in the human and social sciences, following a similar survey on the state of the natural sciences. From the start, Lévi-Strauss makes clear that the 'science' ascribed to the various social and humanistic disciplines is a semantic fiction, more a reflection of their aspiration to science than their actual attainment of it. Moreover, amongst the disparate mass of disciplines gathered together under the rubric of 'human and social sciences', only a few can claim a method approximating that of science (*SA2*, 290, 291; *AS2*, 341, 342). Lévi-Strauss mentions two criteria defining the scientific approach: first, the necessity of the distinction or separation ('dualism') between observer and object of observation; second, the capacity to isolate simple, invariant structures across a range of phenomena (292–3; 343–5). He suggests that linguistics, and to a lesser extent ethnology, have gone some way to meeting the second of these criteria, but in order to properly evaluate the diverse claims to science of the social and human disciplines, he thinks it is first necessary to address the problem of their *classification*. The passage in question merits quotation in full, as it represents a peculiarly 'Lévi-Straussian' solution to the problem:

In truth, this problem of the classification of the social and human sciences has never been treated seriously.

But the brief recapitulation which we have presented in order to point out the ambiguities, confusions, and contradictions in nomenclature, shows that nothing can be attempted on the basis of recognized divisions. We must first start with an epistemological criticism of our sciences, in the hope that, in spite of their empirical diversity and heterogeneity, a small number of fundamental attitudes will emerge. Their presence, absence or combination will make the peculiarity or the complementarity of each one clearer than its goal, openly and confusedly proclaimed. (*SA2*, 297; *AS2*, 349)

[20] The history of the two terms in France is a rather complicated one. The term *sciences humaines* has existed since the seventeenth century, initially designating the study of language, grammar, poetry and rhetoric. It is only in the twentieth century that it acquires a new meaning, close to that of the *sciences sociales*, which appears to have been borrowed from the English language ('Science' in Alain Rey (ed.), *Dictionnaire historique de la langue française*, 2 vols., 13th edition (Paris: Robert, 2000)). Lévi-Strauss uses the ambiguous distinction between the two terms in order to interpolate his own definition of their respective fields of reference.

It is not difficult to see that what Lévi-Strauss is proposing here is a *structural* analysis of the social and human sciences. In *The Elementary Structures of Kinship* and *Totemism*, for example, exactly the same terms are used to describe the state of kinship studies and theories of totemism: a profusion of empirical data and of hypotheses on the data; the necessity of bringing some order to this chaos, of cutting through the complexity of superficial phenomena in order to arrive at simpler, underlying configurations. In the present case, these configurations are the limited set of 'fundamental attitudes' supposed to underlie the diverse orientations of the various disciplines. There is also the implication that these attitudes operate on an unconscious level: what might be consciously but vaguely articulated as the aims and objectives of the different disciplines are subtended by more essential and unconscious tendencies. This is of course one of the central premises of structural analysis, that conscious representations – 'secondary elaborations' – are not necessarily to be trusted and that the truly fundamental structures lie at a deeper level of determination.

Significantly, Lévi-Strauss begins his structural analysis of the social and human sciences by reviving a previous analysis made in *Structural Anthropology* of the relationship between anthropology, sociology and history (*SA*1, 285–6; *AS*1, 313–14). So within the wider community of the human and social sciences, we are returned to the more restricted, 'nuclear' family of history, anthropology and sociology, already examined in 'History and Anthropology'. The criteria for analysis in this case are the following: the presence or absence of empirical observation, the construction of models and (within this category) the use of what Lévi-Strauss terms 'mechanical' or 'statistical' models (*SA*2, 297; *AS*2, 349).[21] He suggests that we 'arbitrarily' assign a positive or a negative to each discipline, in so far as it satisfies one or another of these criteria. The result is a table in which each of the four disciplines (anthropology breaks down into two parts or stages, ethnography and ethnology) has its specific place, distinguished from or associated with its neighbour by a plus or a minus sign (see table 1).

This table could be extended and complicated by introducing further oppositional criteria, and also by applying these to other disciplines. One therefore obtains a kind of periodic table in which each discipline has its assigned place: 'It would then be seen that in relation to all these opposites, the disciplines have their place well marked, positively or negatively' (ibid.). As with the periodic

---

[21] 'A last distinction refers to the relation between the scale of the model and that of the phenomena. A model the elements of which are on the same scale as the phenomena will be called a "mechanical model". When the elements of the model are on a different scale, we shall be dealing with a "statistical model"' (*SA*1, 283; *AS*1, 311). A few pages later, Lévi-Strauss qualifies that 'the social sciences, while they have to do with the time dimension, nevertheless deal with two different categories of time. Anthropology uses a "mechanical" time, reversible and non-cumulative . . . On the contrary, historical time is "statistical": it always appears as an oriented and non-reversible process' (*SA*1, 286; *AS*1, 314).

Table 1

	History	Sociology	Ethnography	Ethnology
Empirical observation vs model building	+	−	+	−
Mechanical models vs statistical models	−	−	+	+

Source: SA2, 298; AS2, 350.

table of the elements, one would be able to predict the place and properties of disciplines which do not as yet exist, represented by the empty spaces that remain in the present table. It would equally be possible to anticipate the future development of existing disciplines (299; 351).[22]

It is perhaps necessary to pause an instant to consider the implications of Lévi-Strauss's structural classification of the disciplines. Apart from the question of the viability of such a classification, which is far from certain (it is not self-evident, for example, that the diverse conceptual, practical and procedural complexes that constitute different 'disciplines' are reducible to binary categorization), one would also need to ask what its logical status might be. Is it legitimate for a discipline to use its own, internal methods of analysis to categorize itself and cognate disciplines? The discipline in question being anthropology, one could imagine a situation in which such analysis would constitute a *critique* of the disciplines, a reflexive questioning of the demarcations and differences, the divisions and dissensions between disciplines, but this is obviously not the case in the present instance. Lévi-Strauss's binary classification of the disciplines is unmarked, he does not declare its affinity with the method which at this point, in 1964, he has perfected in his analysis of mythological systems and kinship structures. It is as if the method itself has now become self-evident, more precisely, that its *application* is self-evident, regardless of the class of phenomena to which it is applied. This problem of level and of logical type is not an isolated one in Lévi-Strauss's work, and we will return to it more than once in the course of the following chapters. For the moment, it is enough to note that Lévi-Strauss considers one of the virtues of his tabulation of the four disciplines in question (history, sociology, ethnography, ethnology) to be that it resolves the state of conflict which has often existed between them (298; 349). Because each discipline has a precisely defined place, both similar to and distinct from its neighbours, their relationship is one of complementarity, of interlocking boundaries, rather than of conflict. Of course, it could be

---

[22] The metaphor of the periodic table in this particular instance is mine, though Lévi-Strauss himself uses the analogy on a number of occasions to describe the finite repertories of linguistic and cultural systems. See for example, *TT2*, 178; *TT1*, 205; *SA1*, 58; *AS1*, 66.

argued that the situation described here is non-conflictual precisely because it essentializes the characteristics (the 'fundamental attitudes') of each discipline and abstracts from the actual history of their conflicts. The ideal and ahistorical situation Lévi-Strauss describes therefore reduces present and previous dissent to an underlying harmony – a description which does not, it should be said, take into account the inherent violence of its own categorization of the human and social sciences. Despite the claimed arbitrariness of the positive and negative signs used in the table above, their application to the disciplines in question, in accordance with the specified criteria, cannot be neutral. Inevitably, a hierarchy is implicit in the relative distribution of these signs. At the top of this hierarchy is anthropology, which combines the empirical strengths of ethnography with the 'mechanical' models of ethnology. Next is history, which is based on empirical observation but whose models are only of the approximate, 'statistical' kind. Finally, there is sociology, which, having two minus signs attached to it, is both deprived of an empirical base and, like history, restricted to the formulation of statistical models. The signs themselves are claimed to be arbitrary, but their effect on our perception of the relative positions of these disciplines is not.

The downgrading of sociology implicit in Lévi-Strauss's tabulation of the disciplines is continued when he widens the focus of analysis to include the exact or natural sciences. It is at this point that the closely knit family of disciplines begins to disintegrate (in the original French, the term repeatedly used is *éclater*, to explode, to break up). In a second moment of his analysis or classification, Lévi-Strauss considers whether the human and social sciences have succeeded in attaining a degree of objectivity comparable to that of the natural sciences, if one accepts that the natural sciences are the ideal model of objective research. His response, predictably, is that only post-Saussurean linguistics can be said to have fully satisfied such criteria. Linguistics is therefore the first amongst the 'confused mass' of the human and social sciences to scale the interdisciplinary wall separating them from the exact sciences (299; 351–2). The problem remains, nonetheless, as to how the remainder of disciplines might be categorized: who, asks Lévi-Strauss, is to be the judge? (300–1; 353, 354).[23] His conclusion is that the interdisciplinary bridge between the exact and the human sciences is selective, concerning only the most progressive research programmes (*les recherches 'de pointe'*): 'Thus, in the five cases considered, we are dealing with a research which implies a close collaboration between certain social and human sciences (linguistics, ethnology, psychology, logic, philosophy) and some of the hard sciences (mathematics, human anatomy and physiology, zoology)' (305; 358). On the strength of this close collaboration – for example, the ethnologist and linguist have more in common with

---

[23] This question confirms the reader's suspicion that Lévi-Strauss's categorization, like all categorization, also possesses a certain performative (legislative) force.

the neurologist and ethologist than with the economist or political scientist – Lévi-Strauss is able to propose a further subdivision: what he has been referring to more or less conjointly as the human *and* social sciences now breaks down into the human sciences on the one hand, and the social sciences on the other. Detaching from the human and social sciences the arts and literature, which have no aspirations to scientific status, he defines the social sciences as including law, economics, politics and 'some branches of sociology and social psychology', and the human sciences as including prehistory, archaeology and history, anthropology, linguistics, philosophy, logic and psychology. Working from this definition, the one basic criterion for the distinction between the social and human sciences becomes apparent, though the distinction itself is based on a difficult truth which is not always willingly acknowledged: the social sciences are firmly established within the society that has produced them, they prepare their students for a practical and professional life in the service of that society, and in this way quite happily serve the status quo. The human sciences, on the other hand, though possessing the same object as the social sciences (humanity and society), offer an external perspective on that object (306–7; 359–60). The terms used by Lévi-Strauss to describe this extra-social viewpoint are interesting: he claims that the human sciences refuse any 'complicity' with or 'indulgence' towards their object of study; they are 'intransigent' in their refusal to involve themselves directly in the affairs of their own society. By virtue of this detached perspective, the human sciences share a greater affinity with the exact sciences than do the social sciences. If the social sciences use technical procedures borrowed from the exact sciences, then such borrowings are 'extrinsic', whereas the human sciences are inspired by the actual methodology of the exact sciences.[24] The human sciences have learnt from the exact sciences that one must pass behind appearances in order to understand (and eventually change) the world, whereas the social sciences accept the world as it is (307–10; 360–3).

Lévi-Strauss's table of disciplines is therefore redrawn in that one now has on the one side the exact and human sciences, and on the other, the social sciences. What before was a 'correlation' between the human and social sciences now becomes, in Lévi-Strauss's words, an 'opposition' (307; 360). Of course, this is all framed in a general description of the various disciplines, but it is clear that in describing the distinctive approach of the human and social sciences, Lévi-Strauss has again placed anthropology and sociology on opposite sides

---

[24] The distinction between 'external' and 'internal' is essential to Lévi-Strauss's conception of interdisciplinarity, which does not consist in the superficial borrowings that characterize the normal mode of exchange between various disciplines, but implies a more radical assimilation of new methodologies. Doubtless the future convergence of the sciences – exact, human and social – which Lévi-Strauss so frequently predicts in his earlier texts, depends on such 'internal' communication.

of a disciplinary fence. In fact, this realignment of disciplines echoes other statements he has made on the distinction between sociology and anthropology. The idea of the sociologist's essential implication in society, as opposed to the anthropologist's habitual detachment, was already being put forward in *Structural Anthropology*:

If a French sociologist of the twentieth century works out a general theory of social life, it will inevitably and quite legitimately (for this attempted distinction is in no way a criticism)[25] reveal itself as the work of a twentieth-century French sociologist; whereas the anthropologist undertaking the same task will endeavour, instinctively and deliberately ... to formulate a theory applicable not only to his own fellow countrymen and contemporaries, but to the most distant native population. (*SA*1, 362–3; *AS*1, 396–7)

He goes on to conclude that the distanced or defamiliarized perspective offered by anthropology, with its observation and description of 'strange and remote societies', means that its analyses are of a greater level of generality than those of sociology: 'We see therefore why sociology can be regarded, and rightly regarded, sometimes as a special form of anthropology ... and sometimes as the discipline which occupies first place in the hierarchy of the social sciences; for it undoubtedly occupies not merely a particular position but a *position of privilege*' (363; 397). This is an interesting manoeuvre: on the one hand, sociology is a special case of anthropology, a subset of that discipline; on the other hand, it is a privileged case in that in regional terms (within the social sciences) it is the master discipline. It has the internal rigour of Euclidean geometry, if one accepts its limited perspective, while anthropology would be comparable to a non-Euclidean geometry.[26] The point is that this manoeuvre places anthropology above sociology but at the same time apart from it, so that one could say of Lévi-Strauss's anthropology that its circumference is everywhere but its centre nowhere.

This description of the place of anthropology, within a certain topography of the human and social sciences, needs to be qualified. The fact that in both volumes of *Structural Anthropology* Lévi-Strauss conceives of anthropology as a more general science of humanity and society than sociology does not mean that anthropology is simply a more abstract moment of socio-anthropological thought. If, as defined above, anthropology as a human science is considered to be closer to the natural sciences, by virtue of its supposed detachment from its object, then it is again more scientific in comparison with the social sciences in that ethnography, the collection of data in the field, anchors anthropology firmly

[25] The remark in parentheses is omitted in the translation.

[26] The analogy is Lévi-Strauss's. Lévi-Strauss is frequently given to comparing what he considers the novel or non-conventional (decentring and generalizing) perspective of structural anthropology to the perspectival revolutions in the history of the exact sciences: the Copernican revolution, general relativity or, as is the case here, non-Euclidean geometry. See also, *CLS*1, 17–18; *EC*, 17–18.

in the concrete. Anthropology is therefore, via ethnography, closer to the 'real' and the particular, while at the same time providing a more powerful description of humanity in general. The insistence on the concrete basis of anthropological knowledge is an important component in Lévi-Strauss's demarcation of anthropology from sociology and other disciplines. In the passage quoted above, for example, he reminds us that 'In some countries, particularly in continental Europe ... sociology follows the tradition of a social philosophy, in which knowledge (acquired at second or third hand) of concrete research carried out by others serves merely to buttress hypotheses' (362; 395–6). A similar critique is implicit in his distinction between the study of *realia* and *generalia*:

All the disciplines dealing with a concrete subject – be this subject total or partial – are grouped in the same category if we want to distinguish them from other branches of the social and human sciences, which seek to reach less *realia* than *generalia*. For example, social psychology, and no doubt sociology also – if we want to assign to it a specific aim and style which would clearly isolate it from ethnography. (*SA2*, 296; *AS2*, 348)

Contemporary sociology is thus, in Lévi-Strauss's mind, more philosophical and speculative than empirical and objective. Anthropology, on the other hand, subsuming as we have seen the empirical moment of ethnography and its synthesis in ethnology, is a truly objective science. If it is given to abstraction and speculation, then this is only as the result of a faithful and arduous apprenticeship of the concrete (24; 35).[27]

From the texts considered in this chapter, covering the period 1949–64, there emerges therefore a coherent and consistent picture of the place of anthropology and of its specificity as a discipline. However, if the ensemble of texts dealing with the question of the disciplines and the relations between disciplines presents an apparently unified perspective, then this is not entirely without its complications. While, in accordance with the nebular metaphor described above, Lévi-Strauss's apparent ambition for anthropology is for it to occupy a place at the gravitational centre of the human and social sciences, then at the same time his desire is that it should remain somehow *eccentric* in relation to these other disciplines. In this respect, perhaps a more precise metaphor for the place of anthropology is that of the statue or monument described in *Structural Anthropology*: 'It has, as it were, its feet planted on the natural sciences, its back resting against the humanistic studies, and its eyes directed towards the social sciences' (*SA1*, 361; *AS1*, 395). In the light of the 'structural' analysis of the disciplines, examined above, the meaning of this analogy is at first quite

---

[27] 'Since the traditional social sciences (sociology, political science, law, and economics) seem incapable of dealing with anything but abstractions, anthropology feels increasingly aware of its traditional calling, which is to constitute a *study of man* in the true sense of the word. Its mission, then, is, in the first place to observe and to describe; secondly to analyse and classify; finally to isolate constants and formulate laws' ('Panorama of Anthropology (1950–1952)', *Diogenes* 2 (Spring 1953), 90; 'Panorama de l'ethnologie (1950–1952)', *Diogène* 2 (April 1953), 121).

clear: anthropology belongs to the human sciences, while it has its feet firmly on the bedrock of the natural sciences (it is based on empirical observation and remains resolutely detached from its object). A problem arises, however, when one considers the third term of the analogy. What does Lévi-Strauss mean when he says that anthropology has its eyes 'directed towards' the social sciences? This image could be said to express the present separation of the human sciences and the social sciences, but also their future reconciliation. Using another of Lévi-Strauss's topographical metaphors, the social sciences are in this sense the *horizon* of anthropology: the terrestrial globe of knowledge being round, the human, exact and social sciences are all destined one day to converge (*SA2*, 311; *AS2*, 364).

But the look cast by anthropology in the direction of the social sciences is a fundamentally ambivalent one. The horizon of convergence projected by Lévi-Strauss is arguably never reached, even by the general anthropology proposed in the two volumes of *Structural Anthropology*. This is not necessarily because of any essential disjuncture between the different disciplines in question, though in retrospect Lévi-Strauss's confidence in the potential of interdisciplinary exchange between the human and natural sciences might seem exaggerated; rather, it is due to Lévi-Strauss's own vision of the place of anthropology as being at the same time a central and a marginal one. From the epistemological and methodological point of view it is central: by comparison with sociology and the social sciences, anthropology is both a more universal and a more down-to-earth (concrete, empirical) discipline. From the point of view of utility or function, on the other hand, anthropology is a marginal discourse. It will be remembered that Lévi-Strauss thinks sociology and the social sciences are essentially conservative in function: their role is not to change or modify the society they describe. Anthropology, by contrast, is more *authentic* than its social scientific cousins in that it is also a potentially radical discourse, a quality which sets it apart from the conventional community of disciplines.

We will be examining Lévi-Strauss's conception of the moral missions of anthropology in chapter 4. In the present context, it is interesting to note that his construction of this decentred anthropology is reflected in his view of the institutional placement of the discipline, briefly set forth in *Structural Anthropology*. On the institutional level, he argues, anthropology cannot merge with the social sciences, which are on the point of gaining independent status within the university system; nor can it attach itself to the arts or science faculties. As he sees it, anthropology falls somewhere between these three faculties, in a kind of institutional no-man's land. The ideal solution, he concludes, would be the school or institute (*SA1*, 361; *AS1*, 394–5). That this effectively places anthropology on the margins of the traditional centres of academic teaching and research in France is no accident. At this point, in 1954, Lévi-Strauss was himself writing from such a position, as a member of the Ecole Pratique des Hautes Etudes in

Paris. Five years later, his election to the first chair of social anthropology at the Collège de France achieved the institutional visibility he sought for anthropology. Historically, both the Ecole Pratique des Hautes Etudes and the Collège de France have been primarily research institutions, separate from the university, and hence free from the constraints and obligations of normal university teaching and administration. Their teaching programmes are based on the research activities of their members rather than on the traditional university syllabus. This position of marginality is also a position of power, as Pierre Bourdieu points out. While members of these institutions might be more or less excluded from the normal decision-making processes in the university, and while the Ecole Pratique des Hautes Etudes, for example, was until recently dependent on the university for the validation of its qualifications, both institutions possess considerable symbolic capital in that their members are viewed as constituting the vanguard of knowledge rather than its simple reproduction.[28]

Bourdieu cites Lévi-Strauss as an exemplary case of the intellectual who has pursued a career outside or on the margins of the traditional French university system.[29] Our more general question here is what this might mean for his own discipline, anthropology. If Lévi-Strauss himself comes to occupy the positions of marginal power he projects as being the ideal placement for anthropology, does this express something that is essential to anthropology itself? Again, this is a question which will be treated in subsequent chapters, both in the context of Lévi-Strauss's conception of the missions of anthropology, and in the context of his autobiographical work: the institutional marginality of anthropology noted above also seems, rather paradoxically, to be a reflection of the personal history of the individual Lévi-Strauss. The 'singular crossroads of disciplines at which anthropology stands' in 1954 is equally the singular position of the individual who in the same year will begin writing *Tristes tropiques*.

This chapter has focused on texts dealing with what could be termed the external aspect of anthropology, that is, questions concerning its *interface* with other disciplines rather than the detail of its internal constitution. It has shown Lévi-Strauss's increasing role during the postwar period as the principal spokesperson for French anthropology, who provides a coherent and wide-ranging programme for his discipline and a vision for its future development. As we have seen, this kind of overview does not simply describe the place of the new discipline within a given interdisciplinary context, it also projects the *ideal* place of that discipline in such a context. Inevitably, this process of self-definition entails the redefinition of boundaries with adjacent disciplines. In the specific historical

---

[28] Bourdieu, Pierre, *Homo academicus* (Paris: Editions de Minuit, 1984), pp. 140–8; *Homo academicus*, trans. Peter Collier (Cambridge: Polity Press, 1988), pp. 105–12. See also Victor Karady, 'Durkheim, les sciences sociales et l'Université', 298 n.60, and 'Stratégies de réussite', 62–3.

[29] *Homo academicus*, pp. 142–3; p. 108.

context of postwar France, anthropology's adjacent disciplines are history and sociology. But Lévi-Strauss goes further than simply attempting to free French anthropology from its historical subordination to sociology: he also challenges the place of sociology and history as the traditional centres of social scientific enquiry. It is important in fact to emphasize the extent to which Lévi-Strauss appears to be dictating the terms of the debate between the disciplines at this point. The responses of his counterparts in history and sociology, Braudel and Gurvitch, examined above, would seem for the most part to be reactions to an agenda that he, Lévi-Strauss, has already set. It should also be remembered that what is at stake here is not simply the internal balance of power between disciplines within the university, but their sphere of influence in the wider intellectual constituency which has traditionally been so important in France.[30] In the 1950s and 1960s, for a number of reasons, not the least of which is Lévi-Strauss's astute promotion of his discipline, anthropology becomes in effect one of the essential reference points of intellectual discourse in France. The rise of structuralism, it could be argued, is historically inseparable from the prestige of anthropology as the most theoretically advanced of the human sciences.

The question of the more general field of influence of anthropology brings us to a discipline which has been largely absent, if virtually present, in Lévi-Strauss's definition of the place of anthropology – that is, philosophy. In spite of the apparent rivalry existing between the three 'nuclear' disciplines of history, sociology and anthropology, such competition is nevertheless conducted *en famille*, so to speak. The family, to continue the metaphor, is that of the social and human sciences; despite their quarrels, the aspiration of each is to the scientific treatment of their object, whether that object be society in particular or humanity in general. Braudel, it will be remembered, normally refers to this family as *les sciences de l'homme*, the sciences of man. Lévi-Strauss, more exclusively, prefers to regard sociology as a distant cousin, and thus makes a rigid distinction between the social and human sciences. Hence anthropology is defined as a *science humaine*, but, if one reviews the membership of this side of the family as enumerated above, so is philosophy. One might pause to ask (which Lévi-Strauss, in his somewhat summary classification of the disciplines, does not) whether philosophy is a 'science' in the same way as history, sociology and anthropology have been defined as 'sciences', each of them dealing in its own manner with a determinable body of 'facts'. The response would probably have to be in the negative. The object of philosophy has traditionally included the entirety of what is human, but its style or approach has by no means been restricted to the strictly 'scientific'. In the more circumscribed context of

---

[30] In his interview with Didier Eribon, Lévi-Strauss twice refers to the preoccupation of French historians during the 1960s with the popularity of anthropology in this wider, extra-academic sphere (*CLS2*, 65, 123; *PL*, 96, 172).

postwar France, and in the intellectual milieu described above, on the other hand, it is easy to see how anthropology and philosophy become competing discourses, to the extent that Lévi-Strauss's reconstruction of ethnology as anthropology not only displaces sociology but also threatens to absorb philosophy. This is particularly evident if one reconsiders his twofold demarcation of anthropology from sociology, according to which anthropology is both a more objective and a more authentic discipline than sociology because it is not complicit with the social systems it describes. However problematic this assertion may be – at the most simple level the equation between 'distance' and 'objectivity' could be questioned – it is clear that anthropology's claim to a certain critical and ethical status places it on terrain already occupied by philosophy. The virulence of some of the exchanges between the participants in the debate around structuralism in the 1960s owes something at least to the implicitly philosophical programme of Lévi-Strauss's anthropology, as will become apparent in the following chapters.

As stated above, this chapter has focused primarily on the external aspect of anthropology's relations with other disciplines, how Lévi-Strauss's construction of anthropology affects the status and identity of proximate disciplines. This does not mean, of course, that Lévi-Strauss's contribution to sociological theory is of secondary importance; on the contrary, it is an integral part of his determination of the rightful place of anthropology within the human sciences. The claims of anthropology to scientific interest would mean nothing if they were not matched by a coherent theoretical framework. It is to Lévi-Strauss's construction of this framework that we will now turn.

2   The model of exchange

> La théorie de la réciprocité n'est pas en cause. Elle reste aujourd'hui, pour
> la pensée ethnologique, établie sur une base aussi ferme que la théorie de
> gravitation l'est en astronomie.
> (It is not the theory of reciprocity which is in doubt. In anthropology this the-
> ory continues to stand, as soundly based as the gravity theory in astronomy.)[1]

In his earlier work, like many anthropologists of his generation, Lévi-Strauss
draws attention to the necessary and urgent task of maintaining and extending
the empirical foundations of anthropology in the practice of fieldwork. This
is seen as especially critical in the case of France, given the relatively late
development of the discipline in the country. As his more empirically minded
critics have never tired of pointing out, Lévi-Strauss's own fieldwork experience
was a comparatively limited one, and he is by inclination a theorist rather
than a fieldworker.[2] This personal bias is freely acknowledged by Lévi-Strauss
himself; in his mind, the imperative of data collection is matched by the necessity
of bringing some order and coherence to the abundance of material it has
generated. The idea of the infinite extension of data and the problem of its
synthesis is a constant leitmotif of Lévi-Strauss's structuralism. Biographically,
it might be traced back to his post-fieldwork experience in North America,
where over a period of several years he assimilated the mass of anthropological
literature deposited in the New York Public Library.

Of course, the synthesis which Lévi-Strauss began to envisage in the
1940s required a theoretical framework, a framework not immediately to hand
in Anglo-American anthropology, despite the decisive influence of the latter in his early formation. There are numerous echoes of Boas, Lowie and
Radcliffe-Brown in Lévi-Strauss's earlier work, but for the fundamentals of
his theoretical work on social organization, he returns to the French sociological tradition, to the school of Durkheim and Mauss. While Lévi-Strauss's
relationship with the work of Durkheim was a qualified and often ambivalent one, his allegiance to Mauss was from the start more immediate and less

---

[1] *SA*1, 162; *AS*1, 179–80.
[2] For example, Edmund Leach, *Lévi-Strauss* (Glasgow: Fontana, 1974), pp. 18–19.

reserved.[3] His familiarity with the work of Marcel Mauss, and more specifically with the theory of exchange elaborated in *The Gift*, must date from the early 1930s at least, and is clearly discernible in the monographs based on his early fieldwork in Brazil. It therefore predates that other decisive influence, the encounter with Jakobson and structural linguistics in 1942, by up to ten years. In the very first phase of Lévi-Strauss's work, therefore, the predominant theoretical influence is Mauss, and his 'structuralism' is an implicit one. As he himself puts it: 'I was a structuralist without knowing it'.[4] In this chapter I will be concentrating on Lévi-Strauss's original mediation of Mauss, and also on how he attempts to articulate and assimilate the model of exchange with the linguistic model. However, in order to properly understand the nature and detail of this mediation it is first necessary to examine the main elements of Mauss's theory of exchange, as it is set forth in *The Gift*.

The paradigm of the gift

The Gift was first published in 1924 in the *Année sociologique*, the journal founded by Emile Durkheim, though Mauss's interest in the gift dates back to the early 1900s at least.[5] Despite the frequent tendency among anthropologists – Lévi-Strauss included – to contrast Durkheim's rather abstract style of reasoning with Mauss's more concrete approach, there are inevitably strong thematic and conceptual links between Mauss's work and that of his teacher and

---

[3]   In his 1945 review of French sociology, dedicated to Mauss, while recognizing Durkheim's fundamental contribution to the discipline, Lévi-Strauss is critical of his methodology, for example, his tendency to resort to historical as opposed to functional explanations, and his neglect of the link between psychological and sociological processes. Despite the mitigating circumstance of context (Durkheim had not benefited from subsequent advances in linguistics and psychology), the contrastive portrait Lévi-Strauss gives of Durkheim and Mauss is visibly biased in favour of the latter. Durkheim is of the old school; rhetorically, his work is heavy and pedantic, weighed down by laborious demonstration and dogmatically stated conclusions. His training in philosophy means that he always approaches sociological and anthropological material from an external perspective. By contrast, Mauss combines phenomenal erudition and a basic intellectual curiosity with an intuitive feel for material and the capacity for imaginative insight. Whereas Durkheim shows a marked preference for synthetic reconstruction and the drawing of universal conclusions, Mauss restricts himself to the integrated analysis of a limited set of cases. Unlike Durkheim, Mauss is aware of the problem of the relationship between sociological and psychological phenomena and sensitive to developments in contemporary psychology (*Sociology in the Twentieth Century*, pp. 515–30; *La Sociologie au XX*ᵉ *siècle*, pp. 520–37). Lévi-Strauss's relative evaluation of the two men remains more or less the same in his inaugural lecture at the Collège de France in 1960 (*SA2*, 5–9; *AS2*, 13–18), though by this stage his attitude towards Durkheim has softened somewhat (see also in the same volume, which is dedicated to Durkheim, 'What Ethnology Owes to Durkheim', *SA2*, 44–8; *AS2*, 57–62).

[4]   *CLS2*, 41; *PL*, 62–3.

[5]   Marcel Mauss, *Essai sur le don. Forme et raison de l'échange dans les sociétés archaïques*, in *Sociologie et anthropologie* (Paris: Presses Universitaires de France, 1950), pp. 143–279; *The Gift. The Form and Reason for Exchange in Archaic Societies*, trans. W.D. Halls (London: Routledge, 1990). Page references will henceforth be given in the main text.

collaborator. In *The Gift* Mauss is still working very much within the framework of Durkheimian sociology, a fundamental concern of which was the problem of social solidarity or social cohesion. Historically, this can be situated in the context of Third Republic France, where the disappearance of traditional forms of morality such as those sanctioned by religion and the family was prompting questions as to how social solidarity could be maintained in a modern secular and industrial state. The question, as it was formulated in sociology, was how do different groups, different sections of a society manage to coexist and cooperate so that those groups still constitute a society? One finds a preliminary response to this question in Durkheim's work *The Division of Labour* (1893), where he distinguished between the 'mechanical' solidarity of traditional societies, based on kinship and shared religious belief, and the 'organic' solidarity of secular, industrial societies, where the individual's social affiliations were more and more determined by membership of occupational or professional groups. In his later work, and in his last publication, *The Elementary Forms of Religious Life* (1912), Durkheim turned more directly to ethnology as the primary source of his data, and came to formulate the idea of collective representations that are created and reaffirmed in moments of social 'effervescence', that is, moments of ritual and ceremonial significance. The social bond – social solidarity – derives from the heightened sense of a shared existence experienced on such occasions.

I am dwelling on the example of Durkheim because *The Gift* is very much a continuation on the theme of social cohesion. The gift, as Mauss defines it in his essay, is a mechanism for the structuring and maintaining of relations within and between different social groups and, indeed, between different so-cieties. It could be said that Mauss's model of cohesion is more dynamic and also more comprehensive than Durkheim's – it is a synthetic view of social relations. But, ultimately, it is guided by the same preoccupation; in *The Gift* Mauss is still working squarely within the Durkheimian paradigm of social cohesion.

In Mauss's essay the gift is not really a gift but rather reciprocal gifts, the exchange of gifts. Mauss's preferred term for such exchange is *prestations* and *contre-prestations*,[6] denoting the back and forth movement, or *circulation* of presents between participants. The function of the gift, as it emerges in the essay, is to bind together different social groups in circuits of reciprocity. For Mauss the act of donation is therefore never disinterested and never arbitrary. The gift is never a pure gift: it is always motivated, consciously or unconsciously, by this primary function of *articulation*, the joining or relating of what is distinct.

---

[6] The English translation of Mauss's essay renders 'prestations' as 'services'. As this seems an unnecessary narrowing of the sense of the French, I will be following Marshall Sahlins's practice of retaining the original term (Marshall Sahlins, 'The Spirit of the Gift', in *Stone Age Economics* (London: Routledge, 1972), pp. 149–84).

This is an essential feature of how Durkheim and Mauss conceptualize social morphology, that is, society as a confederation of distinct but related (articulated) groups.

The preceding definition gives a general but rather abstract idea of Mauss's conception of the gift. It would therefore be useful at this stage to detail the different elements of his model of exchange, so as to give some substance to the definition. Probably the most effective way to do this is to follow the order of exposition of the essay itself, as it is from this exposition or 'demonstration', as Mauss calls it, that a definite model of human relations can be seen to emerge.

Mauss's first major point in *The Gift* is that exchange in 'archaic', non-Western societies is never simply the equivalent of the exchange of goods in industrial, capitalist economies. First, because it is not individuals that exchange, but groups, even if those groups are mediated through their chiefs: 'The contracting parties are [moral] entities: clans, tribes, and families that confront and oppose one another either in groups who meet face to face in one spot, or through their chiefs, or in both these ways at once' (5; 150–1). The exchange Mauss refers to is therefore a collective and not a private phenomenon – it is distinct from individual economic transaction. A second distinction Mauss makes between 'archaic' and utilitarian economies is that it is not simply tangible goods, goods with a calculable use-value, that are exchanged, but also dances, rituals, hospitality, different types of services and so on. Mauss calls this phenomenon the *'system of total prestations'* (5–6; 151). The effect or function of this system of mutual prestation is to set up relations of complementarity and collaboration between the groups involved. Mauss describes this as a complex web, a network of interrelations maintained through the constant circulation of gifts (6; 152). It is at this point, in connection with the notions of interaction, interrelation and circulation, that Mauss introduces the first properly ethnographic example in *The Gift*, that of the native American Indians of the Northwest coast. He refers briefly to the Tlingit and the Haida as examples of total prestation, but very quickly moves on to cite the Kwakiutl custom of potlatch. He admits that this custom is a rare and developed form of the total prestation, but at the same time he insists, rather paradoxically, that it is a 'typical' form of exchange. There follows a description of the potlatch ceremony. What is remarkable about the potlatch, says Mauss, is the agonistic nature of the ceremonies dedicated to the exchange of gifts. There is intense rivalry between the exchanging parties as to who can give the most, and in some instances objects are actually destroyed.[7] On the

---

[7] Later in *The Gift* Mauss gives the well-known example of emblazoned copper plates that are thrown into the sea, proving that the donor is not attached to these valuable objects and that he is powerful enough to destroy without calculation (44–5; 221–6).

other hand, the rivalry characteristic of this form of exchange can in some cases lead to open conflict or even the putting to death of the chiefs or nobles representing particular 'clans' or 'tribes'.[8] What Mauss is describing then is total prestation, that is, ceremonial exchange between two parties, but with the additional element of conflict and competition: 'This act of prestation on the part of the chief takes on an extremely marked agonistic character. It is essentially usurious and sumptuary. It is a struggle between nobles to establish a hierarchy amongst themselves from which their clan will benefit at a later date' (6; 152–3). Mauss proposes, quite logically, that we call this exceptional form of gift exchange '*total prestations of an agonistic type*' (7; 152–3).

In the following chapters of *The Gift* Mauss performs a geographical circuit around the cultures of the Pacific rim, selecting what he considers to be the relevant ethnographic data, in each case extending and qualifying the initial formulation of the gift. Thus the Polynesian data studied in the first chapter provides an illustration of the compulsory nature of donation, in what Mauss shows to be the threefold obligation for participants to give, to receive and to return presents (13; 161). The sometimes excessive generosity Mauss observes in the total prestation is therefore a socially prescribed attitude and not a contingent aspect of individual psychological disposition.[9] A second qualification offered by the Polynesian data is that objects exchanged are inseparable from the participants, in that these things are seen as representing literally the souls of the participants, so that the gift retains something of the donor even after the act of donation (12–14; 160–4). The implicit counterpoint here is contractual and utilitarian exchange in which the link between exchanging parties is broken once the transaction is concluded.

The next significant features of Mauss's model are provided in the second chapter of *The Gift* by the cultures of Melanesia. The central example is the Trobriand Islanders, for which Mauss's principal source is Malinowski's celebrated *Argonauts of the Western Pacific* (1922). The concept which predominates here is that of circulation. The elaborate and protracted exchange ceremonies named *kula*, which Mauss describes as 'noble' exchange (it seems to be restricted to the chiefs of the different groups involved), represent a continual circuit of gifts between the participants. Malinowski calls this the 'kula ring', characterized by a 'constant giving and taking', so that objects exchanged rarely remain in the same hands for any length of time. The extremely competitive

---

[8] On the problematic history of the use of the term 'tribe' in anthropology, see Richard Jenkins, *Rethinking Ethnicity: Arguments and Explorations* (London: Sage, 1997), pp. 16–18; Gwyn Prins, 'Tribe', in Adam and Jessica Kuper (eds.), *The Social Science Encyclopedia* (London: Routledge, 1989).

[9] The notion of obligation and collective constraint is of course thoroughly Durkheimian. Throughout *The Gift* Mauss keeps the gift firmly within this collective dimension of the obligatory norm.

nature of these ceremonies prompts Mauss to compare the *kula* with the potlatch (21; 176).[10]

Mauss is anxious to underline that though the *kula*-type ceremonies are most often mediated through chiefs, the objects exchanged are not *for* the chiefs. These objects are provided by relatives of a lower rank, and when the *kula* expedition is over, the chiefs redistribute presents received to subordinate village chiefs, to clans and even to the common people of related clans (29; 188). The important point here is that for Mauss the 'noble' exchange of the *kula* is not simply a closed circuit of exchange between chiefs; its result is a differential redistribution of wealth to the community rather than the accumulation of wealth by powerful individuals. Again, there is the idea of the gift as a collective phenomenon engaging the whole group: a few pages later Mauss notes that these societies are incapable of thinking of the chief as separate from the clan; he *is* the clan (32; 193). This point is important because it affects the whole of Mauss's moral interpretation of the gift given in the conclusion to the essay. Mauss consistently avoids discussion of the difficult question of the power relations implicit in ceremonial exchange, and, faithful to Durkheim, emphasizes the redistributive and socially binding rather than the hierarchical aspects of *kula* and potlatch transactions.

At this stage in Mauss's demonstration the model of exchange is virtually complete. To summarize the main elements of the model: first, there is the general concept of total prestation, that is, non-utilitarian exchange involving whole communities and a whole range of non-tangible as well as tangible products. Second is the threefold structure of the obligation to give, to receive and to return: generosity is a social imperative rather than a private or individual virtue. Third, there is the moral and spiritual continuum of donor, object and recipient: in gift economies it is not so much the objects exchanged as the moral and social relations created through exchange that are at stake. Fourth is the phenomenon of circulation, implicitly opposed to accumulation and use-value. For Mauss circulation constitutes a socially binding force to the extent that its corollary is redistribution within the group: objects received do not necessarily remain in the hands of the individual representatives of the group. Finally there is the exacerbated form of total prestation characteristic of the potlatch, total prestation of an agonistic type. It is to the potlatch and to the American Northwest that Mauss returns in the second chapter of *The Gift* to complete the properly ethnographic part of his exposition. Here the different American peoples reviewed – Tlingit, Haida, Tsimshian and Kwakiutl – in their

---

[10] This assimilation is typical of the chapters on Melanesian and Polynesian society. In chapter 2 there is a continual and, it could be argued, tendentious, rhetorical inflection of the *kula* towards the potlatch, even if the violently excessive aspects of the potlatch, as described in the introduction, are clearly absent. See Christopher Johnson, 'Mauss's Gift: The Persistence of a Paradigm', *Modern and Contemporary France* 4.3 (July 1996), 307–17.

turn illustrate the various characteristics of the gift economies treated so far. The difference is that in the societies of the Northwest coast these practices are, he says, more radical and more marked. Two aspects in particular are more in evidence: first the notion of credit, that is, of the deferred return of the gift with interest; second, the notion of honour: it is the ranking and reputation of chiefs which is at stake in potlatch exchange, so much so that in extreme cases a failure to return with interest results in the loss of 'face', the loss of rank, even the loss of one's freedom. As Mauss shows, the combination of these two elements of usurious exchange and competition for social position leads to an escalating contest for honour, where the objective is literally to crush, to flatten the rival. The extreme consequence of such rivalry is the ostentatious destruction of goods described earlier in the essay (35–7; 198–202).

Having demonstrated in the first two chapters the geographical extension of the gift economy in the Pacific rim cultures, in the third chapter Mauss goes on to show the historical extension of these practices in Indo-European cultures. The purpose of this new digression is, it seems, to build a kind of bridge between the alterity of the alternative economies described so far and our own contemporary (industrial, utilitarian) economies, by showing that total prestation is not totally alien to modern society and that it can be retrieved from our own past – hence the title of the third chapter: 'Survivals of These Principles in Ancient Systems of Law and Ancient Economies'. In fact, the separation of the economic from the moral and the social spheres is, according to Mauss, only a comparatively recent event in our history, an invention of ancient Semitic and Greco-Roman culture (47–8; 229). This point leads him, quite predictably, to the conclusion in the fourth and final part of the essay, where he insists that our contemporary societies still rest on the 'bedrock' of a pre-Semitic, pre-Greco-Roman gift economy, that all is not lost, and that we can in a sense 'return' to these practices. The application of ethnographic data to contemporary problems of morality and economics is therefore a mediated one; in order to conclude, Mauss has first to show that we are similar to 'archaic' societies in our own past.

What is perhaps most interesting about Mauss's conclusion is that it is not a single conclusion, but in fact three separate conclusions, each with its own section and title: 'Moral Conclusions'; 'Conclusions for Economic Sociology and Political Economy'; finally, a 'Conclusion Regarding General Sociology and Morality'. The first and second conclusions can be dealt with together, to the extent that they address essentially the same question, which is the distinction between rationalist-utilitarian economies and gift economies. As has been seen, Mauss's proposal is that we return to the spirit of the gift, as it is practised in 'archaic' and ancient economies. Here, he proposes more concretely and more specifically that the narrowly rationalist and utilitarian practices of capitalist economies should be replaced by an organized system of social security, with a shift from state to corporate responsibility, a greater sense of professional

morality, and (in what seems to be an allusion to the Melanesian *kula*) an en-
lightened system of redistribution of wealth (67–8; 260–3). The first lesson that
Mauss draws from his demonstration, his first injunction, is therefore simply to
give: 'Let us adopt as the principle of our life what has always been a principle
of action and will always be so: to emerge from self, to give, freely and obli-
gatorily' (71; 265). While the injunction is a worthy one, the reader is tempted
to think that Mauss's proposals are more a reflection of the liberal-socialist
ideals of Third Republic France than of the customs of the Pacific cultures
studied earlier in the essay. Even his attempt in the second conclusion to compare the relationship between wealth and power in potlatch societies with that
in our own societies seems obvious and rather superficial (74–5; 269–70).[11] So
the first two conclusions to the essay are theoretically weak: Mauss's liberal-
socialist economics appear to be unnaturally superposed on the ethnological
demonstration of the mechanism of gift exchange, and the intervening chapter
on the 'survival' of this mechanism in Indo-European culture seems a somewhat
artificial device designed to bridge the two domains.

The third and final conclusion of *The Gift* is more interesting, and arguably
more convincing, as it is this conclusion which finally explains Mauss's fixation
on the potlatch, the fascination which this custom appears to exercise upon him.
It is preceded by what is probably one of the most quoted passages of the essay,
where he explains the heuristic principle on which his analysis has been based.
This has consisted in treating the different societies studied in the essay as
'total social facts', which means that his analysis has attempted to take into
account the totality of these societies and their institutions, at all levels and
dynamically, as they actually function. The type of sociological analysis Mauss
is advocating has therefore to be adequate to the overdetermined object that
is the total social fact; it must be a synthetic comprehension rather than an
abstract analysis of separate customs or institutions. The concept of the gift
performs this synthetic function in that it brings out the *integration* between the
different levels of a given social system: morphological, economic, religious,
legal, cultural-aesthetic (78–80; 274–6).

Following this much-quoted discourse on method, Mauss begins what in substance is an extended eulogy of the kind of societies he has been studying. Such
societies, he claims, are less serious, less individualistic and *apparently* (his
own qualification) more generous, more giving than we are (81; 277). He goes
further than this moral generalization, providing a *psychological* description
of the state of mind in which different groups make contact. It is at this point
that the demonstration moves from a sociological to a philosophical register.

---

[11] Mauss's point is that the individual is not attached to material objects in themselves but to the
status they confer, and that the motivation is therefore 'noble' rather than utilitarian, but he
provides no discussion of the moral or political ramifications of this.

He argues: 'Over a considerable period of time and in a considerable number of societies, men approached one another in a curious frame of mind, one of fear and exaggerated hostility, and of generosity that was likewise exaggerated, but such traits only appear insane to our eyes' (81; 277). This description of psychological ambivalence, worthy of Freud, goes some way to explaining the prominence given to the potlatch in *The Gift*. In its violent exaggeration of the act of donation, the potlatch seems to reveal the essence, the truth of social relations of this type, which is that they are the regulation of a relation potentially even more violent. The very excess and violence of the potlatch is a symptom of the potential conflict which it displaces.[12] The excessive, even aggressive generosity of the potlatch could thus be seen as part of a psychological and behavioural continuum the other extreme of which is total conflict. Mauss expresses this quite brutally when he says that there is no alternative, no middle way between exchange and conflict: 'This was because they had no choice. Two groups of men who meet can only either draw apart, and, if they show mistrust towards one another or issue a challenge, fight – or they can negotiate' (82; 277). It could be said then that the sociological model of exchange constructed in *The Gift* is accompanied in the conclusion by an *existential* model of human contact that would be logically prior to the empirical detail of the different ethnographic and historical cases reviewed in the essay.

From Mauss to Lévi-Strauss

Both in France and internationally, the influence of Mauss's essay on the gift is considerable, extending well beyond the academic disciplines of sociology and anthropology.[13] Indeed, the extent of diffusion of his theory of exchange is such that it could be said to have achieved the status of a paradigm, a more or less stable set of premises and assumptions within which successive generations of thinkers in the human and social sciences have worked. A number of the articles Lévi-Strauss publishes in the 1940s and also parts of his 1948 monograph on the Nambikwara are a direct application of Mauss's model.[14] However, the

---

[12] This is one of the conclusions of Sahlins's commentary of Mauss's essay, i.e., that the reason for the gift lies in its negation and regulation of a Hobbesian state of war underlying all human relations (*Stone Age Economics*, pp. 171–83).

[13] Outside of anthropology, the history of the multiple influences of *The Gift* is a complex one, but in France significant mediators include Bataille and Caillois, via the activities of the Collège de Sociologie. Bataille is especially important for his theory of expenditure (*dépense*), derived from Mauss's description of the North American potlatch ceremonies, a theory which in its turn has visibly influenced the post-existentialist generation of French thinkers.

[14] 'Guerre et commerce chez les Indiens de l'Amérique du Sud', *Renaissance* 1.1–2 (January–March 1943), 122–39; *La Vie familiale et sociale des Indiens Nambikwara* (Paris: Société des Américanistes, Gonthier, 1948); 'La Politique étrangère d'une Société Primitive', *Politique Etrangère* 2 (May 1949), 139–52. In all of these texts the essence of inter-tribal relations is seen to reside in the regulation of conflict through various forms of reciprocal exchange.

appearance of *The Elementary Structures of Kinship* in 1949 seems to mark a
new departure in this respect. Mauss's model of exchange is definitely at the
centre of the theoretical edifice Lévi-Strauss constructs in this imposing book,
but at the same time the model is given a new inflection. As its title suggests,
the main programme of the *Elementary Structures* is an attempt to reduce the
diverse forms of kinship systems found in non-Western societies to a limited
set of elementary structures, from which all observable cases could then be de-
duced or predicted. What is interesting about the book is that this contribution
to an extremely specialized branch of anthropology is accompanied by a more
general contribution to sociological theory. Lévi-Strauss is concerned not simply to bring some kind of order to the mass of data accumulated on kinship
relations, but also to determine the theoretical foundations of his analysis. This
leads him back to the properly Durkheimian question of social cohesion. For
society to exist, he claims, humans must transcend the merely biological relation between individuals. To integrate the biological group into the larger,
social sphere, it is necessary that its members do not marry within the immediate group, but with members of other groups. This is the function of the
prohibition of incest, the quasi-universal trait of human society which forbids
the sexual union of biologically proximate individuals. The reason for this
prohibition, argues Lévi-Strauss, is not a biological but a social one. What appears to be a wholly negative rule also has a positive dimension, the reverse
side of the prohibition of incest being the prescription of exogamy, ensuring
integration through intermarriage with other social groups. From this perspective, the prohibition of incest would be the most fundamental of rules, the first
rule of social integration; in Lévi-Strauss's somewhat philosophical phrasing,
it represents the passage from 'nature' to 'culture'. If, as follows from this,
the kinship ties established through exogamy are the most elementary form
of social bond, then they are not the only form. This is where Mauss's model
of exchange is introduced. After Mauss, Lévi-Strauss sees exchange or reciprocity as the most important mechanism of social cohesion, and he combines
this with his interpretation of the incest prohibition by considering exogamy
as the exchange of women. In the traditional societies studied by ethnologists,
the 'donation' of a sister or daughter to another social group creates the obligation in that group to return a sister or daughter, thus creating a lasting bond
between the groups. A more complex configuration would involve a less direct transaction, whereby the donor would receive a wife not from the second
group, but from a third party, and so on; the overall effect, i.e., social integration, would, however, be the same. Lévi-Strauss terms this 'general' as opposed
to 'restricted' exchange. As in Mauss's model, the exchange of women would
therefore be one of a number of reciprocal transactions binding together distinct
social groups, but for Lévi-Strauss it is a special category of exchange in that
its 'object' (women) is of the highest social value, and the relations it establishes the most permanent and pervasive ones. Indeed, in the conclusion of the

Principle of reciprocity
•
Prohibition of incest/Exogamy
(restricted or general exchange)
•
Cross-cousin alliance/Dual organization

Fig. 2.1

Elementary Structures exogamy is described as the *archetypal* form of exchange (481; 551).[15]

The above summary provides the essence of what might be termed the theoretical infrastructure of the *Elementary Structures*, mostly contained in the two densely argued chapters of the book's Introduction, 'Nature and Culture' and 'The Problem of Incest'. However, the element of theoretical exposition does not end with the Introduction, and continues well into the first part of the book, which is devoted to examples of restricted exchange. Exogamy, the positive aspect of the incest prohibition, is seen as a special case of exchange, its archetypical form, but logically prior to it is what Lévi-Strauss calls 'the principle of reciprocity' – a term which does not, significantly, appear in Mauss's text. The principle of reciprocity is the universal mechanism underlying all forms of exchange, including the exchange of women. In this sense, the different forms of exogamy examined in the *Elementary Structures*, restricted or general, whether it be a question of the different modalities of cross-cousin marriage or dual organization,[16] are simply 'expressions' of the principle of reciprocity. The reader is therefore presented with a hierarchy of logical types which diagrammatically could be represented as in figure 2.1.

What we will be focusing on in the following discussion is less the second and third levels of this hierarchy than its first level. The third level is relevant to the ethnological part of the *Elementary Structures*; while it might have been the occasion of much debate in the specialized domain of kinship studies, it is not of immediate concern to us here. The second level is part of the general sociological theory on which the third level is based – the theory of exogamy

---

[15] From the beginning, Lévi-Strauss has been much criticized for the androcentric bias of this interpretation of exogamy.

[16] Cross-cousin marriage refers to the rule which proscribes marriage between the children of same-sex siblings (parallel cousins) and prescribes marriage between the children of different sexes (cross cousins). Lévi-Strauss defines dual organization as 'a system in which the members of the community, whether it be a tribe or a village, are divided into two parts which maintain complex relationships varying from open hostility to very close intimacy, and with which various forms of rivalry and co-operation are usually associated' (*ESK*, 69; *SEP*, 80). The two parts, or moieties, do not necessarily play a role in matrimonial alliances, and cross-cousin marriage very frequently exists where there is no system of dual organization (S. Dreyfus: 'L'Organisation dualiste', in Pierre Bonte and Michel Izard (eds.), *Dictionnaire de l'ethnologie et de l'anthropologie* (Paris: Presses Universitaires de France, 1991)).

as a modality of exchange, summarized above. The first level belongs to what is essentially the philosophical component of the *Elementary Structures*, in that it is concerned with a *principle*, what Lévi-Strauss presents as a basic and universal trait of human behaviour. The three levels are of course not necessarily always distinct in the text itself, but in certain passages one or another of the two non-ethnological modes can be seen to predominate. Hence in the two introductory chapters discussed above, it is the second level of sociological analysis which is predominant. Later in the book, the first level is foregrounded as we are presented with what amounts to a *demonstration* of the principle of reciprocity. It is to the detail of this demonstration that we will now turn.

In the fifth chapter of the *Elementary Structures*, 'The Principle of Reciprocity', having established and illustrated the notion of exogamy as a modality of exchange, Lévi-Strauss turns to the principle of reciprocity itself. His intention is not simply to state the universality of the principle, but, as he puts it, to show how and why it works (*ESK*, 51; *SEP*, 60). The chapter begins with a standard and straightforward summary of Mauss's theory of exchange, as set forth in *The Gift*. He accepts Mauss's interpretation of the potlatch, which in spite of variations and gradations is a 'universal mode of culture' (53; 62). But, he insists (and this is the first of a series of qualifications and modifications of Mauss's model), the mentality at work here is not restricted to well-defined institutions such as the potlatch; it extends to profane as well as ceremonial instances of exchange (53; 62–3). So Lévi-Strauss's first move is to show the social relevance of gift exchange beyond the institutional and ceremonial instances concentrated on by Mauss: in traditional societies, it informs all levels of everyday life. His next qualification is to question the restriction of socially symbolic gift exchange to these so-called 'traditional' societies. Mauss, it will be remembered, had begun to do this in the conclusion of *The Gift*, but the parallels he made were for the most part elliptical and brief. In 'The Principle of Reciprocity', Lévi-Strauss provides a much more elaborate illustration of non-utilitarian exchange in Western societies, instancing the giving of flowers and other luxury articles, and finally comparing the collective phenomenon of Christmas to a giant potlatch. In this last example, there is a point-by-point correlation with Mauss's model: excessive expenditure permanently affecting family budgets; lavish Christmas cards and the superfluous duplication of presents, similar to the prestige-related destruction of goods in the potlatch; the magical quality of the present (56; 65–6).[17]

While the assimilation of a Western custom (Christmas) with a culture-specific institution such as the potlatch, like the example of gambling which follows, appears somewhat stretched and not entirely convincing, its interest to

---

[17] For a more elaborate treatment of this theme, see 'Le Père Noël supplicié', *Les Temps Modernes* 7.77 (March 1952), 1572–90.

us here lies less in the rigour of the parallel than in the desire which inspires it, that is, to establish the universality of a principle. This desire is equally evident when Lévi-Strauss moves on to the characteristic example of the offering of food (*prestations alimentaires*).[18] Again, he alternates between ethnographic material and everyday examples the (Western) reader will recognize as analogous (57–8; 67–8). However, the series of examples provided – ethnographic and non-ethnographic – all concern ceremonial forms of exchange (*repas de cérémonie*, ceremonial meals). Again he finds it necessary to qualify, to reduce or rather to relativize the collective and ceremonial aspect of reciprocity, underlining that it is not only in ceremonial meals that the ritual of exchange is present (58; 68). At this point, what hitherto has been a macroscopic (sociological) perspective is suddenly scaled down to the dimension of individual interaction. What follows is the longest and most developed example of the principle of reciprocity, an example which very quickly transcends the status of mere illustration to become more precisely a *demonstration* of that principle. Structurally and thematically, it could be said to constitute the centre of the chapter.

In cheap restaurants in the south of France, we are told, there is a whole ritual surrounding the consumption of wine. The bottle served to each customer as part of the meal may be small, and its content often undrinkable, but it is nevertheless the object of special reverence, a kind of 'rich food'. While the food itself, the solid component of the meal, meets the immediate necessity of bodily sustenance, the liquid element of wine is seen as a luxury, a non-essential celebration of the body. Each customer eats for himself (*pour soi*), but the consumption of wine is a social act. Though the content of each bottle is identical in both quantity and quality, it will be poured into one's neighbour's glass and vice versa. Materially, the participants have gained nothing from the exchange, but it is the fact of exchange rather than what has been exchanged which is important (58–9; 68–9).

Up to this point, the example of the provincial restaurant seems no more than a rather picturesque illustration of Mauss's thesis of the symbolic and non-utilitarian dimension of gift exchange. It shows a reciprocity which is almost mechanical in operation in that it is a part of received custom in the milieu in question. The illustration becomes more interesting when, still within the socio-cultural context of the restaurant, the focus is further narrowed to a situation which, one could say, is less 'structured' and for which there is apparently no immediately available code of behaviour. Two strangers are obliged to share a table in a cheap restaurant, and are facing one another, less than a metre apart. They share a certain anxiety and apprehension at this enforced intimacy, while

---

[18] According to Mauss the essential meaning of 'potlatch' is 'to feed', 'to consume' (*The Gift*, p. 6; *Essai sur le don*, p. 152).

their silence is mutually embarrassing, even if there is no sign of hostility on either side. The exchange of wine resolves this difficult situation and dispels the mutual uncertainty by creating a relation between the two individuals. Lévi-Strauss stresses the irreversibility of the process once this first step has been taken. The relationship between the two strangers has so far been one of random encounter and of indifference. The offer of wine inevitably elicits a response – the other person must either accept or refuse. In either case, refusal or acceptance, there is no possibility of return to the *status quo ante*; henceforth, the relationship can only be one of either cordiality or hostility. In the case of acceptance, reciprocation will ensue, thus inaugurating a series of exchanges, in addition to that of wine, between the two participants. Also stressed is the asymmetrical nature of the situation: the process described necessarily requires an initiator; one of the participants must open negotiations, as it were. The risk this initiative entails confers on the agent a certain prestige, a certain advantage over his initially more passive partner (59–60; 69–70).

One might ask what the exact status of this passage is within Lévi-Strauss's general demonstration of the principle of reciprocity. On the one hand it belongs to the category of non-ethnographic material mobilized in this chapter to illustrate the universality of the principle, which is not confined to so-called 'primitive' societies. Unlike the properly ethnographic data used here and in the rest of the book, it assumes in the (French, Western) reader an implicit knowledge and recognition of the described cultural configuration – the situation of the two men in the restaurant is, the author claims, a common and banal occurrence. On the other hand, within this potentially problematic category of non-ethnographic illustration, the passage has special significance in that it operates at a level of description hitherto absent in the general exposition of the principle of reciprocity. The *structure* of the relation established between the two diners is broadly coincident with that described in Mauss's model of exchange: inaugural offer; binary option of acceptance/refusal, cordiality/hostility; in the case of acceptance, the resultant circuit or cycle of reciprocal gesture. There is even an allusion to the potlatch in the reference to risk, prestige and competition, though again the parallel seems rather stretched. The *scale* of the transaction, however, is clearly not the same as in Mauss. It will be remembered that for Mauss, it is between collectivities rather than individuals that relations of exchange and contract are formed, and in this he is thoroughly Durkheimian. In the present instance, and in contrast with the preceding, non-ethnographic examples, the reader is brought down to the micro-level, the 'microscopic scale', as Lévi-Strauss puts it, of individual interaction. This 'drama', with its face-to-face confrontation of the two protagonists, is formally equivalent to Mauss's description of group interaction, but the perspective is visibly biased towards the psychological rather than the sociological. Lévi-Strauss emphasizes that the example presents us with a 'total social fact', whose implications are, in the following, precise order, psychological, social and economic (60; 70).[19]

Transposed into the micro-drama of the *Elementary Structures*, the ritual and ceremonial dimension of exchange described in *The Gift* therefore becomes an entirely profane item of everyday life. It is as if Mauss's attempted demonstration of the universality of gift exchange, by way of the chapter on 'survivals' and the contemporary examples briefly evoked in his conclusion, were seen by Lévi-Strauss to be insufficient. It is as if the *extravagance* of the ethnographic part of Mauss's demonstration (and, in particular, his presentation of the potlatch) needed to be flattened out and reduced to a more immediately plausible and intuitable level of description. This is what Lévi-Strauss implies later in the book, at the start of chapter 7, when he pauses to justify his repeated references to contemporary, Western examples: 'in the setting up of our hypothesis we have so far purposely avoided exceptional examples, or examples which, because their realization in some native society or other has been pushed to a very high degree of perfection, appear exceptional' (84–5; 98–9).

Whether the fictional reconstruction of the relation of reciprocity offered in the fifth chapter of the *Elementary Structures* constitutes authentic verification of the principle is open to discussion. For one thing, one could ask to what extent it is simply a projection of the Maussian model – the point concerning the risk and consequent prestige of initiation, for example, comes across as an unnatural inflection towards the potlatch. This problem of projection apart, it is clear, as we have already noted, that Lévi-Strauss is concerned to investigate the psychological basis of reciprocity as well as its sociological significance. His description follows through the different stages of the formation of a social relation as experienced by the participants, noting the successive affects of anxiety, apprehension, tension, potential hostility, eventual cordiality and commensality. In terms of content, this psychological description seems to be a practical application of the methodological approach prescribed in the *Introduction to the Work of Marcel Mauss*: that one should seek the ultimate verification of sociological laws in the lived experience of individual subjects (*IM2*, 27–8; *IM1*, xxvi–xxvii). In terms of style, the description reads more like a piece of existentialist philosophizing than conventional anthropology. The vivid, present-tense evocation and dramatization of the commonplace situation, in order to illustrate a more general, essentially philosophical point – all this seems only a step away from the famous waiter of Sartre's *Being and Nothingness*, something like a Maussian variation on the theme of the *pour soi* and *pour autrui*. The prospect of a 'structuralist' Lévi-Strauss speaking the language of existentialism is by no means a paradox. His appropriation of this language, here as in other passages

---

[19] The English translation reverses the order of the first two terms: 'social, psychological and economic'.

of the *Elementary Structures*, is perfectly natural in the context of late 1940s France, and seems adequate to his object. It does, however, raise the question of the intended readership of the book, or at least of certain parts of the book. While the highly technical analysis of kinship systems was probably beyond the competence, and indeed interest, of most non-anthropologists, from the opening chapter on nature and culture to the present chapter on the principle of reciprocity the *Elementary Structures* seemed to be addressing an intellectual audience wider than that of specialists in anthropology. The reception given to the work by Simone de Beauvoir, one of the leading figures of the existentialist movement, is an indication of this wider interest. In 1949 de Beauvoir published an enthusiastic review of the book in *Les Temps Modernes*.[20] The same year, in the second volume of *The Second Sex*, she draws on the book for elements of her account of the prehistorical origins of the unequal relations between male and female.[21] Inevitably, de Beauvoir's reading of the *Elementary Structures* is a selective and partial one, which in retrospect makes both her and Sartre's subsequent reaction against structuralism less surprising.[22] Nevertheless, one can observe during the period of the late 1940s and early 1950s a respectful cohabitation of philosophy and anthropology, and what could be described as the 'existential' narrative of the restaurant scene in the *Elementary Structures* is visibly a gesture towards what was then the dominant philosophical movement.[23]

[20] *Les Temps Modernes* 5.49 (1949), 943–9.

[21] *Le Deuxième sexe I* (Paris: Gallimard-Folio Essais, 1976), pp. 122–7; *The Second Sex*, trans. H.M. Parshley (London: Vintage, 1997), pp. 96–9. See also Simon Clarke, *The Foundations of Structuralism. A Critique of Lévi-Strauss and the Structuralist Movement* (Sussex: Harvester Press, 1981), pp. 66–7; Howard Davies, *Sartre and 'Les Temps Modernes'* (Cambridge University Press, 1987), pp. 35–6. Sartre himself makes extensive use of the *Elementary Structures* in the first volume of the *Critique of Dialectical Reason*. Earlier in this text, he cites with approval Lévi-Strauss's description of the provincial restaurant (*Critique of Dialectical Reason I*, trans. Alan Sheridan-Smith (London: NLB, 1976), p. 107 n.12; *Critique de la raison dialectique 1* (Paris: Gallimard, 1961), p. 219 n.2).

[22] In his 1972 interviews with Jean José Marchand, Lévi-Strauss makes the following observation on the reception of the *Elementary Structures* in philosophical circles in France: 'I think that the positive responses were mostly based on a misunderstanding, especially in the French intellectual community, where the feeling, wrongly, was that the book contributed to what was then the dominant philosophy in France, existentialism, basically because of the sharp distinction I made at the start of the book between the order of nature and the order of culture. It was as if they saw me as doing my bit for the philosophical project of setting up the human domain as one completely separate and detached from the rest of creation, something which was neither in my intentions nor my thoughts. For me the distinction was much more a methodological artifice than a philosophical proposition' (*Archives du XXe siècle*, part 3, my translation). On Lévi-Strauss's critique of the kind of philosophical humanism espoused by existentialism, see chapter 4.

[23] Between the late 1940s and mid-1950s Lévi-Strauss publishes four articles in *Les Temps Modernes*: 'Le Sorcier et sa magie' (1949), 'Le Père Noël supplicié' (1952), 'Diogène couché' and 'Des Indiens et leur ethnographe' (1955). On the importance of anthropology in *Les Temps Modernes*, see Howard Davies, *Sartre and 'Les Temps Modernes'*.

So far we have covered a number of related points concerning Lévi-Strauss's use of Maussian theory in the *Elementary Structures*. First there is his extension of Mauss's demonstration of the universality of the principle of reciprocity. In his alternation between ethnographic data and everyday experience, Lévi-Strauss compensates for the weaker and less plausible elements of Mauss's demonstration, for example the chapter on 'survivals' and parts of the 'moral' conclusions. Second, in the example just treated, Mauss's collective psychology is complemented by an existential analysis of individual psychology in a given micro-situation. Third, the net effect of these two inflections of Mauss's theory is a kind of *desacralization* of the mechanism of exchange, as Mauss had formulated it. Lévi-Strauss is concerned to demonstrate the universal operation of the principle of reciprocity, not simply during certain privileged instants of collective convergence, but at each moment and every level of social life. The exchange of women, for example, which he defines in the *Elementary Structures* as *the* fundamental level of exchange, is a continuously effective agent of social cohesion. While Mauss had in a sense shown a social universe given only periodic impetus, on occasions of ritual or ceremonial significance,[24] Lévi-Strauss shows this universe as being endowed with perpetual motion.

Lévi-Strauss is therefore not content simply to state and illustrate the universality of a principle, and this is why the *Elementary Structures* are something more than a conventional ethnological treatise. Whereas ethnologists and sociologists might normally be prepared to adopt Mauss's model of exchange as a useful instrument for social analysis, Lévi-Strauss feels compelled to *explain* the mechanism of reciprocity at lower levels of determination. This is the importance of the example of the restaurant scene treated above. It is qualitatively different from the other examples given in the chapter – ethnographic or non-ethnographic – in that it deals with the formation of what might be termed an elementary structure of reciprocity. Lévi-Strauss himself is aware of the generic singularity of the example, and anticipates the reader's judgement that he has given it disproportionate attention. His justification is that it offers to

---

[24] The extent to which Mauss's model of gift exchange depends on the Durkheimian notion of social convergence, concentration and effervescence is perhaps best appreciated if one reads his other classic essay, the *Seasonal Variations of the Eskimo*, which provides on the level of social morphology a virtual image of the configuration described in the essay on the gift. The dual morphology of Eskimo society, corresponding with a pattern of seasonal dispersal and return, means that there is a marked difference in social activity and behaviour between the summer and the winter months. In summer, according to Mauss, the dispersed groups have little or no sense of religious or social ties, living a secularized and more individualistic existence. During the winter months, when the groups come together again, there is by contrast intense religious and ceremonial activity, at which time the social consciousness is revived and reinforced (*Essai sur les variations saisonnières des sociétés eskimos*, in *Sociologie et anthropologie*, pp. 445–50; *Seasonal Variations of the Eskimo*, trans. J.J. Fox (London: Routledge, 1979). The American Indian peoples of the Northwest coast described in *The Gift* also conform to this model of dual morphology (*The Gift*, p. 34; *Essai sur le don*, p. 196).

sociological speculation the case of the spontaneous formation of a social relation from a non-structured and critical situation. The situation itself, he suggests, presents us with a psycho-social experience whose origins are probably very primitive, and seems to be the distant but recognizable analogue of 'primitive' groups encountering each other for the first time (60; 70–1).

The narrative of the two strangers in the restaurant therefore has the status of an experiment, or rather a thought-experiment. It shows Lévi-Strauss's interest, expressed here and earlier in the *Elementary Structures*, in non-structured, 'non-crystallized' forms of social experience, prior to or outside of social institutions. It permits an existential description of the free interaction of two individuals and the necessary emergence of a structure (reciprocity) from that interaction. Whether one agrees or not with the framing of this experiment, it is clear that Lévi-Strauss is endeavouring to demonstrate the necessity of the relation of reciprocity at a level more fundamental than in Mauss's model. In Mauss, as we have seen, it is not until the conclusion of his essay that he provides any general formulation of the principle of exchange, and here, it will be remembered, the transition from an ethnographical and sociological register to a psychological and philosophical one is as brief as it is swift. Lévi-Strauss's existential drama can therefore be viewed as an extended elaboration of what Mauss had already described as a universal situation, though universal only at the level of collective behaviour and psychology. The critical situation of the two men facing one another over the restaurant table represents literally the psychological *elements* of the social relation described in Mauss. It reduces Mauss's collective psychology of ambivalence to the immediately lower level of individual psychology and shows the principle of reciprocity to be equally operative at this micro-level. Whereas Mauss's demonstration of the universality of the gift relation required the hypothesis of 'survivals' in the West's archaic past, Lévi-Strauss's existential description gives concrete demonstration, here and now, of its 'vestiges' in individual interaction.

The tendency to reduction apparent in this example, which is typical of Lévi-Strauss's approach, does not, however, end here. Within the extended demonstration covering the first part of the *Elementary Structures*, there is a further stage of reduction. In the following chapter, 'Dual Organization', he argues that the frequent division of a 'tribe' or village into two halves or moieties, linked by a network of mutual transactions, does not produce reciprocity; rather, this dual organization is a result of the principle of reciprocity (70; 81). The same applies in the case of cross-cousin marriage, treated in a later chapter. Though they might differ in their degree of definition or complexity, both forms of social relation are viewed by Lévi-Strauss as representing a 'translation' or a 'codification' of the basic, 'regulatory' principle of reciprocity (100–3; 117–20). This basic principle is not simply an emergent structure, as the example of the restaurant scene might lead us to believe; it is, Lévi-Strauss proposes, part of the 'fundamental structures of the human mind' (75; 87–8). Visibly conscious of how nebulous such a formulation must appear, he begins the subsequent chapter, 'The Archaic Illusion', with an attempt to delineate the components of the mental structures referred to. It is worthwhile quoting this passage in full, as it contains the essence of Lévi-Strauss's thinking on the gift:

What are the mental structures to which we have referred and the universality of which we believe can be established? It seems there are three: the exigency of the rule as rule; the notion of reciprocity regarded as the most immediate form of integrating the opposition between self and others [*l'opposition de moi et d'autrui*]; and finally, the synthetic nature of the gift, i.e., that the agreed transfer of a valuable from one individual to another makes these individuals into partners, and adds a new quality to the valuable transferred. The question of the origin of these structures will be taken up later. Whether or not they can account for the phenomena can only be answered from the whole work. Our sole intention at this point is to find out if they do exist, and to grasp them in their concrete and universal reality. (*ESK*, 84; *SEP*, 98)

At first sight, this analysis seems circular and tautological, simply the reformulation in a philosophical, and again partly existential register (for example, the 'opposition' of self and other) of what the reader has already learnt from the argumentation and exemplification of the preceding chapters. The only addition would be that the social relations described in those chapters are restated in mentalist terms. At the same time, the performative effect of this change of focus is to prepare the next stage of Lévi-Strauss's reduction. His concern has been to establish the reality and universality of the structures in question, and this he has done, as was noted earlier, by avoiding what might be considered the more exceptional ethnographic examples and selecting the most everyday of examples from contemporary Western society. But this comparative analysis of customs, Western and non-Western, is, it seems, insufficient to Lévi-Strauss's desire to demonstrate the deep-level determination of the principle of reciprocity. If the interpersonal situation described in the restaurant scene, for example, allowed the reader to observe the actual formation of a structure of reciprocity, it does not, apparently, go far enough. However 'unstructured' the situation involving the two strangers, the individuals in question are not socially and culturally blank slates. The situation may be, as Lévi-Strauss suggested, less codified than other areas of social intercourse, but the interaction described is nevertheless between two already socialized (male) adults of a specific culture.

Given what seems then to be the inadequate depth of the existential description of reciprocity, Lévi-Strauss's gesture in 'The Archaic Illusion' is to propose a more fundamental level of determination. The proposition is that child psychology provides a more universal verification of the structures in question than the comparative analysis of custom and behaviour. This is because, he claims, in all societies the child bears the imprint of his or her particular culture less than the adult, and so offers the example of mental structures that should be common to all cultures (85; 99). The main substance of the exposition that follows is taken from the work of the English child psychologist, Susan Isaacs.[25] What is interesting is how, as with the example of the provincial restaurant, Lévi-Strauss concentrates on the *formation* of a structure as he works through Isaacs's description of the psychological development of the child. The combination of quotation and paraphrase that follows appears to be an accurate mediation of Isaacs's text, but at the same time a process of selection and inflection is evident.

Lévi-Strauss first notes the tendency in all children under five to want exclusive and immediate possession of an object. He qualifies that this impulse is present not only in relation to material objects, but also in relation to non-material activities such as singing or listening to a song. Whatever the object, the young child finds it difficult to have to wait or tolerate others' possession of it. This is not necessarily because of any fundamental, instinctual need for the object in question; the value of the object is rather a mediated one, determined by the fact of another's possession of or desire for it. In order to be secure, in order not to feel impotent, the child must ensure that the other does not enjoy exclusive and permanent possession of the object. The solution to this psychological complex of desire and apprehension and the potential conflict it entails is given in Isaacs's example of two children who are disputing the use of a tricycle. Equal in strength and determination, and refusing external arbitration, the two infants experience the practical impossibility of imposing their own individual wills. They are therefore forced to recognize the principle of an equal right to possession (85–6; 99–100). Lévi-Strauss's gloss of this first part of Isaacs's analysis is again a Maussian and existential one: 'It can thus be said that the capacity for sharing or "taking turns" is a function of the growing feeling of reciprocity, itself the result of a living experience [*expérience vécue*] of the collective fact, and of the deeper mechanism of identification with another [*identification à autrui*]' (86; 100). The reference to lived experience and identification of self and other on the one hand, and to reciprocity and the collective fact on the other, is clearly not in Isaacs, but this inflection towards a phenomenology of reciprocity allows Lévi-Strauss to make the transition to the gift itself, which is treated somewhat later in Isaacs's text. Isaacs remarks that it is not so much the nature of the gift as the act of donation itself which creates the bond of mutual friendship between children. Giving signifies love, and is confirmation that the recipient is worthy of love. Conversely, the failure to receive a gift signals the latter's present or past hostility to the donor. Added to this is the asymmetry of the gift relation: it is better to give than to receive because the capacity to give is indicative of a position of power and

---

[25] Susan Isaacs, *Social Development in Young Children. A Study of Beginnings* (London: Routledge, 1933).

non-dependence. Thus the child's desire to give enormous presents is basically a desire for power. Continuing his quotation of Isaacs, Lévi-Strauss underlines that the donor's apparent generosity is only a transposition of a more fundamental affect governing relations between children, as indeed between adults – hostility. Love is a transform of the hate felt for a potential rival, and in fact children often oscillate between the two extremes. The establishment of a stable friendship is possible only on condition of enmity towards an excluded third party (86–7; 100–1).

Again, the extent to which this excursion into child psychology is prepared and programmed by the Maussian paradigm of exchange is evident. The Maussian model seems to provide a plausible framework for Isaacs's observations on child behaviour, or at least those that Lévi-Strauss has selected for comment and quotation.[26] It is useful to recall here the purpose of his digression, which is to demonstrate the existence of mental structures ensuring the universal operation of the principle of reciprocity. This demonstration is based on the premise that the behaviour of children is less conditioned and restrained by cultural norms than that of adults and therefore more representative of fundamental traits of human behaviour. Whatever one may think of this premise, or of the subsequent inflection of Isaacs towards Mauss, Lévi-Strauss himself takes the demonstration no further, or rather, the demonstration takes another direction. He justifies his digression into the subject of child psychology by evoking the innumerable parallels one finds in ethnographic literature, but this assimilation immediately requires qualification, as it may be misconstrued as supporting the age-old prejudice linking so-called primitive mentality with child mentality (87–8; 101–2). From this point, the argument of the chapter appears to bifurcate. The central part of the chapter is devoted to a refutation of the illusion that non-Western societies represent an archaic stage of human development, comparable to the level of psychological development found in children – hence the chapter's title. While this critique (which has some harsh words for Piaget) is an effective one and is doubtless necessary in its context, what is interesting for our present analysis is the conceptual configuration which emerges from it. Lévi-Strauss argues, convincingly, that all cultures are 'adult' and that the difference between adult and child is the same in all cultures. He also argues (again citing Isaacs) that the psychological differences between child and adult are often exaggerated (91–2; 106–8). This having been established, however, he feels compelled to *explain* these differences:

---

[26] What Lévi-Strauss does not mention in his selective paraphrase of Isaacs is the extent to which her analysis draws on psychoanalytical theory. For example, the child's desire for exclusive possession of an object is said to derive from the 'ultimate situation' of the infant at the breast, which in turn is the prototypical gift (*Social Development in Young Children*, pp. 225, 273).

Adult thinking is built around a certain number of structures which it specifies, organizes, and develops from the single fact of this specialization, and which are only a fraction of the initial summary and undifferentiated structures in the child's thought. In other words, the mental schemata of the adult diverge in accordance with the culture and period to which he belongs. However, they are all derived from a universal resource which is infinitely more rich than that of each particular culture. Every newborn child provides in embryonic form the sum total of possibilities, but each culture and period of history will retain and develop only a chosen few of them. Every newborn child comes equipped, in the form of adumbrated mental structures, with all the means ever available to mankind to define its relations to the world in general and its relations to others [*ses relations au Monde et ses relations à Autrui*]. But these structures are exclusive. Each of them can integrate only certain elements out of all those that are offered. Consequently, each type of social organization represents a choice, which the group imposes and perpetuates. In comparison with adult thought, which has chosen and rejected as the group has required, child thought is a sort of universal substratum the crystallizations of which have not yet occurred, and in which communication is still possible between incompletely solidified forms.

Can this hypothesis be verified? We shall merely indicate the direction in which we believe it could be verified. (*ESK*, 92–3; *SEP*, 108–9)

As can be seen, Lévi-Strauss's explanation of the difference between child and adult psychology is presented as merely an 'hypothesis', but again, its interest for us lies in the conceptual configuration it reveals rather than its ultimate verifiability. What we have here is a quasi-Leibnizian conception of mental structures, according to which the child represents the infinite *compossibilities* of human behaviour, what in a somewhat existentialist turn of expression Lévi-Strauss describes as the totality of possible relations with the world and with others. Individual cultures would be the actualization of a restricted number of these compossibles, a process described, rather problematically, as the 'choice' of each particular social group. So what one might be tempted to view as the complication of adult psychology in relation to child psychology is for Lévi-Strauss a simplification. The choice made by each individual culture is among structures which are mutually exclusive, or which can only combine ('integrate') with certain other structures, which seems to suggest an even deeper-level 'syntax' of combination that would restrict the modality of choice. The term used by Lévi-Strauss to describe this restriction of the multiple and incompatible mental structures found in the child is 'crystallization' (93; 109).[27]

The manner and level at which the hypothesis on the relation between child and adult psychology is argued means that the hypothesis itself is virtually unverifiable, or verifiable only by means of analogy. This is precisely what Lévi-Strauss does, using what he considers to be the parallel example of language acquisition. Language acquisition, he claims, presents us with the same

---

[27] The semantic and conceptual field covered by this term in Lévi-Strauss's work is considerable, as will be seen in the following chapters.

'problems' as the psycho-sociological development of the child, and these problems have been resolved in the same way. The subsequent description of the child's learning of a language's phonological system is based on Jakobson:

> The variety of sounds that the speech organs can articulate is almost unlimited. However, each language retains only a very small number of all the possible sounds. During the prattling period, before the introduction of articulated language, the child produces the total range of sound realizable in human language while his own particular language will retain only some of them. In the first few months of life every child has been able to emit sounds which later he will find very difficult to reproduce, and which he will fail to imitate satisfactorily when he learns languages very different from his own. Every language makes a selection and from one viewpoint this selection is regressive. Once this selection is made, the unlimited possibilities available on the phonetic plane are irremediably lost. (*ESK*, 93–4; *SEP*, 109)

The comparison proposed here between an essentially digital system (speech sounds) and an analogue complex (the integration of individual psychology and collective norm) is to say the least a problematic one. It is all the more suspect because instead of functioning as a possible verification of Lévi-Strauss's previous hypothesis, the example of speech acquisition in fact reveals its conceptual basis. It is only by analogy with the process of selection noted by Jakobson in the learning of a phonetic system that Lévi-Strauss is able to conceptualize the restriction of possibilities he claims to be the basis of the psychological integration of the individual into a given society. The notion of mutually exclusive structures and of their elective combination with a limited number of elements is visibly premised on phonological theory, though the latter is presented as confirmation of this notion rather than its origin. The wholly circular movement of the demonstration becomes apparent when the main hypothesis on the difference between child and adult psychology is restated:

> Likewise, the multifarious structures outlined in the thought and attitudes of the child in the realm of inter-individual relations still have social value, since they constitute the raw material for the formation of heterogeneous systems. However, each of these systems can only retain a small number of them to have any functional value. It is through the child's incorporation into his particular culture that this selection takes place. (*ESK*, 94; *SEP*, 110)

I have insisted on this particular passage because the mode of conceptualization it reveals appears to be a persistent trait of Lévi-Strauss's thought and a basic feature of his version of structuralism. The quasi-Leibnizian concept of an infinity of possibilities, of their selection and elective combination, the notion of the 'integration' or 'crystallization' of traits or structures – these are conceptual complexes which extend beyond the present problem of psycho-social development and inform the whole of Lévi-Strauss's work. We have already seen a weak version of the model in his 'structural' analysis of the disciplines, examined in chapter 1. It will be remembered that the different positions of disciplines in his table of the social and humanistic sciences is a function of their chosen 'attitude' concerning objects and methodology. Like the 'choice' different cultures appear to have made in their selective restriction of the possibilities observed in the child, the various disciplines will have made a similar selection, visible in their own specific, individual orientations.[28]

In the following chapters it will be seen that Lévi-Strauss's reflex is to revert to this model each time he is faced with the problem of structure formation or transformation. In the more immediate context of the *Elementary Structures*, the concept of regressive selection is used, as we have seen, to explain the difference between child and adult psychology, but this in turn serves the more general argument concerning the question of archaism. Again, for Lévi-Strauss it is not enough to argue the relativist case of the equal 'maturity' of all cultures; he must also explain the logic of our frequent misperception of the 'infantile' status of exotic cultures. Because these cultures have made their own original synthesis of the universal traits which, it is claimed, are integrally present in the child, we perceive in them certain infantile features our own cultures will have suppressed in the normal transition from childhood to adulthood. The symmetrical case is also true: non-Western cultures equally perceive Western people to be childish – the example cited is the Navajo perception of the White (95; 111). This is doubtless an elegant, even sophisticated explanation of the possible distortions of cross-cultural perception, but as an explanation it is only partially convincing. Though on a superficial level there may be a certain symmetry in the mutual perceptions of Western and non-Western cultures, this takes no account of the history of their relations, more precisely of the power relationship which habitually constructs the subordinate other as child; nor is there any mention of nineteenth-century evolutionary theory, which added pseudo-scientific sanction to this construction. The Western representation of the infantile nature of non-Western cultures, it could be argued, is more the product of asymmetrical power relations than of some universal phenomenology of cross-cultural perception, as is claimed by Lévi-Strauss.

At this point we seem far from the principle of reciprocity, initially our (and Lévi-Strauss's) point of departure. In fact, as one approaches the end of the chapter in question, there is a noticeable drift in the argument. To recapitulate: Lévi-Strauss opened the chapter with an attempt to define the basic mental structures which might explain the phenomenon of dual organization. His definition isolated three elements: the necessity of the rule as rule; reciprocity as the most immediate form of integration of self and other; the gift as the symbolic agent of this integration. The example of the psychological and social development of young children provided a form of experimental

[28] See chapter 1, p. 21.

verification of the depth and universality of these structures. However, the demonstration is inflected and complicated as the author notes the moral and ideological problems raised by the striking similarities between the infantile behaviour described and ethnographic descriptions of so-called primitive cultures (curiously, the non-ethnographic examples of the universality of reciprocity given in previous chapters are not mentioned here). The subsequent refutation of the archaic prejudice allows Lévi-Strauss to develop, via an exploration of the differences between child and adult psychology, the idea of the regressive selection of mental structures as a model explaining the formation of qualitatively different social organizations, and therefore to explain the 'logic' of the prejudice.

As the preceding analysis shows, Lévi-Strauss's exposition in 'The Archaic Illusion' is an overdetermined one, combining as it does a number of different trains of reflection and argument. Despite the increasing involvement of the exposition, he nevertheless manages to bring its different strands together in the chapter's concluding paragraphs. The theory of regressive selection that emerges from the refutation of archaism also provides him with a final methodological justification for the chapter's almost exclusive concentration on child psychology: such research is important for ethnological studies as it gives direct access to the common mental structures and 'institutional schemas' on which all social organizations are based. It is by placing oneself at this very elementary level that one is able to understand apparently bizarre social formations (95; 111). As proof of this, Lévi-Strauss refers to a personal experience, citing the observation of an individual who had never heard of dual organization, following a lecture he had given on the subject. The example is of a four-year-old child whose parents live in different geographical locations, and who has constructed what is essentially a dualist system or mythology based on the distinction and opposition of two imaginary countries. When questioned on this a few years later, at the age of seven, the subject ('Johnny') is embarrassed and says that he can't remember. The point, we are told, is that had Johnny been a member of, for example, an indigenous Australian society, this kind of representation would have seemed entirely natural, and would have been assimilated into the collective dualism of the social group, whereas such representations are rejected and repressed (*abandonné et refoulé*) in societies like our own, which do not use binary structures to express relations of antagonism and reciprocity, or at least do so in a less systematic fashion (96; 112).

With this concluding example, the chapter is brought back to its point of departure. We return to the question of dual organization, but (according to Lévi-Strauss) at the most elementary level possible, in the example of a pre-school child. The subject 'Johnny' also appears to provide living confirmation of the hypothesis of regressive selection, which is used in the final lines of the chapter to distinguish between infantile, pathological and 'primitive' mentality.

The problem is that in the complicated circuit which leads Lévi-Strauss to this conclusion, the principle of reciprocity which he had defined as the basis of dual organization, indeed of all social organization, has now receded into the background. In essence, what Lévi-Strauss finally advances in this chapter is a theory of socialization premised on a linguistic, or more precisely, a phonological (Jakobsonian) model of the child's integration into a given linguistic group. The progressive selection of sound-elements enabling this integration is 'regressive' in that it involves the elimination of the multitude of other sound-configurations of which the child is capable. Similarly, in Lévi-Strauss's final illustration, dual organization is one potential social form which has been 'selected' by, for example, indigenous Australian societies, and (relatively) 'repressed' by Western societies.

The question is, where does this leave the principle of reciprocity itself? As has been seen, the success of the 'demonstration' of the deep-level determination of the principle in the social development of young children is a qualified one; it is superficially plausible but is also too closely programmed by the Maussian paradigm. The implicit but not stated position in the ensuing digression on the question of archaism is that the principle of reciprocity is not part of the diverse 'attitudes' available to the young child and subject to social selection. The difference lies, it seems, in the distinction between 'system' and 'structure'. In the young child there coexist a number of 'systems', and the child (unlike the normal adult) is able to move without contradiction between these different systems: 'But there are systems. The further we penetrate towards the deeper levels of mental life, the more we are presented with structures diminishing in number but increasing in strictness and simplicity' (94; 110). Lévi-Strauss does not go on to specify what these deeper and more elementary structures might be, preferring to concentrate on the question of the child's social 'polymorphism', but it seems clear that they must be equivalent to the mental structures detailed at the start of the chapter, at the centre of which lies the principle of reciprocity. Unlike the systems inhabiting the socially polymorphous child, this structure would not (could not) be subject to any culture-specific selection: rather, it would form the universal 'bedrock', to use Mauss's term, of social organization.

Exchange and communication

Despite the extended digression on child psychology in 'The Archaic Illusion', we are as distant at the end of the chapter from an understanding of the principle of reciprocity itself as we were at its start. Indeed, at the beginning of the chapter Lévi-Strauss leaves aside the question of the origin of universal mental structures such as reciprocity, intending to return to it at a later stage

(84; 98). Perhaps unsurprisingly, he does not return directly to this question, either in the *Elementary Structures* or elsewhere in his work. At most, there is a lateral response in his subsequent generalization of the principle of reciprocity under the category of *communication*. This is where the model of exchange, which we have seen to be so important to the theoretical infrastructure of the *Elementary Structures*, joins the linguistic model normally considered to be the essential component of Lévi-Strauss's structuralism. On a superficial level the incidence of linguistics in the *Elementary Structures* seems minimal, considering the prominent role given to the discipline in other early programmatic texts – Jakobson for example is mentioned only three times in the book. Despite such low visibility, the presence of structural linguistics in the book is a definite, if diffuse, one. Briefly, the elements of the linguistic inspiration can be summarized as follows:

• On the methodological level, the main project of the *Elementary Structures* – the isolation of a small number of elementary, invariant structures from which the diversity of observable kinship structures might be derived – is directly inspired by the work of Jakobson and Trubetzkoy in phonology.
• On the conceptual level, there are at least three areas of influence. First, the notion of the unconscious operation of social norms, by analogy with the implicit rules of language. The analogy was already well-established in anthropology, since Boas at least (to whom Lévi-Strauss refers), but Lévi-Strauss clearly also has more contemporary developments in linguistics in mind (108–9; 126–7). Second, the conception of agent and object of exchange as arbitrary and differential sign. Lévi-Strauss argues that the matrimonial prohibitions which are the condition of exogamy are logically prior to their object. In other words, an individual woman is not *essentially* inappropriate for marriage within her own group; rather the necessity of exogamic exchange with a second group constructs her as 'other' and therefore alienable from the 'same' of her original group. Similarly, antagonistic relations between moieties are not based on any intrinsic difference between them, but simply on the structural necessity of establishing a distinction between interacting parties (113–14; 132–3). Again, the linguistic model is not mentioned here, but the argument is clearly based on the concept of binary opposition. Finally, there is the idea of the culture-specific socialization of individuals as the regressive selection and combination of universal traits, compared with the process of language acquisition: this was the example treated earlier.

In spite of Lévi-Strauss's mention of Jakobson's 'inspiration' in the preface to the first edition of the *Elementary Structures*, the linguistic model is only fully acknowledged in the final chapter, where he attempts to bring together the different theoretical components of the book into a coherent statement of method. There is first a reiteration of the basic thesis of the book: exchange as the mechanism underlying different rules of marriage, in other words, exogamy, the positive aspect of the incest prohibition, as the primary (archetypal) agent of social cohesion, representing the passage from 'nature' to 'culture', from the indifferent biological relation of individuals to their social relation; without this properly *dialectical* sublation of the natural in the social, society could not exist.[29] Despite his unacceptable hypothesis on the origins of the incest prohibition, the Freud of *Totem and Taboo* is credited with having indicated and explained an important psychological impulse, the unconscious desire to commit incest. Such a desire is not, however, the phylogenetic residue of a historical action, as Freud argues, but is a permanently operative disposition, part of the basic structure of the human mind. Contrary to Freud's thesis of a historically repressed act, Lévi-Strauss attributes the power of this myth precisely to its expression of a desire which has never been satisfied, because society has always opposed it (490–2; 562–4). It is this methodological demarcation *vis-à-vis* Freud which introduces linguistics. Like ethnology, Freud's psychoanalysis is a social science, but it has not entirely freed itself from the traditional but now outdated method of historical reconstruction – the attempt to explain the workings of a present system in terms of its distant origins. For Lévi-Strauss, only linguistics (another social science) has managed successfully to combine synchronic and diachronic explanation, adopting the more scientific approach of explaining both the future and the past of a system in terms of its present state. This is the method of analysis used in the *Elementary Structures*, the result of which has been a reduction of the historical and geographic diversity of kinship rules to three elementary structures (bilateral cross-cousin marriage and matrilateral and patrilateral cross-cousin marriage) based on two forms of exchange (restricted and general) (492–3; 564–5).

Our intention here is not to discuss the validity of Lévi-Strauss's reduction of kinship practices or the comparison he makes between his methods and those of phonological analysis. This ground has been more than adequately covered in more specialized commentaries. Of more immediate interest to the present study is the fact that for Lévi-Strauss it is not sufficient to note the methodological affinity between phonology and (structural) anthropology: he must also explain its necessity. Indeed, the similarity of method is possible precisely because, according to Lévi-Strauss, the two disciplines deal with the same object: the 'reality' they treat is not as different as one might expect, in that both exogamy and language share the same fundamental function of communication and social integration (493; 565). The diagram of logical types used earlier to distinguish the different levels of Lévi-Strauss's analysis could therefore be extended, as in

---

[29] The term 'dialectical' is Lévi-Strauss's (489, 490; 561, 562). Predictably, this aspect of his analysis is underlined by de Beauvoir in her review of the *Elementary Structures*, cited above.

Communication
•
Principle of reciprocity
•
Prohibition of incest/Exogamy
(restricted or general exchange)
•
Cross-cousin alliance/Dual organization

Fig. 2.2

figure 2.2. Obviously, Lévi-Strauss's assimilation of the four terms – exogamy, language, communication, social integration – is extremely problematic. While it is possible to subscribe to his theory of exogamy (the positive aspect of the incest prohibition) as a primary agent of social integration, it is difficult to see how the analogue domain of social contact and interaction can be characterized as simply an aspect of 'communication'. Conversely, while the assimilation of language with communication seems in a general sense acceptable,[30] the role ascribed to it in social integration is less self-evident. The fragility of this second assimilation (language = communication = social integration) is apparent in the insistence with which Lévi-Strauss defends it in the closing pages of the *Elementary Structures*. The ethnographic examples he gives as illustration of the social efficacy of language, of the word as verb, action and power rather than simply a passive vehicle for the expression of ideas, are in themselves and in their respective contexts unexceptionable, but they are clearly not of the same functional order as the principle of reciprocity or its primary expression, exogamy. Similar attempts in texts contemporary to the *Elementary Structures* to assimilate the two levels appear equally limited.[31]

If Lévi-Strauss's concept of communication seems theoretically weak, applicable only in the most abstract and general of senses and questionable in its assumptions, it is perhaps necessary to consider the motives for his insistence on its importance. Parallel to the tendency to reduction, discussed in this chapter, there is also in Lévi-Strauss a consistent desire to *unify* the different elements of his theoretical construction, to give it an overall coherence. As we have seen, there are basically two models which form the conceptual backbone, as it were, of the *Elementary Structures*. The first and most important, Mauss's model of exchange, comes from within sociology; it is a ready-made construct which Lévi-Strauss adopts and adapts in the ways noted above. The second

---

[30] Some would contest this. In *System and Structure*, for example, Wilden insists that language is not communication and that there is in Lévi-Strauss a confusion of the two (Anthony Wilden, *System and Structure: Essays in Communication and Exchange*, 2nd edition (London: Tavistock Publications, 1980), pp. 10–11; 345).

[31] See the articles gathered under the rubric 'Language and Kinship' in *Structural Anthropology*.

model is extraneous to sociology proper, though it does come from what Lévi-Strauss has, perhaps rather tendentiously, designated as another social science, linguistics. So whereas the Maussian model of exchange might be qualified as a 'first-order' model, since it is derived from the observation and comparison of diverse social phenomena, the linguistic-phonological model would be a 'second-order' model to the extent that its primary object is not the social but a subset, albeit a significant subset, of the social. While Lévi-Strauss's application of the first model is restricted to a single, basic function of social systems (reciprocity and exchange), the second, in addition to the methodological inspiration it provides, is applied to different levels of those systems (unconscious norms; exchange between formally differentiated partners; psychological development and socialization). In itself, this use of two distinct orders of conceptualization (sociological and linguistic) should not pose a problem. Methodologically, it would conform to the practice of *bricolage*, as Lévi-Strauss defines it in his later work – that is, an instrumental and provisional approach to concepts and models, adopting and discarding them as and when necessary, in the hope that at each stage they will provide a closer approximation to their object.[32] The problem is that what is effectively a superposition of two models in the *Elementary Structures* is presented by Lévi-Strauss as a fundamental identity. Instead of keeping the two domains apart, he seems to be intent on combining them in a unified theory of social communication. Again, it is as if the methodological and heuristic value of the linguistic model were not enough, as if one needed also to prove the essential necessity of its application to social phenomena. The implicit line of reasoning appears to be as follows: the ultimate basis of the principle of reciprocity resides somewhere in the deep structure of the human mind; language, the essential medium of social intercourse, is equally the product of deep-level determination; therefore, by virtue of their coexistence or continuity at the level of deep structure it is logical and valid to assume the identity of the two from the more general perspective of communication; thus the linguistic model is more than a simple model, applicable to certain social phenomena – more than this, it is a *necessary* model in that its primary object (language) shares the same mental continuum as its secondary object (social relations). An explicit formulation of this idea of a continuity of functions can be found in the 1952 article 'Linguistics and Anthropology', where language and culture are viewed as two parallel modalities of a more fundamental entity, the human mind, whose co-evolution must make them formally and functionally analogous:

If we try to formulate our problem in purely theoretical terms, then it seems to me that we are entitled to affirm that there should be some kind of relationship between language and culture, because language has taken thousands of years to develop, and culture has taken thousands of years to develop, and both processes have been taking place side

---

[32] *SM*, 16–36; *PS*, 26–47.

by side within the same minds . . . Is it possible to conceive of the human mind as consisting of separate compartments so watertight that nothing is able to pass from one to another? (*SA*1, 71; *AS*1, 81)[33]

The intention here is neither to negate nor downgrade the theoretical achievement of the *Elementary Structures*. Placed in its context, the book is a bold work of synthesis, presenting a degree of theoretical sophistication hitherto unknown in French anthropology. Its central thesis – exogamy as the positive (socially binding) manifestation of the incest prohibition; the reduction of the culturally diverse rules governing exogamy to a limited set of basic structures – is a challenging one. The attempt to introduce into anthropology the methods and models of structural linguistics, whatever its limitations, is equally provocative. However, in addition to these important contributions to anthropological theory, the argument of the *Elementary Structures* seems constantly to be seeking justification of its own theoretical foundations – a reflex more philosophical than anthropological. The related attempts at reduction and unification noted above are not in the final analysis essential to the main thesis of the book. As has been seen, the two-stage reduction of the principle of reciprocity (existential and psychological-developmental) is of doubtful validity and does not (cannot) provide conclusive verification of the principle. Similarly, the attempt to unify the systemically distinct levels of social exchange and linguistic expression under the category of communication appears forced and unnecessary. From the point of view of their performative effect, however, both gestures (reduction and unification) respond to Lévi-Strauss's visible desire – his need – to assure the total coherence of his theoretical construction and to motivate at a more fundamental level what might otherwise appear to be non-essential correlations. Again, I am insisting on this particular aspect of Lévi-Strauss's exposition because it is relevant not only to the *Elementary Structures* but to his thought as a whole, as will become increasingly evident in the following chapters. In the context of the development of that thought between the late 1940s and the early 1950s, the attempted grafting of the linguistic-communicational model onto the model of exchange, combined with his preoccupation with the psychological dimension of reciprocity, allows Lévi-Strauss to pass without significant interruption to his second area of specialization, the anthropology of religions, which is the subject of our next chapter.

Reciprocity and authority

Before concluding on the subject of the model of exchange, it would be useful to look at a final aspect of its presentation in Lévi-Strauss's early work, that is, his use of the model to analyse relations of power and hierarchy. Until now we

---

[33] Translation slightly modified. A few pages earlier, language and culture are said to have a similar 'architecture' (*SA*1, 68–9; *AS*1, 78–9).

have been concerned with Lévi-Strauss's treatment of what might be termed the 'horizontal' axis of social cohesion, relations of reciprocity between members of formally homologous groups. At the elementary level of such analysis the question of a 'vertical' axis of hierarchical relations between groups is carefully bracketed. Lévi-Strauss himself is aware of this omission, and recognizes for example the existence of hierarchical structures in cases of dual organization. At the same time, however, he maintains that the mechanism of reciprocity operates even in relations between non-equals:

A perhaps one-sided analysis of the dual organization has too often put the emphasis on the principle of reciprocity as its main cause and result. It is well to remember that the moiety system can express not only mechanisms of reciprocity but also relations of subordination. But even in these relations of subordination, the principle of reciprocity is at work, for the subordination itself is reciprocal: the priority which is gained by one moiety on one level is lost to the other moiety on the other. Political primacy has to be paid at the price of a subordinate place in the system of generations.[34]

One sees here a clear extension of the principle of reciprocity from 'horizontal' to 'vertical' relations, to the perhaps less ponderable and more qualitative category of social position. But the most developed and arguably the most interesting analysis of power relations in Lévi-Strauss's early work is to be found in the chapters of *Tristes tropiques* devoted to the Nambikwara.[35] The analysis is a significant one because while based on the individual example of the Nambikwara, it advances a theory or model of authority more general than this singular, ethnographic case. There is in fact a systematic tendency in the chapters on the Nambikwara to represent their society as constituting a degree zero of civilization. According to Lévi-Strauss, of all the peoples he has encountered in his travels, the Nambikwara possess the lowest level of material culture and the most rudimentary form of social and political organization. More specifically in the chapter on political structures, appropriately entitled 'Men, Women and Chiefs', they are said to represent a perfect specimen, a laboratory case in which social relations can be observed in their simplest form: 'an elementary social structure', 'a society reduced to its simplest expression'. In contrast with the 'over-complicated laws' of other cultures the ethnographer has studied (Bororo, Caduveo), the elementary structure of the Nambikwara polity can teach us something about 'the origins and functions of power' (*TT*2, 314, 316–17; *TT*1, 373, 376–7).[36]

---

[34] 'The Bororo Moiety System, Cerae, Tugaregue', *American Anthropologist* 46 (1944), 267–8. See also *SA*1, 139–40; *AS*1, 154–5, and in the same volume the definition of three 'orders' (312–13; 347–8).

[35] *Tristes tropiques*, chapters 24–9.

[36] In the introduction to an article published in 1944, which 'Men, Women, Chiefs' reproduces, often verbatim, this approach is even more explicitly articulated ('La Théorie du pouvoir dans une société primitive', *Les Doctrines politiques modernes* (New York: Brentano, 1947),

A first remark on Lévi-Strauss's analysis would be that it works on two levels, political and economic. The political aspect is, for the most part, unremarkable. It is first noted that power among the Nambikwara is not hereditary, and that it is the chief himself who nominates his successor, though his choice is normally in agreement with the collective consensus (309; 366–7). On the level of 'external' politics, the chief's foremost privilege is to lead his people into war, which, Lévi-Strauss notes, is reminiscent of Montaigne's cannibals. But he is still more impressed by the native word for chief, which seems to mean 'he who unites' or 'he who joins together', and goes on to explain that the chief's power does not derive from the imposition of authority on an already constituted group, but rather from the expression of the group's desire to constitute itself as a group. The basis of power is therefore consent and not compulsion. As Lévi-Strauss reiterates throughout his description of Nambikwara politics, the chief's position is a precarious one. He has no publicly recognized authority, and his exercise of power is compared to the management of a fragile majority in democratic politics: at every moment, the group is liable to withdraw its consent (310; 368). This description leads in the following pages to more general considerations on the mode of delegation of authority in Nambikwara society, which Lévi-Strauss sees as confirmation of Rousseau's theory of the social contract. Rousseau's insight, he argues, was that cultural phenomena such as consent and contract are not, as some would have it, secondary elaborations, but the very foundation of social life.

What is important in the present context is that the purely political description of leadership, outlined above, is an insufficient characterization of the deep structure of power in the group. Interestingly, at the same time that Lévi-Strauss proposes consent as the foundation of social life, he binarizes this foundation by showing its economic substructure. By itself, the notion of consent is at once too general and too abstract, a psychological attitude rather than a concrete aspect of behaviour: '*consent* is the psychological basis of power, but in everyday life it is expressed by a process of giving and receiving which goes on between the chief and his companions, and which makes the idea of *reciprocity* another fundamental attribute of power' (315; 374). This dual foundation of consent and reciprocity has been described in the pages immediately preceding Lévi-Strauss's reference to Rousseau. In concrete terms, the group's consent is based on the chief's capacity to satisfy the basic needs of the group – the planning of itineraries during the nomadic period, the organization of the various food-gathering activities and the management of relations with neighbouring groups. In all of these activities, the chief has to excel: if he is seen to be less

pp. 41–63; 'The Social and Psychological Aspects of Chieftainship in a Primitive Tribe: The Nambikwara of Northwestern Mato Grosso', republished in Ronald Cohen and John Middleton (eds.), *Comparative Political Systems. Studies in the Politics of Pre-Industrial Societies* (New York: The Natural History Press, 1967), pp. 45–62.

successful than the chiefs of other groups, his people will abandon him and affiliate themselves with the more successful rival group. The basic function of the chief is therefore to serve the group, and he has to be more than resourceful in fulfilling his obligations. The chief's main instrument of policy in the fulfilment of these obligations is *generosity*. However materially poor the group may be, any excess commodities the chief procures must be redistributed to the members of the group. This law of redistribution is so implacable that the chief is frequently generous to the point of expropriation; as the ethnographer observes on a number of occasions, the group is so demanding of the chief that he is often left with nothing. The compensation for this continual self-sacrifice, we are told, is the group's concession to the chief of the right to have more than one wife: polygamy is the chief's exclusive privilege, and in addition to the presumed sexual advantages this gives, it is in actual practice essential for him to have a number of auxiliaries in order to be able to carry out his numerous duties (314; 373). The social cohesion of the Nambikwara group is therefore maintained through a network of mutual obligation and exchange between chief and group: 'The chief has power but he must be generous. He has duties, but he is allowed several wives. Between him and the group there exists a perpetually renewed balance of gifts, privileges, services and obligations' (315; 374–5).

The enquiry into the essence of authority pursued in *Tristes tropiques* thus extends Mauss's model of exchange into the third (vertical) dimension of hierarchical relations, though these hierarchical relations are visibly not of the exploitative kind. As with Rousseau's notion of consent, Lévi-Strauss's use of the Maussian category of generosity does more than simply explain the mechanics of social cohesion: it adds a moral complexion to the facts observed. In the Nambikwara he finds an example of authority that is non-exploitative, based not on a structure of subordination, but on a kind of dynamic equilibrium involving a continuous exchange between chief and people, an 'economy' that is the condition of possibility of political consent. The problem is that despite this finely balanced system of transactions between chief and group, the terms of transaction are not in the end entirely equal. Even taking into account the group's main concession to the chief, the right of polygamy (a privilege apparently only shared with shamans), it appears that there is an imponderable in the equation. As the frequent refusal of those nominated to the office testifies, the privilege of polygamy does not necessarily compensate for what is the onerous and often precarious position of chief:

It can be said that the privilege of polygamy, whatever attractions it may have from the sexual, sentimental or social points of view, would hardly be enough to inspire a vocation. Polygamous marriage is a technical condition of power; in the providing of any deep satisfaction it can only be of secondary importance. There must be some further reason. (*TT*2, 316; *TT*1, 375–6)

It is at this point that Lévi-Strauss passes from an external perspective, an 'objective' description of Nambikwara politics, to speculation on the personal motivations of the chief. His Maussian analysis of reciprocity therefore gives way to, or rather is completed (supplemented) by, a psychological explanation of the function of authority. Having cautioned against the judgement of psychological motivation in cultures very different from our own,[37] he nonetheless proceeds to offer the following interpretation:

When I try to recall the moral and psychological characteristics of the various Nambikwara chiefs and to grasp the elusive aspects of their personalities (which escape scientific analysis but have a certain value, thanks to the intuitive feeling for human communication and the experience of friendship), I am driven to the following conclusion: chiefs exist because, in every human group, there are men who differ from their fellow-beings in that they like prestige for its own sake, are attracted by responsibility and for whom the burden of public affairs brings its own reward. Such individual differences are undoubtedly developed and brought into play to differing degrees by various cultures. But their existence in a society as uncompetitive as Nambikwara society suggests that they are not entirely social in origin, but belong rather to the basic psychological material from which all societies are constructed. (*TT*2, 316; *TT*1, 376)

A number of points need to be made here. First, the conclusion of the psychological irreducibility of leadership meets the deficit observed at the economic level concerning the chief's obligation of generosity and self-sacrifice. It also completes what had risked becoming too 'Durkheimian' an analysis of the function of authority – authority as a mere epiphenomenon of the group, as an impersonal and interchangeable function. Second, this conclusion is arrived at through a process of intuition rather than observation, through the medium of interpersonal contact rather than 'objective' analysis.[38] Finally, the reader is reminded of the *universal* relevance of the case of the Nambikwara: psychological individuation is a basic fact of all societies, and is an essential component in the designation of authority.

At this point it would appear that Lévi-Strauss's analysis is complete. He has examined the political, economic and psychological conditions of authority and demonstrated their necessary complementarity: the notion of consent is in itself an insufficient explanation of the mechanics of social cohesion, its realization being dependent upon the concrete (economic) process of exchange; in its turn the economic explanation fails to account for what is a clear asymmetry

---

[37] To this restriction should be added the ethnographer's imperfect knowledge of the various Nambikwara dialects. On his own admission, this knowledge extended only to a 'a rudimentary kind of Nambikwara', which 'did not allow for the expression of very subtle ideas' (*TT*2, 279; *TT*1, 326–7).

[38] It should be noted that the ethnographer establishes a special relationship with two chiefs in particular, the Wakletoçu and Tarundé chiefs, who are his best informants (308–9; 365–6). A structure of mutual identification is discernible here: the ethnographer is more or less the same age as his hosts and is also the 'chief' of his own group.

between chief and group, and requires another level of explanation, that of the psychological aspect of authority. From the point of view of Lévi-Strauss's analysis, therefore, the exemplary case of the Nambikwara presents a closed and integrated system, a perfect demonstration, one could argue, of Mauss's total social fact. However, outside of this self-contained circuit there remains a residual element, not included but, it could be said, virtually present in the anatomy of power proposed in *Tristes tropiques*: the religious.

In fact, introducing and framing this analysis is a curious episode, related at the beginning of the chapter, concerning the mysterious disappearance of a chief whose group (Sabané) has recently merged with a related, though linguistically distinct, native group (Tarundé). When the chief is finally found, he explains how during the storm of the previous night, he was carried off by the thunder to a remote location, stripped of all his adornments, then returned to his camp. After some discussion within the Tarundé group, it is speculated that the chief has used the pretext of this supernatural occurrence to conceal his negotiations with another party, a third, hostile group camping in the vicinity, plausibly with the intention of betraying his present allies. Shortly after the incident, the ethnographer and the two groups part company, so he never learns of the sequel to these events (306–7; 363–4).

Despite the brevity of this encounter, one effect of the Sabané chief's mystification is precisely to make the ethnographer reflect on the nature and the function of power in the different groups he has observed during his fieldwork with the Nambikwara. Surprisingly perhaps, in the analysis of Nambikwara politics that follows and which we have summarized above, the question of the religious aspect of power does not figure at all. Indeed, it is asserted that while some of the chiefs' functions are approximate to those of a shaman, 'such mystic preoccupations always remain in the background'; magical skills are 'never more than secondary attributes of chieftainship', and there is normally a division of temporal and spiritual power between two individuals (311; 369–70).

It is somewhat paradoxical that while prompting Lévi-Strauss to reflection on power relations among the Nambikwara, the example of the Sabané chief does not seem to contribute to the composite portrait he constructs of these relations. In one respect, this is simply a practical limitation: the ethnographer did not know the Sabané dialect and was therefore closer to the Tarundé group (306; 362). It is nevertheless interesting to note that the Sabané chief combines the two functions of shaman and secular leader (305; 361), whereas the function of Tarundé and Wakletoçu chiefs, the two individuals the ethnographer works most closely with, appears to be an entirely secular one. This difference (or bias) of emphasis would not be so problematic were it not for the fact that Lévi-Strauss is pretending, via the local example of the Nambikwara, to speak of the origin and function of authority *in general*. Is it possible then to detect in the model of authority presented in *Tristes tropiques* a certain suspicion of the sacred? If, as the analysis outlined above suggests, the basis of authority in general is a combination of consent, reciprocity and psychological predisposition, does this mean that the religious attributes of power *in general* are a secondary development, representing a potential *mystification* of power, a possible perversion of authority? Certainly, the episode concerning the Sabané chief's disappearance offers an example of such mystification; another, telling illustration would be the behaviour of the Wakletoçu chief who pretends to master the ethnographer's magic of writing: his subsequent loss of power is an instructive reminder of the strict limits the group places on the chief's use of his authority (296–7, 300; 350, 355).

Whatever the problems of interpretation (and we are, in the final instance, restricted to the mediating testimony of the ethnographer), the analysis of power offered in *Tristes tropiques* could be seen to be formally analogous to the two demonstrations of the *Elementary Structures* treated above, to the extent that in each case the attempt is to show the operation of the principle of reciprocity in the most elementary of configurations. In each case, too, there is a visible attenuation of the ritual and religious dimension: treatment of the profane aspects of everyday life in the *Elementary Structures*; concentration on the secular rather than the sacred basis of power in *Tristes tropiques*. This tendency towards what is in effect a *reduction* of the religious will be a leitmotif of the following chapter.

3   From kinship to myth

Le problème ethnologique est donc, en dernière analyse, un problème de communication.

(In the last analysis, therefore, the ethnological problem is a problem of communication.)[1]

Les problèmes d'ethnologie religieuse relèvent d'une psychologie intellectualiste.

(The problems of religious anthropology require an intellectualist psychology.)[2]

Had Lévi-Strauss ceased writing in 1950, after the publication of *The Elementary Structures of Kinship*, his contribution to anthropology would already have been a considerable one. The work brought to French anthropology an analysis of unprecedented scope and theoretical depth, and its effect outside France was to stimulate debate in kinship studies for the next two decades. It is therefore surprising, and interesting, that shortly after this monumental work appeared, Lévi-Strauss shifted the focus of his research away from kinship studies, to concentrate on the anthropology of religion. The cause of this somewhat abrupt change of specialization, according to Lévi-Strauss, was his move to the Ecole Pratique des Hautes Etudes in 1950, to take the chair in the history of religions previously occupied by Mauss, and more recently by Maurice Leenhardt. In a very short space of time, we are told, he found himself having to begin an entirely new field of study.[3]

Professional and institutional factors were therefore decisive in determining Lévi-Strauss's change of specialization. But in another sense – and this is why the transition is an interesting one – they seem simply to have precipitated what was already a tendency, an internal dynamic of Lévi-Strauss's thinking during this period. Already in the *Elementary Structures*, there is a marked interest in the role played by indigenous representations of kinship relations and the

[1] *IM*2, 36; *IM*1, xxxii.
[2] *AS*1, 227–8. My translation. This sentence does not figure in the original English version of the article.
[3] See *CLS*2, 71; *PL*, 103–4.

'theoretical' nature of such representations.[4] In addition, in the more philosophical passages of this text, there was an attempt to establish the cognitive substratum of the social behaviour (reciprocity) at the base of kinship transactions. Just as importantly, however, it could be said that the reduction attempted in the *Elementary Structures* had reached a kind of impasse. Lévi-Strauss himself says as much when he admits that what he had achieved by more or less 'artisanal' methods could only be pursued in the realm of formal mathematics, and that he himself was not qualified to follow this path.[5] Not qualified, certainly, but also, one could hazard, not willing. The impression here, surprisingly perhaps, is that Lévi-Strauss is simply not interested in formalization by or in itself. It is as if what matters for him is the *possibility* of reduction or, more precisely, the possibility of revealing that possibility, rather than its actuality. Whatever the case may be, it is clear that, while Lévi-Strauss considers Mauss's model of exchange to be a theoretical achievement of next to axiomatic status, as he moves from the study of the 'infrastructures' of social organization to the 'superstructures' of religious representations, the influence and incidence of Mauss in his work is correspondingly reduced. If, according to one of Lévi-Strauss's numerous comparisons with the history of natural science, the theory of reciprocity rests upon foundations as solid as those of the theory of gravitation in astronomy, the work of Mauss as the Newton of anthropology must be superseded and completed by an Einstein – that is, himself.[6]

From reciprocity to symbolism

The problem for Lévi-Strauss was that while a large part of the theoretical infrastructure of his work on social organization had come 'ready-made', as it were, in the form of Mauss's theory of reciprocity, when he turned in the early 1950s to the study of religious representations, no comparable body of theory was ready to hand. In an article published in 1955, in fact, he deplores anthropology's neglect of religious phenomena in the preceding twenty years or so.[7] In the same article, he goes on to give the now classic demonstration of structural analysis as applied to the Oedipus myth. We will return to this important text later in this chapter. However, Lévi-Strauss's first significant negotiation of his new area of specialization is in the *Introduction to the Work of Marcel Mauss*, published in 1950. What is intriguing about this text is that it is in many ways more an introduction to the next phase of Lévi-Strauss's own research than an introduction to Mauss's work. Through his exposition of

[4] *ESK*, 125; *SEP*, 146.
[5] See interview with Catherine B. Clément and Antoine Casanova, 'Un ethnologue et la culture', *La Nouvelle Critique* 61 (February 1973), 29–30.
[6] See *SA*1, 162; *AS*1, 179–80.   [7] *SA*1, 206–7; *AS*1, 227–8.

Mauss's ideas, Lévi-Strauss articulates some of the essential elements of the structuralist programme, in such a way that structuralism seems to emerge as the only logical point of conclusion of Mauss's thought.[8] The elements of this programme can be summarized as follows:

- The notion of the symbolic nature of social customs and institutions (*IM2*, 12; *IM1*, xvi) and the definition of society as an ensemble of different, often incomplete and incompatible symbolic systems (16–18; xix–xxi).
- The idea of a mental unconscious common to all subjects, regardless of cultural variations. This unconscious is not unconscious in the Freudian sense of the term; rather, it is analogous to the deep-level structures of language revealed by structural linguistics (33–6; xxx–xxxi). Such an unconscious would be the transcendental ground which guarantees the ultimate intelligibility of systems of representation radically different from our own.
- The notion of 'surplus' signification and the floating signifier (59–65; xlvii–li).

The hypothesis of a transcendental unconscious will be essential to the structural analysis of myth as practised in the 1955 article and later, most exemplarily, in the four volumes of *Mythologiques*. It is difficult to see how the structuralist programme could function without this hypothesis, but conceptually, it is a simplex, its field of application does not extend significantly beyond its role as the validating condition, verifiable or non-verifiable, of structural analysis. By contrast, the notions of surplus signification and the incommensurability of symbolic systems could be described as conceptual complexes, as they lie at the heart of a network of associations that run throughout Lévi-Strauss's work. It would therefore be useful to dwell an instant on their initial formulation in the *Introduction to Mauss*.

The immediate context of Lévi-Strauss's exposition of his view of the symbolic is his reference to Mauss's essay 'On the Real and Practical Relationships between Psychology and Sociology', and his consideration of the question of the influence of the social on individual psychology and vice versa. From the beginning, he subscribes to the Maussian view that different psychological formations are a translation, on the individual level, of a properly sociological structure, rather than the reverse, and expresses this causality in terms of what he takes to be the *symbolic* nature of society: 'The nature of society is to express itself symbolically in its customs and its institutions; normal modes of individual behaviour are, on the contrary, *never symbolic in themselves*: they are the elements out of which a symbolic system, which can only be collective,

---

[8] See Christopher Johnson, 'From Mauss to Lévi-Strauss', in *Sociology and Anthropology*, special issue of *Modern and Contemporary France* 5.4 (November 1997), 421–32. See also Camille Tarot, *De Durkheim à Mauss. L'Invention du symbolique* (Paris: La Découverte/M.A.U.S.S., 1999), pp. 403–7; Bruno Karsenti, *L'Homme total. Sociologie, anthropologie et philosophie chez Marcel Mauss* (Paris: Presses Universitaires de France, 1997), pp. 278–9.

builds itself' (12; xvi).[9] Abnormal behaviour, Lévi-Strauss continues, gives the illusion of an autonomous symbolic system, whereas in fact it is simply using a system different from that of mainstream society, a distant equivalent (one could hazard here: a transform) of the dominant system. That the pathological is never simply an individual matter is evident in the fact that it is classifiable, and that different social formations produce different classes of disorder. Even the exception of the psychopathological, therefore, is subject to social determination (13–14; xvii). It is this question of the social exception, of the pychopathological, which becomes the focus of Lévi-Strauss's subsequent digression on the question of the shaman's trance and states of possession. He resists the common assimilation of these states with the characteristic forms of neurosis, and argues that even if science were to discover the bio-chemical causes of the latter, this would not invalidate a sociological theory of mental disorder. It is here, in a long passage which takes him far from the main commentary of Mauss, that he outlines what the components of such a theory might be. The passage merits quotation in its entirety:

Every culture can be considered as an ensemble of symbolic systems headed by language, matrimonial rules, economic relations, art, science and religion. All of these systems seek to express certain aspects of physical reality and social reality, and even more, to express the links that those two types of reality have with each other and those that occur among the symbolic systems themselves. The fact that the systems can never achieve that expression in a fully [*intégralement*] satisfying (and above all) equivalent form is, first, a result of the conditions of functioning peculiar to each system, in that the systems always remain incommensurable; second, it is a result of the way that history introduces into those systems elements from different systems, determines the shifting from one type of society to another, and unequal rates of change in the relative evolution of each particular system. So no society is ever wholly [*intégralement*] and completely symbolic, because a society is always a spatio-temporal given, and therefore subject to the impact of other societies and of earlier states of its own development; and because, even in some hypothetical society which we might imagine as having no links with any other and no dependence on its own past, the different systems of symbols which all combine to constitute the culture or civilization would never be reducible to one another (the translation of one system into another being conditioned by the introduction of constants with irrational values, that is, values external to these two systems). Instead of saying that a society is never completely symbolic, it would be more accurate to say that it could never manage to give all its members, to the same degree, the means to apply themselves entirely to the building of a symbolic structure, which for normal thinking is only realizable on the level of social life. For, strictly speaking, the person whom we call sane is the one who alienates himself, since he consents to an existence in a world definable only in terms of the self-other relationship...

Any society is therefore comparable to a universe in which only discrete masses are highly structured. In every society, then, it would be inevitable that a percentage, itself

---

[9] Translation slightly modified.

variable, of individuals find themselves placed 'off system', so to speak, or between two or more irreducible systems ... Their peripheral position relative to a local system does not mean that they are not integral parts of the total system. (*IM*2, 16–18; *IM*1, xix–xx).

This passage, or parts of it, has been much quoted, cited, or paraphrased in commentaries of Lévi-Strauss's structuralism, but none, as far as I am aware, have underlined its essential *overdetermination*, its conceptual complexity. The passage is a veritable Pandora's box, and I will attempt here to unpack some of its contents. First, there is what might be termed the local context of the passage, its treatment of the question of the pathological nature or not of phenomena such as shamanism and possession. Lévi-Strauss's response to the question is to describe individuals such as shamans and the possessed as falling outside of or between the dominant symbolic systems of a given society, but nevertheless as being an integral part of the total system. However, what interests me here is the relative asymmetry between means and ends, that is, the conceptual machinery Lévi-Strauss brings to bear on the 'problem' of the shaman and of possession seems disproportionate to the solution he provides to that problem. This is an example of the tendency, frequent in Lévi-Strauss's work, for theory or speculation to transcend the context in which it is articulated. In other words, the question of shamanism and possession seems almost to be a *pretext* for further theorization on the actual nature of society. The previous, short definition of the symbolic nature of society is here given more development as the principal 'customs' or 'institutions' through which it expresses itself are detailed: language, matrimonial rules, economic relations, art, science and religion. The composition and sequence of this list is not indifferent. On a general level, it could be seen as simply reproducing the traditional categories of anthropological analysis. More specifically, however, Lévi-Strauss gives these categories structure and sequence. Beginning with language (for Lévi-Strauss the *sine qua non* of human society), the first three terms could be seen as designating the most immediate forms of social interaction and exchange, the infrastructure, as it were, of social existence. On the other hand, the final three terms would designate the relatively autonomous instances of creation, intellection and collective representation. Again, this articulation of 'infrastructure' and 'superstructure' is not indifferent; it mirrors the two stages of Lévi-Strauss's own trajectory from social organization to the anthropology of religions, discussed above.

To the extent that it utilizes the notions of expression and translation, Lévi-Strauss's conceptualization of social customs and social institutions as symbolic systems makes this field of enquiry a potentially infinite one. The six instances he mentions are *expressions* of different aspects of the social and natural worlds or the relations between them, and these instances in their turn are viewed as *translations* of one another. The result is a multiplicity of possible relations between different levels or instances. However, the relations of translation between symbolic systems are limited and never integral, as the systems are essentially irreducible. Following Lévi-Strauss's astronomical or cosmological metaphor, these systems are comparable to localized lumpings or concentrations of matter ('discrete masses'), separated by expanses of relatively non-structured material.

I am insisting on the detail of this passage because, beyond the local context of his explanation of the social mechanism of exclusion–inclusion of non-conventional behaviour (shamanism, possession), Lévi-Strauss seems to be attempting to set up the conditions and parameters of structural analysis as he will later practise it: the symbolic nature of the object of analysis; the relative autonomy of different (discrete) symbolic systems. He is also broaching, again on a rather abstract and highly conceptual level, the problem of cultural relativism and cultural change, of the difference between cultures and their relative development, which a few years later will be the subject of *Race and History*. While this theoretical digression is locally subordinate to the question of shamanism and possession and ends with the resolution of that question, thematically it informs the whole of the *Introduction to Mauss*. This can be seen most clearly in another, much-quoted passage on the notion of 'surplus' signification and the floating signifier, in the final section of the *Introduction*.

The context and content of this second passage are as overdetermined as those of the first. While the *Introduction* as a whole is framed as a homage to Mauss, repeatedly insisting on the 'modernity' of his thought, increasingly, as one approaches its conclusion, Lévi-Strauss appears to demarcate and dissociate himself from the master. The process of demarcation begins with his criticism of Mauss's use of the notion of *hau* in *The Gift*. While Mauss recognizes exchange as the common denominator of the different ethnological facts reviewed in his essay, he is curiously unable, according to Lévi-Strauss, to discern its immediate operation in the data available to him. Instead, he perceives only its atomized elements – the threefold obligation to give, receive and return – as they are given to empirical observation. It follows that the only way of explaining how these different moments are articulated is to suppose that there is some force or source of energy which holds them together. This Mauss finds in the Melanesian notion of *hau*, the magical force which ensures that a gift is both received and reciprocated. Lévi-Strauss himself is highly critical of this solution: '*Hau* is not the ultimate explanation [*raison*] for exchange: it is the conscious form whereby men of a given society, in which the problem had a particular importance, apprehended an unconscious necessity whose explanation [*raison*] lies elsewhere' (48; xxxix). Mauss has therefore erroneously taken the indigenous (Melanesian) interpretation as describing the primary reality of exchange, whereas it is merely a secondary elaboration. While this interpretation may be more authentic and more illuminating than our own (Western) interpretations, it remains an interpretation, and as such needs to be reduced to a more fundamental structure: 'Once the indigenous interpretation has been isolated, it must be reduced by an objective critique so as to reach the underlying reality. We have very little chance of finding that reality in conscious formulations; a better chance, in unconscious mental structures to which institutions give us access, but a better chance yet, in language' (48–9; xxxix).[10] It seems, therefore, that Mauss has allowed himself to be mystified by the native interpretation of the *hau*. It is as if his famous intuitive 'feel' for ethnographic data, his much-admired gift for empathetic reconstruction of other mentalities, were now turned against him, becoming a weakness or, at best, a limitation. Such reconstruction looks at the *form* but fails to properly elucidate the *reason* for exchange in the societies studied.[11] It is precisely the task of structural analysis to investigate the reason or reality behind the form.

In essence the same critique is made and the same kind of solution provided in the final section of the *Introduction to Mauss*, where Lévi-Strauss looks at the concept of *mana* in Mauss's earlier work on magic. Durkheim and Mauss used the term *mana* (originally a Melanesian and Polynesian word) to refer to the abstract quality or supernatural force believed, in a number of cultures, to accompany specific forms of human action such as magical practices. Lévi-Strauss thinks that this kind of generalization of a localized term is legitimate if, as he believes is the case, it helps to bring together under a single category different cultural phenomena of the same basic type. However, he questions the restriction of the *mana* complex to so-called 'archaic' civilizations, asking instead whether it is not a universal trait of the human mind (52–3; xlii–xliii). Again, the criticism is that Durkheim and Mauss have described the form but have not explained the reason of the *mana*, that their analysis has stopped short of the elucidation of the deep structure of the behaviour they describe. Again, this criticism is the pretext for Lévi-Strauss to advance his own, structuralist interpretation of the phenomenon: that the social use of terms such as *mana* is part of the unconscious reflex of the human mind to fill the lacunae in its understanding of the world with a signifier of indeterminate and interchangeable value. This reflex is as common in the everyday, non-scientific, behaviour of Western societies as it is in so-called 'archaic' cultures (54–6; xliv).

It would seem that the above critique and correction of Durkheim and Mauss goes far enough, but again, characteristically, Lévi-Strauss's desire is to

---

[10] For a similar critique of Durkheim and Mauss, see *SA*1, 282; *AS*1, 309–10.

[11] The subtitle of *The Gift* is *Forme et raison de l'échange dans les sociétés archaïques* (The Form and Reason for Exchange in Archaic Societies).

elucidate the very foundations of the described phenomenon, and this takes him into an extended speculation on the origin of language and human knowledge:

> Whatever may have been the moment and the circumstances of its appearance in the ascent of animal life, language can only have arisen all at once. Things cannot have begun to signify gradually. In the wake of a transformation which is not a subject of study for the social sciences, but for biology and psychology, a shift occurred from a stage where nothing had a meaning to another stage where everything had meaning. Actually, that apparently banal remark is important, because that radical change has no counterpart in the field of knowledge, which develops slowly and progressively. In other words, at the moment when the entire universe all at once became *significant*, it was none the better *known* for being so, even if it is true that the emergence of language must have hastened the rhythm of the development of knowledge. So there is a fundamental opposition, in the history of the human mind, between symbolism, which is characteristically discontinuous, and knowledge, characterized by continuity. Let us consider what follows from that. It follows that the two categories of the signifier and the signified came to be constituted simultaneously and interdependently, as complementary units, whereas knowledge, that is, the intellectual process which enables us to identify certain aspects of the signifier and certain aspects of the signified, one by reference to the other – we could even say the process which enables us to choose, from the entirety of the signifier and the entirety of the signified, those parts which present the most satisfying relations of mutual agreement – only got started very slowly . . . The universe signified long before people began to know what it signified, no doubt that goes without saying. But, from the foregoing analysis, it also emerges that from the beginning, the universe signified the totality of what humankind can expect to know about it. What people call the progress of the human mind and, in any case, the progress of scientific knowledge, could only have been and can only ever be constituted out of processes of correcting and recutting of patterns, regrouping, defining relationships of belonging and discovering new resources, inside a totality which is closed and complementary to itself. (*IM*2, 59–61; *IM*1, xlvii–xlviii)

Conceptually, there is much to question in this speculation on what Lévi-Strauss calls the 'history of the human mind': the idea of the instantaneous birth of language, as opposed to the gradual acquisition of objective knowledge; the opposition between symbolism and science; the assigning of the Saussurean categories of 'signifier' and 'signified' to the respective realms of the human mind and the 'universe'.[12] However, it is perhaps more appropriate here to formulate our question differently, to ask *why* Lévi-Strauss needs this theory of human knowledge and human symbolization, rather than focusing on its conceptual consistency. Beyond its immediate function as a response to the general question or 'problem' of the *mana*, this passage could be seen as continuing and

---

[12] Derrida addresses some of these questions in his seminal essay, 'Structure, Sign and Play in the Discourse of the Human Sciences', in *Writing and Difference*, trans. Alan Bass (London: Routledge, 1978), pp. 278–93; 'La Structure, le signe et le jeu dans le discours des sciences humaines', in *L'Écriture et la différence* (Paris: Editions du Seuil, 1967), pp. 409–28.

completing the process of mapping which, one could argue, is one of the principal impulses of the *Introduction to Mauss*. Earlier in the text, we have seen, Lévi-Strauss's enumeration of the different symbolic systems constitutive of society contained an implicit division or articulation between 'infrastructural' and 'superstructural' systems: language, matrimonial rules, economic relations (infrastructure); art, science and religion (superstructure). What the present passage is doing, performatively, is separating out the three domains on the second side of this articulation: scientific knowledge is qualitatively different from symbolic systems such as art and religion. In the ensuing text, this division is restated and confirmed as Lévi-Strauss returns (finally) to the question of the *mana*:

I believe that notions of the *mana* type, however diverse they may be, and viewed in terms of their general function (which, as we have seen, has not vanished from our mentality and our form of society) represent nothing more or less than that *floating signifier* which is the limitation of all finite thought (but also the guarantee of all art, all poetry, all mythic and aesthetic invention), even though scientific thought is capable, if not of totally containing it, at least of partially regulating it. Moreover, magical thinking offers other, different methods of channelling and containment, with different results, and all these methods can very well coexist. (*IM2*, 63; *IM1*, xlix)

The floating signifier, which Lévi-Strauss has immediately before defined in *economic* terms as a 'surplus' or 'supplementary ration' of signification,[13] represents the human mind's finitude, its failure to think and describe the world completely objectively, but this limitation also has a positive value, to the extent that it opens up the potentially infinite realm of collective representations (here, interestingly, restricted to myth and artistic creation). So Lévi-Strauss's dialogue with Durkheim and Mauss, while seeming to address and solve the problem of the *mana*, is at the same time and on another level a kind of monologue with himself, an extended reflection on the nature of the object he is interested in at this particular stage. The structure and movement of the *Introduction to Mauss* could therefore be viewed as a progressive narrowing down of the object of analysis, a process of selection and reduction: society as an ensemble of discrete symbolic systems; the distinction between infrastructural and superstructural systems; and finally, at the superstructural level, the relatively autonomous systems of mythic thought and aesthetic production. It is useful to remember, however, that while already in the *Introduction* we can see Lévi-Strauss gravitating towards what will become his major area of specialization, myth, and conceptually preparing the ground for this research, the overall framing of this work of prospection in the final section of the text, as

---

[13] My own impression is that there is an implicit homology in Lévi-Strauss's mind between the surplus production that makes possible the spectacular excesses of the potlatch and the kind of exuberant and 'non-utilitarian' creation one finds in representations such as myth.

the above quotation indicates, is the question of magic. Magical thinking is presented here as a means of semiotic 'containment' analogous to science but also, via the notion of *mana*, as drawing on the same 'surplus' of signification which is the condition of mythical thought. Earlier in the *Introduction*, as we saw, Lévi-Strauss's digression on symbolic systems was framed by the question of the shaman and states of possession. Before proceeding to a consideration of Lévi-Strauss's treatment of myth, it is therefore necessary to look more closely at his thinking on magic and shamanism.

Magical practice and magical thought

'The Sorcerer and his Magic' (1949)[14] is briefly footnoted in the *Introduction to Mauss*, and together with the thematically related 'The Effectiveness of Symbols' (1949),[15] it is Lévi-Strauss's most developed treatment of the subject. A central point made in both texts concerns the relationship between the symbolic and the physiological. 'The Effectiveness of Symbols', for example, is a commentary of an incantation used by shamans to facilitate difficult childbirth. Lévi-Strauss shows how the narrative of the incantation mobilizes the familiar figures of the patient's social and cosmic universe, creating in the patient an internal dramatization of her condition, leading finally to a restoration of equilibrium and a reintegration into the community. The success of the shaman's cure therefore resides in the 'symbolic efficacy' of the incantation, its function as a representation that gives order, coherence and meaning to the patient's suffering, even if it offers no real objective explanation of its etiology (*SA*1, 197; *AS*1, 217–18). Similarly, Lévi-Strauss begins 'The Sorcerer and his Magic' with examples of physiological conditions directly induced by an individual's psychological state: his or her belief that (s)he is a victim of sorcery is confirmed and reinforced by the belief of the entire community in this reality, thus creating the physical symptoms associated with that belief (167–9; 183–5).

In one sense, the explanation Lévi-Strauss gives of magical practice in 'The Effectiveness of Symbols' and 'The Sorcerer and his Magic' is a classically Durkheimian one: society, collective belief is seen in the last instance to sanction and guarantee the sorcerer's power; without such sanction, he is nothing. In their essay on magic, Hubert and Mauss had proposed that 'magic, like religion, is viewed as a totality; either you believe in it all, or you do not... one negative instance topples the whole edifice'.[16] Although they do take into account the individual agency of the magician, for example the possibility of trickery and simulation,[17] in the final analysis they are careful to reduce the appearance of

---

[14] *SA*1, 167–85; *AS*1, 183–203.   [15] *SA*1, 186–205; *AS*1, 205–26.
[16] *A General Theory of Magic*, trans. Robert Brain (London: Routledge, 1972), p. 92; *Sociologie et anthropologie*, p. 85.
[17] Ibid., p. 93; p. 86.

individual contingency to the reality of external constraint. On the one hand, for instance, the magician's simulations are compared to certain states of neurosis in which the individual actually believes in what he or she simulates;[18] on the other hand, the expectations of the group invest the magician with a certain power, and their unconditional belief in that power creates the role that he then finds himself compelled to play.[19]

In 'The Sorcerer and his Magic', Lévi-Strauss consistently underlines the irreducibility of social context in the construction of the shaman's function. However, as he notes at the beginning of the chapter, the object of his study is more psychological than sociological (185, note 3; 185, note 1). His analysis of the other polarity of what he calls the 'shamanistic complex', the psychology of the shaman him- or herself, is an attempt to reconstitute what Hubert and Mauss had tended to neglect, that is, the psychological ambiguity of the shaman and of the social context that supports him or her. With Hubert and Mauss, we have seen, one either believes or does not believe in magic. The process has an almost mechanical quality: between the nervous constitution that predisposes the shaman to spirit possession and states of trance, and the public expectation validating the shaman's power and function, there is little room for psychological nuance, critical reflex or a more empirical attitude.[20]

In contrast to the purely sociological approach of Hubert and Mauss, Lévi-Strauss's study explores the many nuances and ambiguities of individual and collective psychology in relation to magical practices. The first two examples he provides, one of which is based on his own personal experience during his fieldwork with the Nambikwara, are a convincing illustration of how belief in the magical is not a simple affair, that such belief does not exclude a degree of scepticism, a critical attitude or specific practical or political considerations (169–75; 185–92).[21] It is, however, the third example in Lévi-Strauss's study, a native autobiographical account, which probably best illustrates the psychologically undecidable aspect of the shaman's experience. The narrative describes the experience of a Kwakiutl named Quesalid, who does not believe in the power of the shamans in his society. Initially acting through simple curiosity, but also with the intention of exposing their trickery, he succeeds in gaining admission into the group and initiation into their practices. He goes on to learn the techniques, songs and rites of the profession and discovers in effect that

---

[18] Ibid., p. 96; pp. 88–9.   [19] Ibid., pp. 96–7; pp. 89–90.

[20] Hubert and Mauss are categorical on this point: 'while all science, even the most traditional, is still conceived as being positive and experimental, belief in magic is always *a priori*' (ibid., p. 92 [translation modified]; p. 85); 'we have no wish to imply that magic does not demand analysis, or testing. We are only saying that it is poorly analytical, poorly experimental and almost totally *a priori*' (ibid., p. 124; p. 117); 'Magic should be considered as a system of *a priori* inductions, operating under the pressure of the needs of groups of individuals' (ibid., p. 126; p. 119).

[21] The episode involving the Nambikwara is related in chapter 29 of *Tristes tropiques*.

the much-vaunted power of the shamans rests on no more than skilful dissimulation and play-acting. He wishes to pursue his investigations, but now finds that he is no longer free. After a successful cure, he acquires the reputation of a 'great shaman'. Though Quesalid does not lose his scepticism (he attributes the success of his cure to the psychological state of the patient), he does however begin to hesitate when he comes to compare the relative effectiveness of different magical practices. As it happens, his own method appears to be more effective than those of his colleagues in neighbouring groups. Little by little, the initiate becomes reconciled to his profession. He defends his method against rival practitioners and his initial scepticism gives way to a more nuanced attitude (175–8; 192–6).

It is easy to see that, unlike Hubert and Mauss, who are mainly concerned to give an *external* description of magical practices (the social function of the shaman, the social sanctioning of his role, ceremonies of initiation, etc.), Lévi-Strauss's study gives an *internal* perspective on the same phenomenon. What his predecessors present as critical moments of the shaman's experience, for example, the experience of revelation or initiation, Lévi-Strauss describes from a different point of view and with a difference of emphasis. Quesalid is indeed initiated in his story, but what is significant is not the initiation itself, nor the moment of revelation (there is none), but an intellectual process involving the gradual, almost imperceptible passage from radical scepticism to qualified belief. Lévi-Strauss's analysis therefore paints the tableau of an intellectual apprenticeship; the protagonist's experience becomes a kind of quest. The condition of this quest, its motivation, is not the congenital, physiological or nervous predisposition described in the aforementioned sociological accounts of magic, but *curiosity*, a primarily intellectual attitude. Indeed, it could be said that all that was extraordinary about the figure of the shaman, as he is described in the characterizations of Hubert and Mauss, is here reduced to the obviousness, even the banality of the everyday. The protagonist, Quesalid, experiences neither possession, nor states of ecstasy, nor personality change. There is no point in the narrative at which he loses control: he is a lucid experimenter and not an ecstatic; he compares methods and results and decides on the relative efficacy of different practices, a procedure not unlike that of modern science, Lévi-Strauss reminds us (176; 194).[22] Quesalid thus comes to belief through a series of approximations or negotiations of the real. Revelation, if it occurs at all, comes only through the test of empirical comparison. If, according to Hubert and Mauss, belief in magic is always a priori, in the present example such belief is rigorously a posteriori.

---

[22] In an interview with the French anthropologist Marc Augé in 1989, Lévi-Strauss reasserts his suspicion of the psychopathological interpretation of shamanic behaviour (*Current Anthropology* 31.1 (February 1990), 87–8).

As was remarked earlier, Lévi-Strauss's intention in 'The Sorcerer and his Magic' is not to question or criticize the typology of the magician proposed by his predecessors, nor to minimize the importance of the social in the creation and validation of the shaman's function, quite the contrary. The perspective he adopts has rather the effect of completing a picture that tended to reduce or simplify the psychological element. As Lévi-Strauss points out, the psychology of the shaman is not a simple one. He is neither simply a believer nor a sceptic. At the close of the narrative, he is not an unconditional believer, but is 'conscientious' in the exercise of his professional duties (178; 196).

Placed in its historical context, Lévi-Strauss's choice of focus, that is, the restriction of his study to the lived, conscious experience of the shaman, seems close to certain aspects of existentialist philosophy: its suspicion of individual or collective possession, of the unconscious, of that which undermines the responsibility and reflexivity of the subject. But the choice of focus (as Lévi-Strauss himself pointed out, more psychological than sociological) cannot be reduced simply to this particular philosophical context, nor to the fact, significant as it may be, that the article was first published in the journal founded by Jean-Paul Sartre, *Les Temps Modernes*.[23] Equally important is the extent to which this perspective is in accordance with a common theme or characteristic of Lévi-Strauss's thought. What stands out in the shaman's story, and in the commentary which follows it, is the emphasis Lévi-Strauss places on the *logic* that informs magical practices. In fact, for Lévi-Strauss, such activities are never simply empirical in nature, but are also supplemented by theory: they always need to be articulated in the form of a *system*. As much as the success of the magical cure (which is never certain), what counts here is the *coherence* of the shaman's system. In Lévi-Strauss's commentary of Quesalid's story, it seems that everything turns on this concept of 'system' and its coherence. The protagonist's 'system', for example, begins to form in his mind after his first successful cures. This system becomes more coherent with the collapse of the competing systems of his rival colleagues. Finally, the public support for one or the other system (none of which, we are reminded, has any basis in reality), essential to the success of the shaman, depends on the relative complexity or elaborateness of the system finally chosen, and the intellectual and affective 'satisfaction' the system gives to the public (176, 197; 193–4, 197).

The concept of system appears in fact to be a constant of Lévi-Strauss's thought. Whether it be a question, as in this case, of the shaman and his public or, in later studies, of mythical or 'savage' thought, there seems to be the same requirement of consistency and coherence. This is because for Lévi-Strauss,

---

[23] The rather severe criticism of the psychoanalytical cure given in the concluding pages of the article is in fact in keeping with the anti-psychoanalytical stance of *Les Temps Modernes* during this period. See Howard Davies, *Sartre and 'Les Temps Modernes'* (Cambridge University Press, 1987), pp. 29, 31–3.

the human mind is unable to tolerate experience that is discontinuous and not integrated into an ordered system. In the case of magic, for instance, he suggests that

in contrast with scientific explanation, the problem here is not to attribute confused and disorganized states, emotions, or representations to an objective cause, but rather to articulate them into a whole or system. The system is valid precisely to the extent that it allows the coalescence or precipitation of these diffuse states, whose discontinuity also makes them painful. To the conscious mind, this last phenomenon constitutes an original experience which cannot be grasped from without. (*SA1*, 182; *AS1*, 201)

Interestingly, Lévi-Strauss does not return to the question of magic in his later work. Nor does he repeat the kind of 'existential' analysis provided in his commentary of the story of Quesalid. Nevertheless, in terms of both its approach and its content, 'The Sorcerer and his Magic' represents an important stage in the development of his thought. In terms of approach, it seems to be a working example of his interpretation of the total social fact, advanced in the *Introduction to Mauss*. The total social fact does not, he claims, simply imply a systemic, as opposed to an abstract and analytical, approach to the different levels of a given social reality. To be truly total, it would also be necessary to observe the 'incarnation' of this reality in individual experience, an observation which can be made from two perspectives: the point of view of the individual case history; and the more general (anthropological) point of view of the physical, psychical and sociological conditions of all modes of behaviour (*IM2*, 26; *IM1*, xxv).[24] The 'original experience' of the narrative of Quesalid would appear to offer such incarnation or subjective verification.[25] In fact, it is formally analogous to the passages in the *Elementary Structures* discussed in the previous chapter (restaurant scene, analysis of the psychological development of children) in that it shows the point of precipitation of a structure, the emergence of a system, from the point of view of individual behaviour and psychology. In terms of content, 'The Sorcerer and his Magic', like its sister text, 'The Effectiveness of Symbols', articulates some of the most basic themes of Lévi-Strauss's subsequent work on collective representations: the power of symbolic expression; the essential

---

[24] See also the following passage: 'the proof of the social cannot be other than mental; to put it another way, we can never be sure of having reached the meaning and the function of an institution, if we are not in a position to relive its impact on an individual consciousness' (*IM2*, 28; *IM1*, xxvi).

[25] In his book on Native American autobiography, H. David Brumble questions the status of the analysis offered in 'The Sorcerer and his Magic', to the extent that it is based on the testimony of an individual who is far from being a typical example of 'native' mentality. Although the individual named Quesalid had been raised among the Kwakiutl, his father was a Scotsman and his mother Tlingit. Lévi-Strauss omits to mention the fact that Quesalid's English name was George Hunt and that he had received extensive training from Boas in the methods of fieldwork (*American Indian Autobiography* (Berkeley: University of California Press, 1988), pp. 6–10).

rationalism and coherence of 'savage' thought, which is not as far removed from Western science as some would have us believe.

In a sense, it could be said that the subjective 'verification' of the nature of magical thought provided in 'The Sorcerer and his Magic' is an experiment which for Lévi-Strauss it is simply not necessary to repeat. The impression here, as with similar passages in the *Elementary Structures*, is that the study is a kind of conceptual cell or building block, an element in a chain of reasoning that, once completed, requires no more attention and can be taken as a given. Whatever the case, his psychological, or more precisely, intellectualist treatment of the question of magic, and his subsquent abandonment of this aspect of the anthropology of religions, are a clear enough indication of where his interests are developing, and in this respect his increasing focus on myth and systems of classification comes as no surprise.

Myth and ritual, totemism and sacrifice

We have already commented on the programmatic nature of *Structural Anthropology*, the collection of essays and articles published in 1958. The title itself acts as a kind of performative, stating both the widened scope of the discipline (anthropology, as opposed to ethnology) and its theoretical ambitions (the structural analysis of human society and culture). No less important, however, is the internal structure of the book, its five sections reflecting some of the principal concerns of the new anthropology: 'Language and Kinship', 'Social Organization', 'Magic and Religion', 'Art', 'Problems of Method and Teaching'. The central section, 'Magic and Religion', is dedicated to the anthropology of religions, and contains four chapters. Quite symmetrically, the first two chapters are the texts on magic discussed above, while the second two are devoted to myth. We will be examining the originality of Lévi-Strauss's treatment of myth in more detail below, but before proceeding to this, it is necessary to ask a simple question regarding his demarcation of the field of religious anthropology: where does the symmetrical division of the chapters of 'Magic and Religion' between magic and myth leave the traditional category of ritual?

A cursory glance at the index to *Structural Anthropology* shows that ritual is referred to a number of times in the book, but closer inspection reveals that only a small number of these references are devoted to consideration of the nature of ritual, which is not given anywhere near the same level of theoretical investment as myth or magic. Indeed, most of the references to the topic in the book are made in the context of the analysis of magical practices, so it is mostly a question of ritual as individual application rather than collective participation. In other instances, such as in 'The Structural Study of Myth', ritual is used simply to illuminate aspects of the myth studied, a practice that will become frequent in Lévi-Strauss's later work on mythology. The occasions on which Lévi-Strauss actually does give more direct consideration to the question of ritual therefore merit special attention, as they shed some light on the reasons for his relative neglect of the subject.

The first is in 'Structure and Dialectics', the last chapter of the section 'Magic and Religion'.[26] This short chapter was originally a contribution to a volume dedicated to the work of Roman Jakobson, published in 1956, and bears the traces of this origin. However, rather than being a consideration of the concepts of structure and dialectics, as the title suggests, the discussion centres on what was a standard subject of debate in the anthropology of religions, the relationship between myth and ritual. Lévi-Strauss rejects the traditional tendency to treat this relationship as one of homology, that is, treating myth as a projection of ritual, a kind of template or foundation for ritual, or conversely, viewing ritual as a dramatized illustration of myth. In each case, a one-to-one correspondence between the elements of the two is assumed, without questioning the fact that not all myths have corresponding rituals, or that such homologies can only be demonstrated for a limited number of cases, and without questioning the reasons for such replication (SA1, 232; AS1, 257). The essence of Lévi-Strauss's demonstration in 'Structure and Dialectics' is to prove that even where a relationship of homology can be found between myth and ritual, this is a special case of a more general relationship between the two phenomena. Using the example of Pawnee society and culture, he shows that rather than a direct, one-to-one, 'mechanical' causality between myths and rituals, the relationship is a 'dialectical' or, more precisely, a transformational one: for example, Pawnee myth is not an exact reflection of Pawnee ritual, but a symmetrically reversed version of the initiation rituals of neighbouring plains cultures (Blackfoot, Mandan, Hidatsa) (236–7; 261–2). The detail of Lévi-Strauss's analysis, and the problems it raises, need not concern us here – it is a typical structural analysis of the oppositions, correlations and inversions of the elements constituting the myths and rituals under consideration; the notion of transformation itself will be a guiding principle of his later investigation of myth, and the cross-cultural diffusion of myth in the *Mythologiques* cycle.[27] More interesting in the present context is what one might call the methodological vector of Lévi-Strauss's analysis, to the extent

---

[26] SA1, 232–41; AS1, 257–66.

[27] As Lévi-Strauss himself points out, his conception of transformation was inspired by D'Arcy Wentworth Thompson's *On Growth and Form*, and is essential to a proper understanding of the structuralist method: 'Now the notion of transformation is inherent in structural analysis. I would even say that all the errors, all the abuses committed through the notion of structure are a result of the fact that their authors have not understood that it is impossible to conceive of structure separate from the notion of transformation. Structure is not reducible to a system: a group composed of elements and the relations that unite them. In order to be able to speak of structure, it is necessary for there to be invariant relationships between elements and relations among several sets, so that one can move from one set to another by means of a transformation' (CLS2, 113; PL, 159). A graphic illustration of Lévi-Strauss's understanding of transformation is provided in the final part of *The Naked Man*, which reproduces a diagram from Thompson's

that its postulation of a non-essential and indirect (transformational) relationship between myth and ritual in effect establishes the *relative autonomy* of myth
as a cultural system.[28] The decoupling of myth and ritual is stated in markedly
stronger terms in the lectures given on the subject at the Ecole Pratique des
Hautes Etudes in 1954–5. These lectures cover some of the same ground as
'Structure and Dialectics', but add the following, illuminating statement on the
relationship, or rather, 'opposition', as Lévi-Strauss sees it, between myth and
ritual:

Finally, we thought to have proved that the symbolic value of the ritual is entirely
contained in its instruments and actions [*gestes*]. The words – prayers, incantations,
formulae – appeared meaningless, or at least endowed with only a slight functional
utility. From this point of view, a veritable opposition appeared between the myth and
the rite. Whereas the former is language [*langage*], but draws its meaning from a peculiar
use of that language [*langue*], the ritual uses language in the ordinary way, and elects to
signify at another level. The terms *metalanguage* and *paralanguage* were proposed to
render this distinction.

It is to linguistics that the mythologist should best address himself in order to elaborate
his explanatory modes [*modèles*]; to study rituals, one should rather look for them in the
theory of games. (*AM*, 205; *PD*, 257)[29]

To define ritual as essentially gestural and nonverbal (paralinguistic) and to
assign its theorization to game theory is effectively to confine it to the 'infrastructural' side of the social and cultural complex, as Lévi-Strauss conceives
it. Here, it joins other, similarly formalizable interactions such as matrimonial
exchange and economic relations. Significantly, however, Lévi-Strauss did not
pursue the possibilities of such formalization, and his subsequent efforts are
instead concentrated on the 'metalanguage' of myth and the linguistic model.

book representing the shapes of different species of fish as geometrical transforms of one another
(*NM*, 677; *HN*, 606). Finally, another important source of the notion of transformation in Lévi-
Strauss seems to be Norbert Wiener's *Cybernetics*, discussed below. For an important analysis
of the mathematical and scientific origins of Lévi-Strauss's models of transformation, see Mauro
W. Barbosa Almeida, 'Symmetry and Entropy. Mathematical Metaphors in the Work of Lévi-
Strauss' (*Current Anthropology* 31.4 (August–October 1990), 367–85). See also Jean Petitot,
'La Généalogie morphologique du structuralisme', *Critique* 50.620–1 (January–February 1999),
97–122, especially 108–9.

[28] This is explicitly stated a few years later in the first volume of *Mythologiques*, *The Raw and
the Cooked*: 'Often also it is not sufficiently taken into account that the mythological system
is relatively autonomous when compared with the other manifestations of the life and thought
of the group. Up to a point all are interdependent, but their interdependence does not result in
rigid relations which impose automatic adjustments among the various levels. It is a question
rather of long-term pressures, within the limits of which the mythological system can, in a sense,
argue with itself and acquire dialectical depth: that is, be always commenting on its more direct
modalities of insertion into reality, although the commentary may take the form of a plea in
favor or a denial' (*RC*, 332; *CC*, 338).

[29] See also *SA2*, 66; *AS2*, 84, where the 'metalanguage' of myth and the 'paralanguage' of ritual
are described as being complementary rather than in opposition to one another.

This closing off of the question of ritual does not pass unnoticed by other anthropologists, and in the 'Finale' to the *Mythologiques*, which can be seen as an extended defence of the structural method, it is clear that Lévi-Strauss feels compelled to account for this bias. The accusation, coming mainly from British anthropologists, is that his exclusive concentration on the symbolic and the cognitive has neglected the reality of the extreme affective states experienced during social activities like ritual, which cannot simply be reduced to modalities of the intellect. His response is to question interpretations which place affective states such as superstitious anguish at the centre of ritual activities, whilst accepting, with qualifications, the role played by emotions such as anxiety in their motivation. Ritual in its purest form, considered apart from any verbal gloss or accompaniment, can be defined as the performing of gestures and the manipulation of objects, both of which are submitted to the procedures of fragmentation and repetition. In its obsessive deployment of these procedures, ritual is, claims Lévi-Strauss, working in a direction opposite to that of myth. Whereas myth is the schematic dividing up the continuum of reality in order to create a signifying system based on the opposition of elements, the operations of ritual are a desperate attempt to re-establish the continuity of lived experience:

On the whole, the opposition between rite and myth is the same as that between living and thinking, and ritual represents a bastardization of thought, brought about by the constraints of life. It reduces, or rather vainly tries to reduce, the demands of thought to an extreme limit, which can never be reached, since it would involve the actual abolition of thought. This desperate, and inevitably unsuccessful, attempt to re-establish the continuity of lived experience, segmented through the schematism by which mythic speculation has replaced it, is the essence of ritual, and accounts for its distinctive characteristics. (*NM*, 675; *HN*, 603)

The affective dimension of ritual is therefore not primary, according to Lévi-Strauss. The anxiety experienced on such occasions, for example, is not felt in relation to this or that aspect of lived experience, but rather is a reaction to what symbolic thought has done to that experience. In this sense, such anxiety is epistemological rather than existential in nature (680–1; 608–9).

Lévi-Strauss's response to his detractors is at best a lateral one, and it is doubtful that his definition of ritual and its relation to myth would satisfy their scepticism. What it does achieve is to offer a kind of *post hoc* rationalization of his earlier choice of focus, in that it proposes the epistemological priority of myth over ritual. Under Lévi-Strauss's interpretation, ritual becomes a derived phenomenon, dependent on the mediation of myth and thus by implication of secondary interest.

So what we have in Lévi-Strauss's different negotiations of the field of myth and ritual is a systematic work of demarcation and reduction, which leaves myth as the privileged object of study and linguistics as the privileged model for its analysis. It is as though myth were seen by Lévi-Strauss as being the most *stable* of the diverse concretizations of social and cultural life, and therefore the most susceptible to the rigorous kind of analysis found in linguistics. As the 'solidified' product of collective thinking, as 'thought made object' (*RC*, 10–11; *CC*, 18–19), it is at least seen as the best means of access to the workings of the human mind, much in the same way that Freud viewed dreams as the royal road to the unconscious. Though one might disagree with Lévi-Strauss's framing of the myth–ritual question, it is characteristic of the will to coherence we have noted a number of times in the present study. Indeed, it might be said that Lévi-Strauss himself suffers from a form of epistemological anxiety, a constant need to delineate the precise boundaries of his object of study, to define its relative position with respect to cognate objects and finally to justify the priority given to it. Such is the case with myth and ritual, and a similar impulse can be observed in the case of totemism and sacrifice.

The major part of Lévi-Strauss's thinking on totemism is contained in the two texts published in 1962, *Totemism* and *The Savage Mind*. As Lévi-Strauss himself confirms, these are sister texts, and could have been written as a single book (*AM*, 6; *PD*, 15–16). In terms of the development of his thought and method, they represent the prelude to the *Mythologiques*, a final clearing of the theoretical ground before embarking on this large-scale project. A common concern of both *Totemism* and *The Savage Mind* is to show the rigour and coherence of systems of classification used in nonliterate cultures. Whereas traditional interpretations of these systems saw them as being entirely affective in motivation, expressing the mystical 'participation' of the individual with nature,[30] Lévi-Strauss instead sees such representations as a 'logic of the concrete', processing the phenomena of the natural world into units of opposition in order to construct context-free systems of signification. In the case of totemism, the distinctions established between different animal species, for example, are posited as being homologous with the divisions within and between different social groups. Against the functionalist interpretation that would see the classification of living species as an essentially utilitarian activity, Lévi-Strauss emphasizes the speculative dimension of such thinking, its relative semiotic freedom in comparison with other systems of signification. To use the memorable distinction made by Lévi-Strauss in *Totemism*, natural species are selected not because they are 'good to eat' but because they are 'good to think' (*T*, 89; *TA*, 132).[31]

The intellectualist bias of *Totemism* and *The Savage Mind* is entirely characteristic of Lévi-Strauss's own intellectual preferences, as we have observed so far. Again, as with myth, in the case of totemism there is the concern to

---

[30] The classic example of this kind of reading is the work of the French philosopher and sociologist Lucien Lévy-Bruhl. For Lévi-Strauss's criticism of Lévy-Bruhl, see *SM*, 268; *PS*, 355; *MM*, 16.

[31] For Lévi-Strauss's critique of Malinowski and functionalism, see also *MM*, 15–16.

exhaust the subject, to account for and integrate any residual elements, and for totemism this residual element is sacrifice. In the penultimate chapter of *The Savage Mind*, there is a passage of approximately six pages devoted to the relationship between totemism and sacrifice, a traditional 'problem' of religious anthropology. Lévi-Strauss immediately dismisses the old theory of the totemic origin of sacrifice, and proposes instead that the two 'systems' are mutually exclusive. Whereas totemism is based on the structural homology between natural species and social groups, the basic principle of sacrifice is that of substitution: the species selected for sacrifice is interchangeable, the essential intention being the establishing of a link between the human and the divine, whether the sacrifice is one of expiation or of communion. To use Lévi-Strauss's terminology, sacrifice is *metonymical*, while totemism is *metaphorical*. Whereas totemism is based on a postulated homology between objectively real systems (social segmentation, natural speciation), sacrifice makes the objectively false assumption of the continuity (one could say: the in-difference) of the living world (one animal is substitutable for another) and postulates a relation with a non-existent being. As a system of classification, totemism is a linguistically based code of interpretation, more or less well formulated, but always aiming at coherence; sacrifice is a particular form of discourse which lacks coherence, even though it is repeated many times (*SM*, 223–8; *PS*, 295–302).

One could question the schematism of Lévi-Strauss's point-by-point opposition of totemism and sacrifice. It is not that he is wrong in his attempt to decouple these traditionally associated institutions; his criticism of, for example, the kind of historical-speculative interpretations that saw totemism as a more primitive form of sacrifice, is entirely appropriate. More generally, his questioning of the reality of so-called 'totemism' and his presentation of it as a way of thinking, a system of classification, rather than a religion, is a challenging readjustment of the traditional categories of anthropological analysis. The problem is that this work of reframing and redefinition does not seem to be enough for Lévi-Strauss. Indeed, he seems to be intent on mapping the whole terrain of the anthropology of religions, establishing the respective positions and the relative importance of the ideal objects occupying that terrain. The metaphor of the map is perhaps not precise enough. Given that Lévi-Strauss's mode of intuition, when charting a particular conceptual space, is more frequently tabular than topographical, a more appropriate image would probably be that of the *diagram*. For the anthropology of religions, this diagram would look something like the following:

<pre>
                    MYTH ------ RITUAL
(pensée sauvage) | | (pratique sauvage)
                 CLASSIFICATION -- SACRIFICE
                   (totemism) |
                              MAGIC
</pre>

It is evident from the preceding analysis that Lévi-Strauss's preference is always for *la pensée sauvage*, rather than *la pratique sauvage*. This preference has partly to do with the fact of the relative abstraction of the former: as a code or discourse whose primary means of expression is linguistic it is more susceptible to structural analysis, as Lévi-Strauss conceives it. But we have also seen that in each case Lévi-Strauss feels the need to justify his choice of object, and the insistence with which he pursues and rationalizes the oppositions between myth and ritual, totemism and sacrifice is symptomatic of this concern. Myth is epistemologically prior to ritual, which is a reaction against what (savage) thought has made of the world; sacrifice is epistemologically inferior to totemism, an incoherent discourse which lacks the objective foundations of the latter. The symmetrical subordination of ritual and sacrifice therefore leaves Lévi-Strauss free to concentrate on the ideal objects that are totemism and myth. We will now examine in more detail his treatment of the second of these objects, myth.

Myth, language, information

The 1955 article 'The Structural Study of Myth' is, by all accounts, an important stage in the development of Lévi-Strauss's structuralism. Its centrepiece, a study of the Oedipus myth, is the basic prototype of the kind of structural analysis he will go on to practise in more extended works such as the *Mythologiques* cycle. It is commonly accepted that the model for structural analysis, as set forth in this article, is derived from linguistics, and Lévi-Strauss explicitly indicates this derivation in his presentation of the structural method. The current state of mythological studies, he argues, is precisely analogous to that of linguistics in its pre-scientific phase. Just as philosophers of language sought a one-to-one equivalence between groups of sounds and their meaning in a given language, so theories of myth (such as Jung's theory of archetypes) have tended to attach fixed meanings to specific mythological themes.[32] The emancipation of linguistic theory came with the realization that the signifying power of language does not reside in sounds themselves, but in the manner of their combination, hence in the arbitrary nature of the sign. Lévi-Strauss thinks that the study of myth is in need of a similar revolution of perspective (*SA*1, 208–9; *AS*1, 229–30). The problem here is that not only is myth in principle subject to the same kind of analysis as language, it is also objectively a part of language, which is its primary means of expression. He therefore distinguishes three levels in language: the two, distinct levels of *langue* and *parole*, as defined by Saussure,[33]

---

[32] See also *IM*2, 37; *IM*1, xxxii.

[33] *Langue* is the abstract and invariant system of rules which conditions language, while *parole* is the actual (contingent, variable) production of language in speech and other linguistic acts. See Ferdinand de Saussure, *Course in General Linguistics*, trans. Roy Harris (London: Duckworth, 1983), pp. 13–14; *Cours de linguistique générale* (Paris: Payot, 1986), pp. 30–1.

and a higher level of complexity, at which the myth operates, and which is both dependent on the first two levels and detached from them. Myth is therefore a qualitatively different form of language (in this sense, one could say that myth is an 'emergent' property of language), but it can be analysed in the same way as language. So Lévi-Strauss arrives at the following, basic propositions concerning the analysis of myth:

- Like any language, myth is made up of elements or constituent units, but of a higher order of complexity than the constituent units of language. One can therefore trace an ascending order of inclusion and complexity from phoneme (minimal unit of sound) to morpheme (minimal unit of meaning) to sememe (sequence of morphemes) to the 'gross constituent units' of myth, what Lévi-Strauss calls the *mytheme*.
- The meaning of myth is not to be found in its isolated constituent elements, but in the way in which these elements are combined. (*SA*1, 210–11; *AS*1, 231–3)

There remains the problem of how to identify and isolate the 'gross constituent unit' or mytheme, as it is of a different order to that of the phoneme, morpheme or sememe. Lévi-Strauss's solution to this derives from his practice of treating each myth individually, and breaking up the narrative sequence into the shortest possible sentences, each of which is entered on an index card and given a number corresponding to its place in the sequence. It emerges that each card denotes a linking of a subject and a predicate. The basic characteristic of each individual mytheme must therefore be that of a *relation* (211; 233).

However, this work of identification and isolation does not go far enough. Along the horizontal axis of the myth, the diachronic unfolding of its narrative, the same type of relation can occur at differently spaced intervals, so that if one views the myth along its vertical axis, that of synchrony, this relation will appear in its 'natural' grouping, alongside other, similar relations. The real constitutive elements of myth are therefore not isolated relations, but 'bundles' (*paquets*) of relations, that is, groups of relations of the same type.[34] The 'meaning' of the myth, as Lévi-Strauss understands it, derives not from the diachronic sequence of its narrative (which can often be absurd and senseless), but from the combinations (or more precisely, the binary oppositions) between these bundles of relations (211–12; 233–4).

The demonstration Lévi-Strauss goes on to give of the structural method, as explained above, is a famous one. Provocatively, he selects the Oedipus myth as a preliminary test case, on the grounds that it is known by everybody and thus needs no introduction. He isolates four mythemes, or groups of relations in this myth, and sets them out in a tabular arrangement.

---

[34] The term 'bundle' figures in both Trubetzkoy and Jakobson, and refers to the phoneme as a collection of distinctive sound-features. See Jakobson, *Selected Writings*, vol. I (The Hague: Mouton, 1971), p. 435.

Cadmos seeks his sister Europa, ravished by Zeus			
		Cadmos kills the dragon	
	The Spartoi kill one another		
			Labdacos (Laios' father) = *lame* (?)
	Oedipus kills his father, Laios		Laios (Oedipus' father) = *left-sided* (?)
		Oedipus kills the Sphinx	
			Oedipus = *swollen-foot* (?)
Oedipus marries his mother, Jocasta			
	Eteocles kills his brother, Polynices		
Antigone buries her brother, Polynices, despite prohibition			

Fig. 3.1

If one reads this table (see figure 3.1) like a text, from left to right and top to bottom, then this reproduces the diachronic sequence of the myth, its surface narrative, so to speak. However, if one reads the table from left to right only, one column at a time, half of the diachronic sequencing is lost and one is left with the underlying meaning of the myth. Thus the first column groups together relations in which there is an exaggeration of kinship ties, while the second column reverses this relation into one of undervaluation. The third column denotes relations in which there is a negation of the autochthonous origins of humanity (the destruction of monsters), while the fourth, referring to various impediments to walking properly, affirms these origins. So the relationship between columns 4 and 3 is structurally homologous to that between columns 1 and 2. The fact that the relations expressed in columns 1 and 2, 4 and 3 respectively are mutually exclusive is at least compensated by the fact that it is possible to think of their mutual exclusion as being homologous (214–16; 237–9). Lévi-Strauss concludes:

Turning back to the Oedipus myth, we may now see what it means. The myth has to do with the inability, for a culture which holds the belief that mankind is autochthonous . . . to find a satisfactory transition between this theory and the knowledge that human beings are actually born from the union of man and woman. Although the problem obviously cannot be solved, the Oedipus myth provides a kind of logical tool which relates the original problem – born from one or born from two? – to the derivative problem: born from different or born from the same? By a correlation of this type, the overrating of blood relations is to the underrating of blood relations as the attempt to escape autochthony is to the impossibility to succeed in it. Although experience contradicts theory, social life validates cosmology by its similarity of structure. Hence cosmology is true. (S41, 216; AS1, 239)

It is difficult for the non-specialist to comment on the detail of Lévi-Strauss's interpretation of the Oedipus myth, in particular as it is relies, at a crucial point, on a triangulation with North American Indian mythology. However, even for the reader unfamiliar with the different thought-universes of world mythologies, there are inevitably questions concerning the principles of Lévi-Strauss's interpretation and approach. If one accepts that the system of myth is a kind of second-order language, and that its structure is analogous to that of natural language, and if one accepts that it is therefore susceptible to the same kind of structural analysis as natural language, then there is the difficulty – which Lévi-Strauss recognizes – of determining exactly what the constitutive elements of this system are. His solution, as we have seen, is to fall back on his own practice of isolating instances of subject–predicate relationships, but there is no explanation as to why such relations should constitute the minimal unit of mythical discourse. Similarly, it is tempting to view the oppositions posited between the different 'bundles' of relations (the vertical groupings of mythemes in the table representing the myth) as more a product of Lévi-Strauss's own, peculiar interpretation of the myth than a disclosure of its essential meaning.

Whatever one's doubts as to the appropriateness of the linguistic model as applied to the Oedipus myth, it is for Lévi-Strauss a powerful heuristic tool which allows him to take the study of myth into entirely new dimensions. The basic elements of structural analysis, as summarized above, will remain more or less constant in the more substantial excursions into North and South American mythology that make up the major part of his later work. The main thing that can be said about this analysis is that it is *counter-intuitive*; in other words, by atomizing its object (myth) and by positing another (unconscious) level of organization and signification, it defamiliarizes our common, everyday understanding of what a myth actually is.

From the point of view of the reception of structuralism in France in the 1950s and 1960s, Lévi-Strauss's choice of the linguistic model is by no means indifferent. While the relations that structural analysis uncovers are not immediately available to conscious intuition (in this respect structuralism is a reaction against the predominantly phenomenological bias of French philosophy in the postwar years), it could be said that the means of conceptualizing these relations, as proposed by Lévi-Strauss, is nevertheless intuitively the most assimilable representation of them. To present myth as a kind of language that remains part of language opens the door, in principle, to the analogous treatment of other forms of social discourse. The basic principles of structural analysis, which Lévi-Strauss takes from Saussure, Trubetzkoy and Jakobson, are relatively simple, and can be illustrated by examples taken from any particular language: the unconscious nature of the rules underlying linguistic utterances; the arbitrariness of the sign; the differential and combinatorial basis of meaning.

The above points might be said to constitute the vulgate of structuralism, as it was disseminated in the 1950s and 1960s, and as it is still taught today. But while it is impossible to overestimate the contribution of linguistics to Lévi-Strauss's version of structuralism, to concentrate exclusively on this influence leads to a rather one-dimensional picture of his thinking, and, in the present instance, of how he comes to conceptualize myth. I am thinking here not of the musical analogy, which only begins to be used in any systematic manner in the *Mythologiques* cycle, but of the more general scientific and technological context in which Lévi-Strauss's structuralism is first formulated. Lévi-Strauss has always presented himself as a thinker with a passionate interest in science, who despite his lack of formal training, attempts to keep himself in touch with the most recent developments in scientific research.[35] In the earlier stages of his career, when he begins to formulate the theoretical framework of structuralism, the most prominent and promising areas of new development are in information theory and cybernetics.[36] Compared with the attention given to linguistics, the reference to these disciplines in *Structural Anthropology* is negligible, but their impact on his thinking is clear. The bibliography of *Structural Anthropology* lists some of the most important recent works in the field, Wiener's *Cybernetics* (1948) and Shannon and Weaver's *The Mathematical Theory of Communication* (1950). In an earlier chapter of the book, 'Language and the Analysis of Social Laws' (1951),[37] Lévi-Strauss underlines the revolutionary implications

---

[35] See *MM*, 5; *CLS2*, 111; *PL*, 156.

[36] Roger Smith notes the importance of this science for cognitive psychology in the 1950s: 'Information science, visible in material form in computing technology, became what has been called a defining technology, a technology which gives a culture its dominant models for investigation and understanding and structures the way we think about the world. This "defining" went deep in the domain of psychology. Cognitive psychology was the imagination of the computer age applied to knowledge of the mind. The word "cognitive" connoted interest in information receiving, processing and storing functions, and in the consequent control of human capacities' (*Fontana History of the Human Sciences* (London: Fontana Press, 1997), p. 837). Also to be noted is the influence of information theory in linguistics itself. This influence is clearly apparent in Jakobson's work of the 1950s and 1960s, where he frequently mentions the convergent interests of the two disciplines (see *Selected Writings*, vol. II (The Hague: Mouton, 1971), pp. 556, 570–1). It is possible that it was individuals such as Jakobson and Margaret Mead who alerted Lévi-Strauss to the theoretical potential of cybernetics, through their respective participation in the Macy Conferences, held in the United States between 1942 and 1953. On the interdisciplinary implications of the Macy Conferences, with particular reference to the cognitive sciences, see chapter 3 of Jean-Pierre Dupuy, *Aux origines des sciences cognitives* (Paris: La Découverte, 1994); *The Mechanization of the Mind. On the Origins of Cognitive Science*, trans. M.B. DeBevoise (Princeton and Oxford: Princeton University Press, 2000).

[37] *SA1*, 55–66; *AS1*, 63–75.

of Wiener's book for the future of the social sciences (55; 63). It would therefore be useful to take a closer look at some of the science behind these two texts.

As scientific disciplines, information (or communication) theory and cybernetics were the result of the specific technical and engineering problems of the technologies of communication and control developed in the first half of the twentieth century. Information theory grew out of the very concrete requirements of the telecommunications industry: how to optimize the transmission of information through a given channel and guard against its degradation in the process of transmission. Cybernetics originated in Wiener's collaboration in the construction of control apparatus for anti-aircraft guns during the Second World War. Human gun operators were found to have a relatively low success-rate in hitting a moving target such as an aircraft, whose subsequent movements at any given instant were, moreover, unpredictable. The problem was to devise automatic control systems capable of achieving a more consistent success-rate than a human agent alone.[38] The problems of cybernetics were therefore convergent with those of information theory, to the extent that they were as much communications problems, i.e., communication between human and machine and from machine to machine, as mechanical problems. In both cases, significant advances were made in the formalization and mathematization of the areas in question. However, in each of the texts cited above, the authors also provide a set of basic concepts, expressed in a manner accessible to the non-specialist and not requiring any detailed mathematical knowledge, which seem particularly relevant to the development of Lévi-Strauss's thinking in the early stages of his itinerary. The concepts of information, message, noise, redundancy and feedback, for example, all play a role in his conceptualization of the nature and function of myth.

In information theory, the concept of information refers not, as in everyday usage, to meaning, but to the set of possible alternative messages in a given communication situation.[39] In a simple communication system, the *information source* selects a *message* out of a set of possible messages, a *transmitter* converts the selected message into a *signal*, which is sent through a *channel* to a receiver, which reconverts the signal into a message to be passed onto the *destination*.[40]

---

[38] See Norbert Wiener, *Cybernetics or Control and Communication in the Animal and the Machine*, 2nd edition (Cambridge, Mass.: MIT Press, 1961), pp. 5–6. On Wiener's somewhat exaggerated view of his contribution to the wartime effort, see Jeremy Campbell, *Grammatical Man. Information, Entropy, Language and Life* (Harmondsworth: Penguin, 1982), pp. 30–1.

[39] 'The word *information*, in this theory, is used in a special sense that must not be confused with its ordinary usage. In particular, *information* must not be confused with meaning ... the word information in communication theory relates not so much to what you *do* say, as to what you *could* say. That is, information is a measure of one's freedom of choice when one selects a message' (Claude E. Shannon and Warren Weaver, *The Mathematical Theory of Communication* (Urbana: University of Illinois Press, 1959), pp. 99–100).

[40] Ibid., pp. 98–101.

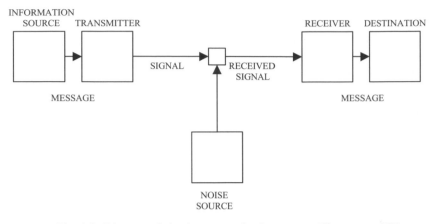

Fig. 3.2: Diagram of simple communication system (Shannon and Weaver, *The Mathematical Theory of Communication*, p. 98).

The diagram used by Shannon and Weaver to represent a simple communication system is presented in figure 3.2.

This model describes an artificially simple communication situation, where the information source chooses only between several definite messages. A more natural and realistic situation would be where the information source makes a sequence of choices from a set of elementary symbols (letters, words, musical notes, etc.), the selected sequence then constituting the message. Of particular interest to information theory is the role of probability in the generation of the message. As successive symbols are chosen, their selection is not totally random, but governed by probabilities dependent on preceding choices, a so-called 'Markoff process':

A system which produces a sequence of symbols (which may, of course, be letters or musical notes, say, rather than words) according to certain probabilities is called a *stochastic process*, and the special case of a stochastic process in which the probabilities depend on the previous events, is called a *Markoff process* or a Markoff chain. Of the Markoff processes which might conceivably generate messages, there is a special class which is of primary importance for communication theory, these being what are called *ergodic processes* ... [where] any reasonably large sample tends to be representative of the sequence as a whole ... Ergodic systems, in other words, exhibit a particularly safe and comforting sort of statistical regularity.[41]

If one now concentrates on the transmission of the message, or more precisely, the signal into which the message has been converted or encoded,[42] then

---

[41] Ibid., p. 102.
[42] '[T]he function of the transmitter is to *encode*, and that of the receiver to *decode*, the message' (ibid., p. 107).

however cleverly one has encoded the message, the channel through which the signal is transmitted will always be subject to interference in the form of *noise*. This shows the applicability, in the domain of information theory, of the second law of thermodynamics, which states that the entropy, that is, the degree of disorder or disorganization of a closed system, increases with time. Stated in informational terms, the message can lose order in the process of transmission, but can never gain it. The result is that at the receiving end of the system of communication, there will always be uncertainty as to the exact content of the original message.[43] The engineering solution to this problem is to build a degree of *redundancy* into the encoded message, that is, to combat the distorting effect of noise by adding non-essential information to the message. In this way, the risk of distortion of the original message is distributed across a wider statistical range, increasing the probability that the message deciphered at the receiving end of the system will be close to the correct one. Shannon and Weaver note:

It may seem surprising that we should define a definite capacity C for a noisy channel since we can never send certain information in such a case. It is clear, however, that by sending the information in a redundant form the probability of errors can be reduced. For example, by repeating the message many times and by a statistical study of the different received versions of the message the probability of errors could be made very small.[44]

Redundancy is therefore the 'cost',[45] the price to pay for the protection of a message, if it is not to be unduly distorted in its transmission through a given channel. It increases the 'weight' of the signal, so to speak, but ensures that the receiver converts the signal into the most likely approximation of the original message.

Wiener's book covers much of the same ground as Shannon and Weaver, but his view of the scope of the new information sciences is a wider one. Indeed, he proposes that the field devoted to the problems of control, communication and statistical mechanics be named cybernetics, after the ancient Greek term χυβερνητής or *steersman*.[46] As the latter term suggests, cybernetics is about regulation, or rather, self-regulation. Central to cybernetics are the notions of the *programme*, for example, the set of instructions that determine the nature and sequence of the operations a given machine is to perform, and of *feedback*, that is, the establishing of a circuit or loop of communication between the system (programme plus mechanism) and its environment, which enables information about its effect on that environment (its output) to affect subsequent operations. Feedback which maintains a system in a steady-state, within parameters determined by its programme, is called *negative feedback*, as it tends to oppose, limit

---

[43] Ibid., pp. 109, 111. As Emmanuel Dion indicates, uncertainty is a central concept of information theory, to the extent that information could be defined as the reduction of uncertainty (*Invitation à la théorie de l'information* (Paris: Points-Seuil, 1987), p. 87).

[44] Ibid., p. 39.   [45] Ibid., p. 43.   [46] *Cybernetics*, p. 11.

or check what the system is already doing.[47] Wiener cites the case of homeostasis in living systems, the automatic regulation of basic organic functions such as body temperature, blood pressure and so on, as a physiological instance of negative feedback.[48]

The above points describe some of the central concepts of communication and cybernetic theory, and we shall presently be tracing the incidence of these concepts in Lévi-Strauss's thought. However, it would be useful first to look at some of the wider implications of information science articulated in the works in question, as it emerges that these have significant bearing on how Lévi-Strauss views his own theoretical practice and its interdisciplinary dimension. In Wiener's work, especially, there are numerous statements on the nature and status of the new sciences, which he sees as being essentially *operational*:

> The science of today is operational; that is, it considers every statement as essentially concerned with possible experiments or observable processes. According to this, the study of logic must reduce to the study of the logical machine, whether nervous or mechanical, with all its non-removable limitations and imperfections.
>
> It may be said by some readers that this reduces logic to psychology, and that the two sciences are observably and demonstrably different. This is true in the sense that many psychological states and sequences of thought do not conform to the canons of logic. Psychology contains much that is foreign to logic, but – and this is the important fact – any logic which means anything to us can contain nothing which the human mind – and hence the human nervous system – is unable to encompass. *All logic is limited by the limitations of the human mind when it is engaged in that activity known as logical thinking.*[49]

Wiener's view of logic as an embedded phenomenon, whether it be in a human or mechanical system, is an expression of his more general scepticism regarding the separation of pure mathematics from its physical instantiations in the real world.[50] It is also a reflection of the high level of reciprocal determination, during this period, between technological development and scientific formalization in the fields of computing and communication. A leitmotif of Wiener's book is the problem of the *design* of machines that are the concrete embodiment of logical processes. Something of this instrumental approach to knowledge is also to be found in Lévi-Strauss. His treatment of myth is operational to the extent that it is seen as a working model of specific processes of human thinking. His presentation of the *Mythologiques* sequence is as a kind of extended experiment, whose 'laboratory' is the geographical zone covered by the two Americas, the ultimate goal of the experiment being to uncover the inner logic of the human mind. In fact, it seems that the very notion of human mind, as Lévi-Strauss understands and uses it, originates in Wiener's reflections

---

[47] Ibid., p. 97.   [48] Ibid., p. 114.   [49] Ibid., p. 125.
[50] See Campbell, *Grammatical Man*, pp. 24–5.

on the limitations of logic, which according to Wiener is reducible, in the final instance, to the workings of the central nervous system.

If elements of Lévi-Strauss's methodology seem close to the kind of operational science described by Wiener, then there are similar points of correspondence regarding the scope of this science. Shannon and Weaver see the relevance of the theory of communication as extending far beyond the field in which it was originally conceived:

The word communication will be used here in a very broad sense to include all of the procedures by which one mind may affect another. This, of course, involves not only written and oral speech, but also music, the pictorial arts, the theatre, the ballet, and in fact all human behaviour.[51]

This is a theory so general that one does not need to say what kinds of symbols are being considered – whether written letters of words, or musical notes, or spoken words, or symphonic music, or pictures. The theory is deep enough so that the relationships it reveals indiscriminately apply to all these and to other forms of communication.[52]

One can see, in statements such as these, the origins of Lévi-Strauss's notion of society as communication, and his initial optimism regarding the possible formalization of social behaviour from this perspective. From the cybernetic point of view, Wiener notes the interdisciplinary implications of the science of communication, applicable not only in fields such as neurophysiology, but also in the study of higher-level organizations such as human society:

It is certainly true that the social system is an organization like the individual, that it is bound together by a system of communication, and that it has a dynamics in which circular processes of a feedback nature play an important part. This is true, both in the general fields of anthropology and sociology and in the more specific field of economics; and the very important work, which we have hardly mentioned, of von Neumann and Morgenstern on the theory of games enters into this range of ideas.[53]

However, hardly has Wiener opened this door onto the possible extension of cybernetic theory to the human and social sciences, than he abruptly slams it shut again. He is in fact sceptical about the applicability of the principles of cybernetics to social and economic problems: to be properly effective, such analyses would have to be based on long runs of statistics under essentially constant conditions, whereas in human affairs the opposite is normally the case. His conclusion is that 'the human sciences are very poor testing grounds for a new mathematical technique'.[54] In the last chapter of his book, entitled 'Information, Language and Society', Wiener expresses a similar scepticism, this time from the point of view of *scale*. Whereas the great advances in the

---

[51] *The Mathematical Theory of Communication*, p. 95.   [52] Ibid., p. 114.
[53] *Cybernetics*, p. 24.   [54] Ibid., p. 25.

exact sciences have been made in fields where there is a high degree of isolation of the object from the observer, in the social sciences the observer is of the same scale as the phenomenon he or she is observing, with the result that the very act of observation will inevitably influence the object observed.[55]

As has already been noted, Lévi-Strauss believes Wiener's book to be of great importance to the human and social sciences, and he certainly does not share Wiener's scepticism regarding the possible applications of cybernetics. In 'Language and the Analysis of Social Laws', he agrees that the cases considered by Wiener (the ethnographic monograph, works of applied anthropology) are indeed not open to precise formalization, for the reasons stated above. However, there is at least one discipline in the social sciences which does satisfy the conditions specified by Wiener, and that is linguistics. As a social phenomenon, language operates at a level which is inaccessible to our everyday consciousness, and as such is an object independent of the observer. Moreover, the data available on language in some cases dates back thousands of years, while in cases where such data is not available, the lack of historical depth can often be remedied by comparative analysis. Lévi-Strauss goes on to suggest that the kind of formalization that has been possible in information science should therefore also be possible in linguistics, some of the problems of which could be solved by the use of modern calculating machines (SA1, 55–8; AS1, 63–6). The more interesting part of this chapter, from our of point of view at least, comes when Lévi-Strauss considers whether the success of linguistics might be reproduced in other areas of the social sciences. If this is the case, if the same method applied in linguistics produces the same kind of results in other areas, then we might be justified in thinking that it is possible to formulate universal laws on the workings of the human mind (58–9; 67). The first testing ground for such speculations is that of kinship studies, and here Lévi-Strauss repeats some of the main arguments of the *Elementary Structures*: kinship relations as a modality of exchange; exchange and language as modalities of communication, both of them being part of the same symbolic function within the human mind. He then asks whether other aspects of social life, such as art and religion, might share the same characteristics, and therefore be open to the same kind of analysis (59–62; 68–71).

What is interesting about these speculations on the possibilities of formalization in anthropology is that the informational paradigm cited at the start of the chapter, which Lévi-Strauss claimed to hold so much promise for the social sciences, is in fact mediated through linguistics. The argument runs as follows: ethnography and the social sciences do not at present satisfy the conditions of scientificity proposed by Wiener; however, the discipline of linguistics does satisfy these conditions; therefore, the methods of linguistics may be extended

---

[55] Ibid., pp. 162–3.

to other social phenomena. The problem is that by focusing on the question of scientificity, Lévi-Strauss fails to engage with the actual science itself. While both here and in other chapters of 'Language and Kinship' there is explanation of the basic principles of linguistics, the only concepts mentioned relating to information theory are the very general notions of 'communication' and 'message'. So despite the enthusiastic homage paid to Wiener at the start of the chapter, the conceptual detail of the science he represents is somewhat lacking, to say the least. However, this does not mean that Lévi-Strauss's references to information science are not to be taken seriously; on the contrary, it could be said that as Lévi-Strauss moves into his second area of specialization, the anthropology of religions, this science is at least of equal importance to linguistics in terms of how he conceptualizes his object of study. This is apparent if we re-examine the analysis of 'The Structural Study of Myth' in the light of what we have learnt about cybernetics and communication theory.

It was noted above that Lévi-Strauss's treatment of the Oedipus myth is the centrepiece of 'The Structural Study of Myth', a working example of structural analysis. However, this illustration of method is preceded and prepared by two examples or comparisons, which Lévi-Strauss hopes will elucidate for the reader his rather abstract explanation of the idea of *bundles* of relations, as explained above. In the first example, he describes the hypothetical situation of archaeologists from another planet visiting earth long after the passing of human civilization, and managing to decipher our systems of writing, but then falling upon some musical scores that clearly belong to a different category of notation. After some false starts, they realize that unlike the linear sequencing of alphabetical writing, the scores should be treated as a complex pattern to be read both horizontally (melodically) and vertically (harmonically). In the second example, an individual who knows nothing about playing cards observes a fortune-teller over a long period of time, noting the different profiles of her customers and the nature of her consultations. If (s)he manages to gather a sufficient body of data relating to this custom (s)he will, like the ethnologist, be able to discern the structure and composition of the deck of cards and the rules of its distribution (212–13; 234–5). Interestingly, the first example makes use of the musical analogy which will be so important in Lévi-Strauss's later studies of myth.[56] But more generally than this, both examples are about information retrieval, the reading of patterns, patterns which emerge through a process of *repetition* – for the alien archaeologist, the periodic repetition of similar harmonic units; for the person observing the fortune-teller, the repetition of cards belonging to the same set. The importance of the principle of repetition is underlined by Lévi-Strauss in the conclusion of the chapter:

[56] Significantly, Jakobson compares the bundle of distinctive features that constitutes the phoneme with a musical chord, which can be broken up into the smaller components of individual notes (*Selected Writings*, vol. I, p. 435; vol. II, p. 105).

First, the question has often been raised why myths, and more generally, oral literature, are so much addicted to duplication, triplication, or quadruplication of the same sequence. If our hypotheses are accepted, the answer is obvious: The function of repetition is to render the structure of the myth apparent. For we have seen that the synchronic-diachronic structure of the myth permits us to organize it into diachronic sequences (the rows in our tables) which should be read synchronically (the columns). Thus the myth exhibits a 'slated' structure, which comes to the surface, so to speak, though the process of repetition. (*SA*1, 229; *AS*1, 254)

This process or principle of repetition may be compared with the notion of redundancy, as explained above: in order for the message of the myth to be transmitted correctly, it must be over-coded, to guard against the possible distortion (noise) that might affect the process of transmission. So if myth, according to Lévi-Strauss's more explicit comparison, is a 'language', it is also, more generally and arguably more essentially, encoded information. What is more, the 'message' of the myth is not contained in a single transmission, so to speak, but distributed across a range of related myths: an important aspect of Lévi-Strauss's methodology in 'The Structural Study of Myth' is not to consider a single, supposedly more 'authentic' version of a given myth, but instead to take the myth as the ensemble of its variants (217–18; 240–2). This is to treat myth as a kind of *time series*, as Wiener describes it: 'The message is a discrete or continuous sequence of measurable events distributed in time – precisely what is called a time series by the statisticians. The prediction of the future of a message is done by a sort of operator on its past, whether this operator is realized by a scheme of mathematical computation, or by a mechanical or electrical apparatus.'[57] This connects with what Shannon and Weaver said above about ergodic processes, that is, processes where a reasonably large sample is representative of the sequence as a whole. Lévi-Strauss illustrates this approach with the example of a room containing furniture arranged in a specific pattern, where our knowledge about the distribution of the furniture depends on two mirrors placed on opposite walls. If the mirrors are perfectly parallel, then the number of images projected will theoretically be infinite. If, on the other hand, one of the mirrors is set at an angle, the number will be dramatically reduced, so that four or five images will be enough to provide adequate, if not perfect, 'information' (Lévi-Strauss's term) on the disposition of the room (218; 242). So even though the time series that is myth is a fragmentary one, it is possible to reconstitute its message through a statistical treatment of a limited number of its variants. In a later text, *From Honey to Ashes*, this notion of the statistical reconstitution of information is illustrated in an example taken, quite appropriately, from the domain of telecommunications:

---

[57] *Cybernetics*, pp. 8–9. See also p. 69. At the close of 'The Structural Study of Myth', Lévi-Strauss briefly considers the possibility of a computerized treatment of the comparison of variants, involving the use of state-of-the-art IBM equipment (*SA*1, 229; *AS*1, 253) – a reference omitted in the French version of the text.

It can happen that myths belonging to different communities transmit the same message, without all being equally detailed or equally clear in expression. We therefore find ourselves in a situation comparable to that of a telephone subscriber who is rung up several times in succession by a caller giving, or repeating, the same message, in case a storm or other conversations may have caused interference with his earlier messages. Of the various messages, some will be relatively clear, others relatively indistinct. The same will be true even in the absence of background noise, if one message is given at great length whereas a second is abridged in telegraphese. In all these instances, the general sense of the messages will remain the same, although each one may contain more or less information, and a person who has heard several may legitimately rectify or complete the less satisfactory ones with the help of the more explicit. (*HA*, 127; *MC*, 106)

The preceding examples show that while the linguistic model may go some way to explaining the combinatorial and differential nature of myth, as Lévi-Strauss conceives it, the informational model provides a number of concepts which are equally essential to his analysis: message, coding, noise, redundancy, statistical distribution. If we now move from the question of the nature of myth to that of its *function*, then again the linguistic model can only give a limited and partial response. To say that myth is a kind of (second-order) language may suggest how one might approach its analysis, but it does not tell us what myth is for. In the analogies treated so far, the analyst of myth is compared to an observer attempting to reconstruct a given message or reality: the alien archaeologist; the observer of the fortune-teller or the furnished room; the recipient of fragmented telephone messages. The position of the mythologist is therefore an external one, to the extent that he or she is not the primary destination of the message, but the interceptor of a message intended for another. In fact, in its original context, the coded information that is myth could be seen to have a *cybernetic* function, to the extent that it is a 'looped' message from a given society to itself, a meta-discourse whose function, according to Lévi-Strauss, is the regulation and resolution of contradiction. Immediately following the passage quoted above, regarding the 'slated' structure of myth, he continues:

However, the slates are not absolutely identical. And since the purpose of myth is to provide a logical model capable of overcoming a contradiction (an impossible achievement if, as it happens, the contradiction is real), a theoretically infinite number of slates will be generated, each one slightly different from the others. Thus, myth grows spiral-wise until the intellectual impulse which has produced it is exhausted. (*SA*1, 229; *AS*1, 254)

What Lévi-Strauss seems to be describing here is a process of negative feedback, that is, the continual self-adjustment of mythical discourse in order to approximate the resolution of (real) contradictions. So as a relatively autonomous symbolic system, myth would be both regulated and regulating, both a reflection (or encoding) of the contradictions of social life and a retroactive regulation of them. In the case of the Oedipus myth, it will be remembered, the different 'bundles' of relations isolated by structural analysis were grouped in pairs of oppositions, each pair expressing contradictory propositions. What the myth did, according to Lévi-Strauss, was not to eliminate these mutually exclusive propositions, but to mediate their contradiction by positing their homology at another level, that is, in relation to other pairs of oppositions.[58] Again, one may question whether this is the real meaning of the Oedipus myth, whether it is an accurate explanation of the (unconscious) mode of thinking behind the myth, but it is clear that Lévi-Strauss views such mediation as serving an essentially homeostatic function, to the extent that it displaces contradictions rather than directly resolving them. This places myth within the same mental continuum as magical thought, in the sense that it possesses a kind of symbolic efficacy that does not necessarily have an objective correlate. More than a language, more than simply information, from the point of view of its function, myth would therefore seem to be a kind of information technology, an instrument, a 'logical model' or 'logical tool', as Lévi-Strauss puts it, that supplements human cognition and permits the intuitively unthinkable to be thought. In the domain of social superstructures, therefore, myth is functional in the same way that infrastructural systems such as kinship are functional: 'But what is true of the rules of kinship is also valid for mythic narratives. Neither are limited to being simply what they *are*: they *serve a purpose* – to solve problems which are sociological in the one case and socio-logical in the other' (*OTM*, 228; *OMT*, 187).

This chapter has followed the different stages of the intellectual trajectory that takes Lévi-Strauss in the 1950s from the study of social organization to the anthropology of religions and finally to the study of myth. Between the *Elementary Structures* and *Mythologiques*, in a range of programmatic texts, he progressively narrows the focus of attention to concentrate on that area of human activity he sees as the most susceptible to a certain kind of scientific reduction, the realm of collective representations and, in particular, myth. It is as if in his negotiation and definition of myth, Lévi-Strauss were responding to Wiener's two conditions for scientific study, discussed above: the isolation of the object from the observer (like language, myth is the articulation of an unconscious structure unavailable to everyday intuition; it is relatively autonomous, part of the social 'superstructure'); and the availability of long statistical runs of data (the distribution of myth across its variants provides a sufficiently wide sample for analysis). Lévi-Strauss's construction of myth as a discrete object of study, his definition of its nature, its function, its relation to other social phenomena and the appropriate method for its analysis, effectively creates a paradigm within which he will work for the next three decades, a kind of 'normal

---

[58] '[M]ythical thought always progresses from the awareness [*prise de conscience*] of oppositions toward their resolution [*médiation*]' (224; 248). See also Lévi-Strauss's analysis of Caduveo face paintings in *Tristes tropiques*, which realize in the realm of plastic art a symbolic expression of ideal social institutions unattainable in everyday existence (*TT2*, 197; *TT1*, 227).

science' whose parameters are less a limitation than a liberation, allowing him unlimited speculation in a field almost entirely of his own making. In a way, the relative autonomy he claims for myth as a symbolic system could equally be applied to his own analysis of myth. Whereas his work on kinship structures was, by its nature, relatively more exposed to the verification and contradiction of his academic peers, his delimitation of the field of myth is such that it forms a closed system, coherent within its own terms of reference perhaps, but elusive as to its ultimate verifiability.

Whatever one's reservations about Lévi-Strauss's theory of myth, like the theory of kinship it is an essential prerequisite to the understanding of other dimensions of his thought. If we have learnt anything about Lévi-Strauss, it is that he is a synoptic thinker, always anxious to validate and unify the various parts of his system. If we turn now to the question of *values*, to the ideological dimension of his thought, it is therefore in the knowledge that this is not separable from the main body of structuralist theory, but continuous with it.

4   Structuralism and humanism

> L'ethnologie n'est ni une science à part, ni une science neuve: c'est la forme la plus ancienne et la plus générale de ce que nous désignons du nom d'humanisme.
>
> (Ethnology is neither a separate science, nor a new one. It is the most ancient, most general form of what we designate by the name of humanism.)[1]

We have seen that one of the essential conditions of structuralism's claim to scientific interest is the restriction of its field of analysis, the reduction of the traditional problems of religious anthropology to an 'intellectualist psychology', as Lévi-Strauss called it, whose privileged objects are classificatory systems and myth. This entailed the relative marginalization of subjects such as ritual or sacrifice, and in general the reduction of the individual or collective experience of religion to their cognitive dimension. This 'desacralization' of the object of religious anthropology is in some respects symptomatic of the general development of the discipline in the twentieth century, but in Lévi-Strauss, it could be said, this tendency is developed to the extreme. For Lévi-Strauss, totemism is not a religion, or a part of religion, but a mode of intellection; the sacred is more a function of the human mind's demand for order and coherence than a spontaneous experience of the transcendent.[2]

Parallel to the desacralization of the object of anthropology is what one might term the dehumanization of the subject. If anthropology's point of departure is the lived experience of fieldwork, the concrete interaction of the ethnologist with the other culture and his or her testimony of that experience, then in Lévi-Strauss the destination of such experience is the abstraction of structural analysis. Here, he never ceases to remind us, we should be cautious of native interpretations of social phenomena, as these are at best secondary elaborations, attempted rationalizations of motivations and mechanisms whose ultimate foundations

---

[1] *SA2*, 272; *AS2*, 319.

[2] See the closing remarks in *Totemism* on the 'dissolution' of both totemism and religion (*T*, 103–4; *TA*, 152–3). See also Denis Hollier, *Panorama des sciences humaines* (Paris: Gallimard, 1973), p. 458; René Girard, *Des Choses cachées depuis la fondation du monde* (Paris: Grasset, 1978), pp. 9–14; *Things Hidden Since the Foundation of the World*, trans. Stephen Bann, Michael Metteer (London: The Athlone Press, 1987), pp. 3–7.

₍fieldwork?.

are unconscious.[3] The kind of subjective verification Lévi-Strauss seemed to be proposing in some of his earlier texts can therefore only come *after* the abstraction of structural analysis; it could never be its point of departure.[4] In the realm of collective representations, the relative autonomy he claims for myth detaches it from the immediate reality of human interaction; as the unconscious articulation of a 'message' whose structure is beyond our immediate intuition, the myth, or the *system* of myth (defined as the ensemble of its variants), quite literally possesses a life of its own. Viewed from this distance, the question of the empirical origin of myth becomes redundant: not only is the individual teller of myths dissolved in the wider context of a collective (and culture-specific) process of myth-making, but the process of myth-making itself is subsumed under the more inclusive and more abstract category of the human mind. As Lévi-Strauss famously asserts in his introduction to *The Raw and the Cooked*, 'I therefore claim to show, not how men think [*pensent*] in myths, but how myths operate [*se pensent*: are thought, literally, think themselves] in men's minds without them being aware of the fact' (*RC*, 12; *CC*, 20).

The effective suspension of human agency one finds in structuralism is of course already present in the discipline Lévi-Strauss sees as its main inspiration, linguistics. In a very Durkheimian passage of the *Course in General Linguistics*, Saussure insists that 'language is not a function of the speaking subject, it is the product that the individual passively reproduces... It is the social part of language, external to the individual, who by himself is powerless either to create or to modify it.'[5] The Saussurean concept of *langue*, a collective construct with its own distinct autonomy, reduces the role of the subject to that of the contingent executor of *parole*. A similar bracketing of individual agency is to be found in the information sciences, the second, less frequently acknowledged source of structuralist theory, investigated in the previous chapter. In his wide-ranging introduction to *Cybernetics*, which traces the scientific genealogy of this new discipline, Wiener designates the great philosopher and mathematician Leibniz as its 'patron saint', and goes on to suggest that contemporary advances in computer technology lie along the continuum of an increasing mechanization of human thought: 'It is therefore not in the least surprising that the same intellectual impulse that has led to the development of mathematical logic has at the same time led to the ideal or actual mechanization of processes of thought.'[6]

---

[3] See, in particular, *SA*1, 18–23; *AS*1, 25–30.

[4] This can be usefully contrasted with the approach of Lévi-Strauss's Africanist contemporary Marcel Griaule, who was elected to the first university chair of ethnology in France at the Sorbonne in 1943. Griaule placed great emphasis on the direct testimony of his Dogon informants, establishing a special relationship with an old hunter named Ogotêmmeli, who initiated him into the secrets of Dogon religion and cosmology. The deference paid in Griaule's work to native interpretations could not be further removed from Lévi-Strauss's approach.

[5] *Course in General Linguistics*, p. 14; *Cours de linguistique générale*, pp. 30–1.

[6] *Cybernetics*, p. 12.

The process Wiener is describing here, that is, the relief and economy of human thought processes through their externalization, whether 'ideal' (mathematical) or 'actual' (calculating machines, etc.), brings to light the already instrumental nature of human thought itself, and this is precisely Lévi-Strauss's conception of myth, as an instrument, a 'logical model' or 'logical tool' which allows the expression of ideas or relations inaccessible to normal intuition.

But the critical question here is that of agency, of who uses what, and to what extent the 'what' may become independent of the 'who'. For the historic importance of Wiener's book is that it describes a new phase in the evolution of human technology, where the previously predominant modes of extension and externalization of human functions, the tool or the machine, requiring direct manipulation or supervision, are being superseded by programmed, 'intelligent' systems where immediate human control is no longer needed. These properly *cybernetic*, or self-governing, systems could be seen to mark the final stage of the delegation of human functions to the automatic and autonomous processes of the machine. It is from this perspective and from this distance, as it were, that Lévi-Strauss seems to view myth. More than the notions of information or information technology, which continue to presuppose an agent, a transmitter of information or a user of technology, it seems that the most appropriate image for his conception of myth is that of the self-governing machine.[7]

An adequate history of the philosophical reception of the information sciences in France, and indeed internationally, remains to be written. What is clear is that in France Lévi-Strauss was one of the first significant mediators of these sciences, and that the various humanist responses to structuralism need to be situated in the more general context of debates concerning the social and cultural effects of information technologies. Already, in *Cybernetics*, Wiener is addressing such issues, and the moral concerns raised by his intervention in this sensitive area prompts him, a few years later, to write *The Human Use of Human Beings* (1950). The principal message of this book was that despite the great progress achieved in the mechanization and automation of production, in the final instance this has to be seen as being secondary to human ends. Whatever the moral reassurances of thinkers such as Wiener, the advance of structuralism and the human sciences in France was in the minds of its humanist critics indissociable from an ambient science and technology which seemed at each step to marginalize and relativize the position of the human subject. Lévi-Strauss himself did little to dissipate such fears, to the extent that he viewed traditional humanism as representing the final barrier to a properly objective understanding of human nature. In an interview with Raymond Bellour in 1967, for example, he protested: 'But at the moment we're having to contend with

---

[7] In *The Raw and the Cooked*, myths are described as being, like music, 'instruments for the obliteration of time' (*des machines à supprimer le temps*) (*RC*, 16; *CC*, 24).

a sort of theological humanism. At each stage of the emergence of modern science people said: what you're proposing places in question the existence of God. Now we're being told that what we're doing is questioning the existence of man.'[8] Typically, Lévi-Strauss viewed the development of anthropology, and by implication, the rest of the human sciences, as analogous to the history of the natural sciences in their emergent phase. His prioritization of the scientific perspective, and his accompanying criticisms of the limitations of philosophical investigation, doubtless contributed to the somewhat ambivalent relationship which existed between philosophy and structuralism in France in the 1950s and 1960s. Inevitably, this ambivalence was greatest in the case of existentialism, the philosophy which under the aegis of Jean-Paul Sartre had become the dominant intellectual movement in France after the war. While, as was noted in chapter 2, there was a degree of mutual recognition and respect in the relations between Sartre and Lévi-Strauss in the late 1940s and early 1950s, it did not take long for substantial differences to emerge in their respective systems of thought. Whereas Sartre's brand of existentialism was primarily concerned with the experience of the subject in-the-world, stressing the importance of historical situation and the necessity of individual choice and responsibility, structuralism focused on the (unconscious) structures that precede individual agency and resist historical contingency, and, at least in principle, remained closed to questions of a moral or ethical nature. Whereas existentialism could be situated within a recognizable tradition of Western philosophy, taking its inspiration from the phenomenology of Husserl and Heidegger, for Lévi-Strauss the programme of structuralism and the human sciences represented a break with metaphysics, a rejection of the traditional problems of philosophy in order to pursue a truly scientific investigation of human behaviour. In *Tristes tropiques*, he attacked the subjectivist bias of existentialism, asserting that a philosophy based on personal experience can never tell us anything essential about society or humanity and is simply a dramatization of the individual (*TT*2, 58; *TT*1, 61). In response, Sartre criticized the abstraction of structural analysis and its objectification of human experience, which ignored the dialectical realities of concrete relations and of the historical process. In his view the priority structuralism gave to autonomous and unconscious structures dehumanized the subject and excluded the possibility of individual agency.[9]

The debates that developed around existentialism and structuralism in the 1960s provide a typical case history, if one is interested in the dialectical counterpointing of schools or movements which seems to be a permanent feature

---

[8] *Les Lettres françaises* 1165 (12 January 1967), 5. My translation.

[9] See 'Jean-Paul Sartre répond', interview in *Sartre aujourd'hui, L'Arc* 30 (1966), 94–5; 'L'anthropologie', in *Situations philosophiques* (Paris: Gallimard Tel, 1990), pp. 283–94. See also François Dosse, *Histoire du structuralisme*, vol. I, pp. 397–8; *History of structuralism*, vol. I, pp. 325–7.

of French intellectual life. In this sense, it is impossible to understand the phenomenal success of structuralism in France without reference to the previous hegemony of existentialism, of which it appeared to be a point-by-point refutation. More fundamentally, however, the advance of structuralism represented a definitive shift in the distribution of intellectual power, a realignment of the relative spheres of influence of different genres of intellectual discourse. We have already looked at the interdisciplinary implications of Lévi-Strauss's pronouncements concerning the scope of anthropology and the human sciences, especially with regard to traditionally proximate disciplines such as history and sociology (chapter 1). Our conclusion was that while a strategic demarcation from these disciplines was an important aspect of his promotion of anthropology, in the wider arena of intellectual debate in France the real adversary was philosophy. For Lévi-Strauss, the traditional role of philosophy as the privileged point of synthesis of human knowledge – both scientific and humanistic – was becoming increasingly redundant. The human sciences had no need of this kind of philosophy, and could think for themselves. Moreover, he thought that philosophy, to its detriment, had become hopelessly out of touch with contemporary developments in the natural sciences. Despite these deficiencies, philosophy still appeared to be aspiring to the federating role it had previously held, even though the conditions justifying this position no longer existed.[10]

The power shift, in terms of intellectual influence, from philosophy to the human sciences is epitomized in the contrasting models of the intellectual presented by Sartre and Lévi-Strauss. While Sartre's notion of the *intellectuel engagé* (the socially and politically committed intellectual) belonged to the post-Enlightenment tradition of the intellectual as both moral consciousness and moral agent, Lévi-Strauss was seen to represent a new generation, a new breed of intellectual, the *savant* (expert, specialist, scientist), who felt no compulsion to pronounce on moral questions beyond her or his specialism, even less to take to the streets in defense of personal ideals.[11] Whereas Sartre represented a species of intellectual who operated in an extra- or para-academic environment, Lévi-Strauss's power base was clearly the university, and within the university, some of the most prestigious of its research institutions.

However, despite this professionalization, so to speak, of the role of the intellectual, in the case of Lévi-Strauss it cannot be said that the intellectual's moral mission has been entirely liquidated; rather, it has been displaced. Lévi-Strauss sees the role of the human scientist as first and foremost one of objective

---

[10] See the critique of philosophy in the 'Finale' of *The Naked Man* (*NM*, 637–43, 684–9; *HN*, 570–5, 612–16). More specifically on philosophy's lack of engagement with contemporary science, see 'Entretien avec Claude Lévi-Strauss', in Raymond Bellour and Catherine Clément (eds.), *Claude Lévi-Strauss* (Paris: Idées-Gallimard, 1979), p. 186.

[11] See *CLS2*, 158; *PL*, 219.

research and detached analysis – this is the principal ambition of structuralis.. Nevertheless, there is an ideological dimension to his thought which is not entirely independent of the structuralist project. All of this has to be viewed in the context of what was, increasingly, the special status of ethnology in France in the postwar period. The decline of the European powers and the wave of decolonization which followed the war had caused many to question the pre-eminence of European culture and consciousness and also to criticize its ethnocentrism. In this context it seemed logical that ethnology, in its special role as mediator of non-Western cultures, should become the special focus of such questioning and criticism. Indeed, in the 1950s and 1960s ethnology came to be regarded as a 'new humanism',[12] with a wider vision of humanity than the traditional philosophical version of humanism, whose conception of the individual subject was culture-specific and thus far from achieving the universality it claimed. Lévi-Strauss himself played a central role in defining this new humanism. While the scientific mission of structuralism seemed to exclude consideration of questions of value or ideology, the origin of structuralism in anthropology is far from indifferent. In this sense, human science and humanism are not antinomical. Our task in the remainder of this chapter is to examine how Lévi-Strauss manages to combine these two registers, the scientific and the humanistic.

Race, history, culture

So far we have been looking at the more narrowly anthropological and theoretical of Lévi-Strauss's texts, the importance of which was to establish his position and reputation both within his own academic specialism, anthropology, and, via the influence of structuralism, in many other areas of intellectual inquiry in postwar France. However, the generic range of Lévi-Strauss's work is much greater than this, and alongside these specialized studies one finds texts of a more general interest, addressing a wider public than the academic and intellectual circles just mentioned. In this category, the most significant early contribution is *Race and History* (1952).[13]

In 1950 Lévi-Strauss had been one of the signatories of a declaration by various experts on the question of race, and it was this declaration which prompted the United Nations Educational, Social and Cultural Organization (UNESCO) in 1951 to call for responses on the question of what modern science has to

---

[12] Lévi-Strauss uses the term *nouvel humanisme* in 'Panorama de l'ethnologie (1950–1952)', *Diogène* 2 (April 1953), 96–123 (96). See also Roger Bastide, 'L'ethnologie et le nouvel humanisme', *Revue philosophique de la France et de l'étranger* 4 (October–December 1964), 435–51.

[13] The essay was republished as the concluding chapter of the final section of *Structural Anthropology 2* ('Humanism and the Humanities') in 1973 (*SA2*, 323–362; *AS2*, 377–422).

contribute to the debate on racism. In itself, this sort of activity was not without precedent – it was not unusual for anthropologists to use their expert status to comment on questions of this kind. Earlier in the century, Boas had made similar interventions in the United States, and there are distinct echoes of Boas in *Race and History*. The difference is that whereas Boas's interventions took place in the relatively circumscribed context of race relations in the US, Lévi-Strauss's contribution is situated in the more global context of postwar decolonization. Another interesting point is that Lévi-Strauss was not the only French anthropologist to involve himself in the debate. From 1950 there was a close dialogue between himself, Alfred Métraux and Michel Leiris on the race question.[14] The exchange of ideas which took place between Lévi-Strauss and Leiris merits particular attention, as Leiris was to write his own contribution to the UNESCO survey, *Race and Civilization*.[15] The collaboration between the two men is discernible in the content of the two essays, which cover more or less the same ground in terms of the arguments they advance against the traditional forms of rationalization of racial prejudice. The core of these arguments may be summarized as follows:

- Both Leiris and Lévi-Strauss reject biologistic explanations of 'racial' difference: there is no scientific proof of a genetic correlation between so-called racial types and moral or intellectual characteristics. Leiris emphasizes that these kind of scientific explanations are simply an attempt to justify political oppression and economic exploitation.
- The observed differences between different human groups are the result of cultural factors which are themselves the effect of different paths of historical development.
- Cultural development is impossible without culture contact. Truly isolated societies remain in a state of relative cultural stagnation (both Leiris and Lévi-Strauss speak here of a 'cooperation' between cultures; Lévi-Strauss also refers to a 'coalition' of cultures – we will return to this term later).
- There is no such thing as a society living in a 'state of nature'. So-called 'primitive' societies with a low level of technological development nevertheless possess a high level of cultural development or 'civilization'.
- Western pre-eminence in the field of technology is based on a longer-term development over a period of several millennia and is also the product of more recent exchanges with other civilizations.
- Our judgements of other cultures are always conditioned by the values of our own culture and can therefore never be absolute judgements.

In view of the previous dialogue between the two anthropologists on the race question, it is not surprising to find so many points of convergence in their

[14] Aliette Armel, *Michel Leiris* (Paris: Fayard, 1997), p. 515.
[15] Michel Leiris, *Race et civilisation*, in *Cinq Etudes d'ethnologie* (Paris: Gallimard Tel, 1969), pp. 9–73; *Race and Culture* (Paris: UNESCO, 1951).

two essays. Both mobilize the same range of disciplines (biology, genetics, history, prehistory and archaeology, as well as anthropology) and sometimes even use the same examples (the Tasmanians as an illustration of the dangers of cultural isolation; the Eskimos as an example of technological sophistication at least equal to that of Western science). More generally, it could be said that these arguments and these examples belong to an already well-defined body of anthropological discourse on the question of race, dating back to Boas at least, and that in this sense the possible repertory of reponses to the question is a limited one. On the other hand (and this is why the comparison with Leiris is so instructive), while the two essays might draw on the same repertory of reponses, their use of this repertory differs in several important respects. It would be use-ful here to work through some of these differences, as this will give us a clearer idea of both the originality of Lévi-Strauss as a thinker and, in the context of the present chapter, his thinking on humanism and the human sciences.

In many ways, Leiris's essay is the more immediately accessible of the two texts, in that it is more focused on the central issues concerning racism. From the opening pages of the essay, the question of race is firmly contextualized in recent history, with particular reference to the racist ideology of Nazism. This very immediate moral concern, and the awareness of the necessity to resist ideologies such as nazism, inform the entire essay. Biographically, they may be seen as a direct expression of Leiris's personal experience of the war, as a member of the French Resistance. A good part of the first half of the essay is devoted to the refutation of biological or genetic explanations of cultural difference, and it is only towards the middle of the text that Leiris introduces anthropology, or more precisely, ethnography, to counter the idea of a supposed 'state of nature' attributed to so-called 'primitive' cultures.[16] Anthropological facts and anthropological theory form the basis of the argument in the remainder of the essay, in passages on the definition of culture, the relationship between culture and personality, culture contact and cultural change, and the relativity of categories applied to other cultures. The title of the conclusion, 'Racism is not an innate attitude', sums up the combative tenor of the essay and the sense of urgency Leiris gives to the question. It argues not only that racism is a product of specific social and cultural factors, rather than a natural reflex, but also that it is possible to localize it historically, as the product of European colonial expansion and the political and economic exploitation that were its corollary. One may disagree with Leiris's historical localization of racism, and his singularizing of the European case, but what does emerge from his diagnosis is the imperative of action. It is here that one feels most strongly the presence

---

[16] 'The knowledge of anthropology [*ethnographie*] (now a systematic discipline) possessed by Western science of the middle twentieth century warrants the assertion that there is no extant group of human beings today which can be described as being "in the natural state" ' (*Race and Culture*, p. 19; *Race et civilisation*, p. 35).

of the author as an individual with a moral mission, and not simply as an expert (anthropologist) called upon to pronounce on the question of race. Leiris calls for the radical transformation of the exploitative political and economic structures which he believes to be at the heart of the colonial problem. For Leiris, the political imperative seems therefore to take precedence over a purely anthropological point of view: anthropology might help us in the understanding and explanation of the race question, but in the final instance it is useful only as a prelude to action, in the service of human emancipation.

When one passes from Leiris's contribution to that of Lévi-Strauss, the differences between the two texts are not simply compositional or stylistic, that is, the kind of differences one would expect to find between any two authors or experts writing on the same subject. Instead, it could be said that Lévi-Strauss takes the question of race and raises it to a higher level of abstraction. As has been noted, all of the elements of Leiris's text are present, in one form or another, in Lévi-Strauss's essay, but the relations between these elements and the relative emphasis placed on them are completely transformed.

The first significant point to make about *Race and History* is how quickly and summarily in the introduction Lévi-Strauss dismisses racist theories on the biological or genetic determination of cultural differences – theories which Leiris spends more or less the first half of his essay refuting – in order to situate the debate on another level, that of the *diversity* of cultures. Even if one succeeds in refuting racialist theories, there remains, according to Lévi-Strauss, the fact and the problem of cultural diversity, and its apparent corollary, the inequality of cultures. The task Lévi-Strauss sets himself in his essay is therefore to determine whether such diversity represents an advantage or a disadvantage for humanity (*SA2*, 325; *AS2*, 379). Whereas Leiris does not introduce the anthropological perspective on cultural difference until approximately the middle of his exposition, in Lévi-Strauss's essay this perspective is present from the beginning of the text.

The second important difference between the two essays is the fundamentally speculative register of Lévi-Strauss's text. While Leiris's response to the UNESCO question brings together and deploys an already constituted body of facts and theories, it seems that Lévi-Strauss uses the question as the point of departure of a more abstract speculation on culture and history. Very early on, in the second section of the text, one finds the following formulation: 'When studying these facts...one ends up wondering whether human societies are not defined (with regard to their mutual relationships) by a certain optimum diversity beyond which they could not go, but below which they should not go either without endangering themselves' (327; 381). And shortly afterwards, on the question of what Lévi-Strauss terms 'internal diversification', that is, the differentiation, within a society, between classes, castes, professional or religious groups, he writes: 'We can wonder if this *internal diversification* does not tend to increase when the society becomes, in other ways, larger and more homogeneous' (ibid.).

These opening speculations set up, in a very classical manner, the 'problem' that will be the guiding thread of *Race and History*, and in a manner very characteristic of Lévi-Strauss, the essay attempts to construct a conceptual framework adequate to the resolution of the problem. Thus in the fourth section of the essay, there is the essential distinction between 'cumulative' and 'stationary' histories. The first would apply to those societies which progress through an accumulation of technical inventions and discoveries, continually building on previous knowledge to form great civilizations such as our own. The second would refer to societies no less ancient or gifted, but which never manage to synthesize their discoveries in the same way as cumulative societies, oscillating around a more or less fixed level of development (335; 391). The big question, as the essay unfolds, is how the cumulative societies, in particular, Western civilization, came to exercise the global influence they now enjoy. On the one hand, Lévi-Strauss relativizes the technological achievements of the West: in the ensuing sections of the essay, much is made of the fact that Western technological culture represents only a fractional moment in the total history of human culture, and that the industrial and scientific revolutions of the past two or three centuries owe their existence to the no less significant event of the neolithic revolution. Moreover, two of the immediately quantifiable advances of modern civilization – an increase in available energy per capita and an increase in life expectancy – are accompanied by an increased incidence of war and inequality (346–7; 404–5). On the other hand, he needs to explain the singularity of the Western variant of cumulative history, and to do this he introduces the notion of probability. He says that the problem of the singularity of technologically 'cumulative' cultures, cultures like our own and before it the neolithic, is a statistical problem, that is, the problem of a relatively more complex 'combination' (353; 411). It is at this point that the famous analogy of the game of roulette is introduced, in which the gambler would have to bet on infinitely long sequences of numbers before winning, and would run the risk of bankruptcy before reaching the required combination of numbers. The solution to this dilemma is to increase the number of players so as to pool resources and thereby increase the probability of a successful combination (354; 412–13). If one accepts this analogy, what Lévi-Strauss is proposing is that the singular event of cumulative cultures is made more probable if it is understood that these cultures are in fact the result of a 'coalition' of cultures.[17] Only a high level of interaction between a number of different cultures over a long

---

[17] This section of the essay is visibly inspired by the game theory of von Neumann and Morgernstern, but the roulette metaphor is also combined with a concept of interactive exchange derived from Mauss. Lévi-Strauss's assertion that 'the exclusive fatality, the unique fault which can afflict a human group and prevent it from completely fulfilling its nature, is to be alone'

period of time can account for the existence of cumulative civilizations such as our own.

In its simplest formulation, the idea of the cultural coalition, analogous to Leiris's idea of cooperation, is unobjectionable. It is difficult to assert that prolonged contact and exchange between different cultures does not in any way contribute to a measure of cultural development, though the concepts of 'exchange' and 'development' would always need qualification, and would probably be impossible to quantify. What is less certain is Lévi-Strauss's basic conceptualization of culture as a combination of traits, where combination is conceived in a linguistic-informational and even biological manner, and of cultural contact as a kind of game. The latter analogy seems to be taken directly from the game theory of von Neumann and Morgenstern, and while it is rhetorically effective, providing a concrete image of the ideas Lévi-Strauss is trying to communicate, it is misleading to the extent that it reduces the overdetermined histories and modalities of cultural contact to the strategies of abstract players. The combinatorial conception of cultural systems is consistent with the structuralist approach investigated in the previous two chapters, but whereas in the social and cultural systems of kinship and myth this approach might lay claim to a certain pertinence, it is difficult to see how it can be effective at the macro-level of the historical interaction of cultures. An additional complication is that the combinatorial model of culture is also, implicitly, a biological one: throughout *Race and History*, the problem of diversity is posed as being quite literally vital to the progress of the human race, in the same way that genetic diversity is essential to the adaptive potential and survival of a species. This implicit analogy is made explicit in a later essay on the same subject, again commissioned by UNESCO and published in 1971. The second essay, entitled *Race and Culture*,[18] reproduces many of the arguments of the first, but it also refers back to the previous essay in a passage which brings together the various concepts discussed so far:

Over [twenty] years ago . . . I used the notion of coalition to explain that isolated cultures cannot hope to create by themselves the conditions for a truly cumulative history. For such conditions, I said, diverse cultures must voluntarily or involuntarily combine their respective stakes, thereby giving themselves a better chance to realize, in the great game of history, the long winning series that allows history to progress. Geneticists now express similar views on biological evolution . . . in the history of populations, genetic recombination plays a part comparable to that of cultural recombination in the evolution of the ways of life, the techniques, the bodies of knowledge, and the beliefs whose distribution distinguishes the various societies. (*VA*, 17–18; *RE*, 39–40)

(356; 415), echoes the conclusion of Mauss's *The Gift*, where gift exchange is seen as a mechanism for regulating conflict between groups but also a means of avoiding 'isolation and stagnation' (*The Gift*, p. 82; *Sociologie et anthropologie*, p. 278).

[18] *VA*, 3–24; *RE*, 21–48.

It will be noticed that there is a paradoxical reversal of the direction of reference or causation in this passage. What Lévi-Strauss appears to be saying is that in the twenty years separating the two essays the successive discoveries in genetic science have confirmed his own previous model of cultural development, whereas, as a close reading of *Race and History* shows, that model was already implicitly biological.[19] The first essay was written a few years before the major advances in molecular biology in the 1950s, but the necessary elements for Lévi-Strauss's model of cultural interaction and adaptation were already present in neo-Darwinian genetics.[20] Whatever the problems of influence or precedence, it is evident that by way of the homology suggested between genetic and cultural, Lévi-Strauss is more generally proposing a *stochastic* model of historical change. The genetic recombinations he refers to in *Race and Culture* are the products of random mutation; there is no pre-programmed direction to the process: evolution is teleonomic but not teleological.

Again, rather than dwelling on the question of the consistency of Lévi-Strauss's models, it is perhaps better to focus on the reasons for his choice of these models, as this choice seems to be motivated not simply by their explanatory potential, but by his thinking about the future of cultural diversity and the possibilities of influencing that future. For it is clear that Lévi-Strauss does not view the evolution of world culture neutrally, that for him the present world order does not represent the best of all possible worlds. In this sense, the most essential question is the technological (economic, military) predominance of the West and the accompanying globalization of Western culture, rather than the more restricted question of race. Significantly, the various models (combinatorial, statistical, mutational) used to explain the mechanisms of this success also point to its contingency, and this leaves the door open to the possibility of change. In the last section of *Race and History*, he argues that the cultural diversity which is the strength of the European coalition must in the long term tend towards homogenization. Again, the metaphor used is that of the game: the longer the game lasts, the greater the tendency towards an equalization of the resources of each player and a reduction in the chances of obtaining a winning combination (358–9; 418). Again, the explicit metaphor of the game

---

[19] See, for example, the passage on the encounter of the Old and New Worlds in section 7 of the essay. For a criticism of the biological analogy in *Race and History* and *Race and Culture*, see Emmanuel Terray, 'Face au racisme', *Magazine Littéraire* 223 (October 1985), 55.

[20] In his later work, Lévi-Strauss sees the development of molecular biology as providing an important confirmation of the methods of structural analysis. See, for example, his preface to Roman Jakobson's *Six Lectures on Sound and Meaning*, trans. John Mepham (Sussex: Harvester Press, 1978), pp. xxi–xxii; xxv–xxvi; *Six Leçons sur le son et le sens* (Paris: Editions de Minuit, 1976), pp. 14–15, 17–18; and, especially, the concluding section of *Mythologiques* (*NM*, 675–6, 684–7; *HN*, 604–5, 614–15). See also Christopher Johnson, 'Structuralism, Biology and the Linguistic Model', in J. Wolfreys, J. Brannigan and R. Robbins (eds.), *The French Connections of Jacques Derrida* (Albany: State University of New York Press, 1999), pp. 135–9.

is accompanied by a second, more implicit analogy, in this instance the thermodynamic or informational concept of entropy. As was noted in the previous chapter, the second law of thermodynamics states that the entropy, that is, the degree of disorder or disorganization of a closed system increases with time. Stated in bio-informational terms and in the closed system of cultural exchange Lévi-Strauss is describing here, the intermixing of what at the beginning are a diversity of cultural traits would lead in the long run to an equalization, a flattening out of the initial diversity. The solution to this dangerous but inevitable process of homogenization, he argues, is to actively promote diversity. Normally, the process can be countered in two ways. The first is to diversify the internal structure of a given society, in other words, to introduce hierarchical differences between its constituent groups, leading to the exploitative structure of, for example, our modern industrial societies. The second solution, dependent on the first, is to introduce new players, new partners into the initial coalition of cultures. Historically this is what happened with Western imperialism and colonization (359–60; 418–19).

It is clear that Lévi-Strauss's preferred solution to the problem of cultural homogenization is the second option, that is, the opening up of the closed system of cultural exchange, though in the postwar, and what is rapidly becoming the postcolonial context of *Race and History*, the agent responsible for promoting such cultural diversity would not be a colonizing state or coalition of states, but rather the anonymous 'international institutions' alluded to in the closing pages of the essay. The mission or responsibility of these institutions would be to oversee the liquidation of obsolete forms of cultural collaboration while selecting others better adapted to present conditions:

Institutions must first assist humanity and make the reabsorption of these defunct diversities as painless and safe as possible. These diversities are the valueless residues of modes of collaboration which exist as putrefied vestiges and constitute a permanent risk of infecting the international body. They must be pruned, amputated, if need be, to facilitate the birth of other forms of adaptation. (*SA2*, 361; *AS2*, 420–1)

So if, as was mentioned earlier, the process of cultural recombination described by Lévi-Strauss is a stochastic one, this does not exclude the possibility of a certain agency. To continue his roulette metaphor, the game is not over. Just as in biology, artificial selection and, more recently (more powerfully), biotechnology are possible modes of human intervention in the process of evolution, so Lévi-Strauss appears to believe in the possibility of intervention in the sphere of cultural interaction and cultural evolution. The problem is obviously how the 'institutions' he refers to might distinguish between the obsolete and the vital, on what criteria the distinction might be made, and indeed *who* would provide the relevant data. It is at this point that the reader can perceive or at least suspect another possible instance of judgement or decision behind these institutions, that of the ethnologist, the ethnologist whom Lévi-Strauss will later describe as the conscience and consciousness of the West, the witness and mediator of cultures radically different from our own.[21] One could go even further here, and suggest that the quest for diversity is delegated not simply to the ethnologist, but more specifically and more narrowly still to the *structural* anthropologist. I say this because the imperative that Lévi-Strauss articulates in the closing lines of *Race and History* is a curiously Leibnizian one. He says that 'we must... encourage secret potentialities' held in reserve by history, that 'the diversity of human cultures is behind us, around us and ahead of us' (362; 422). This idea of potentiality, of a virtual reality of cultural alternatives, should be related to the repertorial or tabular model of classification mentioned at the start of Lévi-Strauss's essay. Here he suggests that in order to properly address the question of diversity, it would first be necessary to make an inventory, not only of the different societies or cultures existing at the present time, but also of all the cultures which would have preceded them in past history. The problem with this is that apart from the limitations of historical analysis as compared to the study of contemporary cultures, many cultures have no written or recorded history, so that even indirect experience of their past is impossible. The most faithful inventory would therefore have to include a number of blank spaces or entries corresponding to unknown or extinct societies, and the number of these blank spaces would inevitably be infinitely greater than those which one would be able to fill (325–6; 379–80).

The concept of the inventory is a recurrent feature of Lévi-Strauss's structuralism, a frequent point of comparison being the periodic table of the elements. In Mendeleyev's table, each element which has been discovered has its assigned place in the table, but it is also possible to predict the existence of new, hitherto undiscovered elements. One of the main characteristics of the inventory mentioned in *Race and History* is precisely the idea of virtuality, of a kind of compossibility, to use the Leibnizian term, that is greater than actuality. In the essay's concluding remarks, there is therefore a certain optimism in the belief that the threatened closure of world civilization can be countered by the mediation of alternative cultural realities. This is not so straightforward as it may sound, since it is not simply a question of the empirical observation and recording of qualitatively diverse cultures. A leitmotif of Lévi-Strauss's work is the lament, common among ethnologists of his generation, of the rapid disappearance of the object of ethnographic study, and the importance of extending and intensifying the practice of fieldwork wherever possible. At the same time, the plethora of data that has been generated on exotic cultures is useless if it is not matched by an adequate theoretical framework within which to understand it. It is from this perspective that Lévi-Strauss seems to be approaching

---

[21] See *TT2*, 389–93; *TT1*, 465–71; *SA2*, 31–2; *AS2*, 43–4.

the question of diversity in the conclusion of *Race and History*, that is from a structuralist understanding of the nature of culture and of the treatment of information on culture. It will be remembered that the procedure for analysing myth, examined in the previous chapter, was to treat it as a virtual construct, as the ensemble of its variants, and that this methodological approach owed as much to information theory as it did to linguistics. The myth was like a message whose content was distributed across a range of separate transmissions. Whatever the degree of distortion or noise to which the signal was subjected, it was, in principle, possible to reconstruct more or less accurately the original message. In *The Naked Man*, Lévi-Strauss expresses this possibility of recuperation in explicitly informational terms:

> The second law of thermodynamics is not valid in the case of mythic operations: in this field, processes are reversible, and the information they convey is not lost; it is simply converted into a latent state. It remains recoverable, and the role of structural analysis is to look beyond the apparent disorder of phenomena and restore the underlying order. (*NM*, 216–17; *HN*, 190)

As we have seen, a similar optimism is expressed in the concluding pages of *Race and History*. Whereas the general diagnosis of the rest of the essay points to the destruction, dispersal or extinction of cultures in the wake of Western expansion (a few years later, in *Tristes tropiques*, anthropology is ironically redefined as an 'entropology'),[22] the virtual reconstructions of structuralism are a possible means of information retrieval. The seemingly detached and abstract activity of structural analysis therefore becomes a task, a labour, a kind of mission, the reincarnation of lost mental worlds.

To return to our original point of comparison, despite the obvious merits of Leiris's text – its clarity of exposition, its pedagogical concern, its sense of moral purpose – the speculative drive of Lévi-Strauss's contribution, its mobilization of models and concepts external to the field of anthropology and the human sciences (theory of relativity, probability theory, information theory, genetics), gives his argument a rhetorical force of a quite different order. As we have discovered a number of times already, whatever the object of study may be, Lévi-Strauss is never content simply to describe its phenomenal aspect. In the case of *Race and History*, therefore, he attempts to explain not simply the fact of cultural difference and cultural change, but also its underlying mechanisms. So while, as we have seen, Lévi-Strauss draws from the same basic repertory as Leiris in his treatment of the question of race, his approach leads him to a quite different conclusion than Leiris. What is above all apparent in Leiris's conclusion is the *voice* of the author as a moral presence: his role as expert, as anthropologist,

---

[22] 'Anthropology could with advantage be changed into "entropology", as the name of the discipline concerned with the study of the highest manifestations of this process of disintegration' (*TT*2, 414; *TT*1, 496).

seems subordinate to this. For Leiris, anthropological knowledge is finally only an auxiliary in the fight against racism and colonial exploitation, and the mission of anthropology, if there is one, would pass through the intermediary of the ethnographer, his or her first-person testimony of colonial oppression. With Lévi-Strauss, it cannot be said simply that there is a lack of moral intention. One finds in his text, for example, an acerbic critique of racist theories, of Western ethnocentrism and the destructive effects of colonialism. However, it seems that the voice of Lévi-Strauss is a mediated one, that between the individual Lévi-Strauss and the question of racism there is, necessarily, the intermediary instance of the discipline of anthropology. It has been noted that at the beginning of his essay Lévi-Strauss very quickly shifts the focus of discussion onto the anthropological plane, in effect displacing the question of race onto the problem of cultural diversity. The formulation of this problem and the subsequent conceptualizations of cultural change one finds in the essay are circular and self-contained to the extent that the solution to the problem can only be an anthropological (more precisely, a structural anthropological) one, in what we have described as the structuralist imperative of recuperation, articulated at the close of the essay.

The impression then – and this is not an isolated instance in his work – is that Lévi-Strauss has used the occasion of the UNESCO survey on race to widen the question, in effect turning the debate on racism and colonialism into a philosophical dissertation on diversity.[23] In the process, there is a kind of strategic positioning of (structural) anthropology as the repository and mediator of diversity. This drift from the political and ideological centre of the debate did not pass unnoticed. There is evidence that, in spite of the close collaboration and dialogue between Lévi-Strauss and Leiris prior to the publication of their UNESCO contributions, after 1952 there was a growing tension in their exchanges, especially in relation to political questions. For Leiris, the race question was inevitably and irreducibly a class question, and he was visibly frustrated with Lévi-Strauss's resistance to the idea of the ethnologist's political responsibility and his or her involvement in political issues.[24]

The frustration of colleagues such as Leiris with this kind of philosophical detachment is understandable. The distanced perspective from which Lévi-Strauss approaches the question of race in *Race and History* is consistent with his general view of anthropology as a human science, whose applications, in whatever sphere, are secondary to the imperative of scientific enquiry. His call

---

[23] This is also Pierre-André Taguieff's evaluation of the essay: 'Lévi-Strauss's approach [in *Race and History*] is more aesthetic than moral or political. It implies neither a synthesis or fusion of cultures, nor their segregation, and seems to be based on the Leibnizian norm of maximum variety within the formal unity (cognitive or epistemological) of humankind' (*Les Fins de l'antiracisme* (Paris: Michalon, 1995), p. 409, my translation).

[24] Aliette Armel, *Michel Leiris*, pp. 516, 534–5.

for the promotion of cultural diversity in the final pages of the essay does seem curiously abstract, in view of the urgent moral and political questions at stake. Rather than offering any convincing response to these questions, it seems simply to provide an external validation of the research mission of modern anthropology, as he conceives it, permitting the infinite extension of the inventories of structural analysis.

Leaving aside the local question of the ideological divergence between Lévi-Strauss and Leiris, the interest of Lévi-Strauss's reflections on world culture and world history in *Race and History* is obviously not restricted to this text alone. Again, it is as if the text were a testing ground for ideas which will later become central to his thought. The distinction between stationary and cumulative history, the valorization of the neolithic period, the notion of a possible intervention in the course of cultural development, all of these are thematic units that will be developed and deployed in subsequent texts with a specific ideological effect, constituting what one might term the lesson, or rather, *lessons* of anthropology.

The lessons of anthropology

When, in the mid-1940s, existentialism was criticized for its alleged 'anti-humanism', one of the key elements of Sartre's defence of his philosophy was the notion of authenticity. For Sartre, the individual was the product of his or her acts rather than the expression of some predetermined nature. Existence preceded essence, and the individual was fundamentally free in his or her choice of action. Inauthenticity, or 'bad faith', described the situation of those individuals who refused to recognize their freedom, and consistently shifted the responsibility for their own failings or feelings of failure onto external factors over which they had no control. Authenticity, or 'good faith', referred to individuals who exercised their freedom without reference to any external moral or political authority and who accepted total responsibility for their actions. According to Sartre, existentialism was a humanism to the extent that there was no conflict between individual self-determination and the collective good: the ultimate goal of individuals acting in good faith is a search for freedom, and freedom is the essential foundation of all values.[25]

As was noted earlier, Sartre's philosophy of freedom takes as its point of departure the fact of individual consciousness, of the individual's immediate experience of the world, his or her situation in the world. Lévi-Strauss, on the other hand, is faithful to the Durkheimian tradition of sociology which views the individual's character, his or her choices and behaviour as variable functions

---

[25] *L'existentialisme est un humanisme* (Paris: Gallimard/Folio-Essais, 1996), pp. 69–70; *Existentialism and Humanism*, trans. Philip Mairet (London: Methuen, 1973), pp. 51–2.

of social norms, rather than the reverse. At the qualitatively different level of social institutions and collective representations, the Sartrean categories of individual responsibility, choice and freedom simply make no sense. As we saw, for Lévi-Strauss existentialism represents a false dramatization of individual psychology, and exhibits all the limitations of an approach he generically refers to as 'phenomenological'. But while he would see no scientific interest in the question of individual authenticity, as Sartre formulates it, there is an interesting appropriation of the term in his reference to different forms of social organization. In the 1954 article 'The Place of Anthropology in the Social Sciences', Lévi-Strauss argues that while the kind of societies studied by anthropologists are normally classified in a privative manner – *non*-civilized or *non*literate societies, *pre*- or *non*-industrial societies – the apparently negative associations of these descriptions in fact conceal a positive reality. Because of the relatively low population count in these kinds of societies, relationships between individuals are more concrete and more direct, and in the case of larger or more geographically extended societies, systems of kinship ensure the preservation of these intimate links (*SA*1, 365; *AS*1, 400). In fact, claims Lévi-Strauss, it is our own society which should be described in privative terms, and here the vocabulary is visibly Sartrean:

Our relations with one another [*avec autrui*] are now only occasionally and fragmentarily based upon global experience, the concrete 'apprehension' of one person by another [*d'un sujet par un autre*]. They are largely the result of a process of indirect reconstruction, through written documents. We are no longer linked to our past by an oral tradition which implies direct contact with others (storytellers, priests, wise men, or elders), but by books amassed in libraries, books from which we endeavour – with extreme difficulty – to form a picture of their authors. (*SA*1, 366; *AS*1, 400–1)[26]

While it might be possible to identify 'levels' of authenticity in modern societies, their overall characteristic is one of inauthenticity, where relationships between individuals in literally every sphere – interpersonal, administrative, political – are intermediate rather than immediate. The extension of the mass media has only added to the catastrophic loss of autonomy experienced by the modern individual. So if one accepts Lévi-Strauss's previous definition of society as a system of communication, then his diagnosis of modern industrial society is that it is characterized by a *pathology* of communication.[27]

This counterpointing of 'modern' and 'primitive' society is continued and developed in a series of radio interviews with Georges Charbonnier in October–December 1959. Predictably, Charbonnier asks Lévi-Strauss what his discipline has to teach us, more specifically, what the essential difference is

---

[26] See also *CLS*1, 51–4; *ELS*, 60–3.
[27] Lévi-Strauss cites Wiener's *Cybernetics* and *The Human Use of Human Beings* on the alienation of communication in modern communities (*SA*1, 366–7; *AS*1, 401–2).

between so-called 'primitive' and 'modern' cultures. In his response, Lévi-Strauss is careful to qualify that, in addition to the questionable designation of 'primitive', the societies in question are infinitely varied in type. But he nevertheless goes on to provide a scientific analogy to explain what he sees as the main difference between 'us' and 'them', 'modern' and 'primitive' society. The first could be characterized as 'hot' societies, working in a manner analogous to the steam engine, producing their energy through a basic disequilibrium or difference of potential. These are societies based on the hierarchical differentiation between groups and the exploitation of one group by another, and it is this type of class exploitation which contributed to the rise of Western civilization. The second category, 'cold' societies, would function like clocks, requiring only a small initial input of energy to set them in motion, and periodically returning to a central point of equilibrium. These societies Lévi-Strauss describes as inherently more 'democratic', in that their political organization is based on the principle of unanimity, on the conscious or unconscious avoidance of the kind of inequalities or dissensions characteristic of Western industrial societies. In such societies, if a vote is taken on any important issue, it is not enough that a majority vote determines the final decision: any source of disagreement would be seen as compromising that decision, so everything is done to ensure total unanimity. He gives the example of certain Pacific island societies, where a kind of ritual combat is organized prior to any important political deliberation, so that old enmities and differences may be purged, thereby ensuring common assent when the decision is finally taken (*CLS*1, 32–6; *ELS*, 37–42).

The distinction between hot and cold societies seems to revive, and complement, the distinction made in *Race and History* between stationary and cumulative history. Whereas in *Race and History*, the distinction was based on differences in technological development (the success of Western civilization being based on the accumulation and exchange of technical knowledge), in the interviews with Charbonnier the hot/cold distinction is based on sociological and political differences. Lévi-Strauss brings these two levels together in his subsequent development of the machine metaphor, where he qualifies that society is both a machine and the work that this machine produces, which is equivalent to the distinction between society and culture. Society is defined as the different modes of relations between individuals, whereas culture is defined as the ensemble of relationships between society and the world. The central concept here is that of entropy. In hot societies, analogous to the thermodynamical machine (the steam engine), the social by-product is a high level of entropy (disorder) or social inequality, whereas in the cultural realm the result is a low level of entropy, or a highly structured material environment. Conversely, in cold societies, which are compared with the mechanical machine (the clock), there is a relatively low level of technological development but also a low level of social entropy, so that these societies enjoy, to use Durkheim's term, a higher degree of social cohesion or social solidarity (*CLS*1, 40–2; *ELS*, 45–7).

Despite the appealing symmetry of Lévi-Strauss's distinctions, it is not certain how far the metaphor of the machine advances our understanding of cultural difference, or whether it provides an adequate representation of the qualititative variations between different forms of society. The concept of entropy itself is used in a manner which bears little resemblance to its original, scientific formulation, and in this sense is more likely to confuse than to enlighten a reader unfamiliar with the subject. In general, like the speculations of *Race and History*, the interviews with Charbonnier bear the mark of Lévi-Strauss's reading of Norbert Wiener,[28] and the implicit comparison, in the series of distinctions between 'stationary' and 'cumulative', 'hot' and 'cold', etc., is with mechanisms of control and modes of feedback. The societies Lévi-Strauss calls 'cold' or 'stationary' would be what Wiener termed *homeostatic* systems, that is, systems where the control mechanism is one of negative feedback, maintaining the system in a 'steady state', between well-defined variables. On the other hand, 'cumulative' or 'hot' societies would present the case of systems where there is no overall control mechanism, characterized by a process of *positive* feedback. Whereas in the negative feedback circuit, information on the output of the system is fed back to its input, to ensure that subsequent output is maintained within a limited set of parameters, in the case of positive feedback there is no such check, and the system is subject to an exponential growth that knows no limits.

The negative feedback characteristic of cold societies can also be interpreted as *resistance*, resistance to change, resistance to the kind of historical development that Western societies have experienced. In Lévi-Strauss's inaugural lecture at the Collège de France, given in January 1960, he gives the following elaboration:

Although situated in history, these societies seem to have developed or retained a particular wisdom which impels them to resist desperately any modification in their structure that would enable history to burst into their midst. Those which, recently still, best protected their distinctive character appear to be societies inspired by the dominant concern to persevere in their existence. The way in which they exploit the environment guarantees both a modest standard of living and the conservation of natural resources. In spite of the diversity of their marriage rules, a demographer can recognize in them the common characteristic of rigorously limiting the birthrate and keeping it constant. Finally, a political life, based on consensus and allowing no other decisions than those taken unanimously, seems conceived to exclude that driving force [*moteur*] of collective life which makes use of the contrasts [*écarts différentiels*] between power and opposition, majority and minority, exploiters and exploited. (*SA2*, 28–9; *AS2*, 40)

---

[28] In particular, the final chapter of *Cybernetics*, 'Language, Information, Society'.

Of the three forms of equilibrium mentioned here, we have already discussed the last two, demographic stability and political unanimity. The first, however, the idea of ecological balance, merits further analysis, as it extends Lévi-Strauss's thinking on social and cultural authenticity to the question of humankind's relationship with nature. In a paper written in 1961, 'Cultural Discontinuity and Economic and Social Development',[29] he identifies three sources of the resistance of traditional societies to modern, industrial civilization: the desire for unity (which reproduces his previous remarks on political consensus), the rejection of history and the respect for nature. As was noted above, Lévi-Strauss defines culture as the ensemble of relationships between human society and the world, and it is along this nature–culture axis that he pursues the question of our attitudes towards nature. While noting that all human societies recognize a distinction between nature and culture, as that which separates the human from the animal, he argues that it is only in industrial society that an unconditional priority is given to culture over nature. In so-called 'primitive' societies, nature has a much more ambivalent status. On the one hand, as is universally the case, nature is perceived as being prior and subordinate to culture; on the other hand, nature is also above culture, *super*natural, to the extent that it is the realm in which the individual may make contact with ancestors, spirits and gods. In contrast to this essential relationship with the supernatural, there is a kind of devalorization of material, manufactured objects, and a strong and deep resistance to what Lévi-Strauss calls 'instrumentality'. This sort of resistance would also be a common feature in the past history of our own civilization (*SA2*, 320–1; *AS2*, 373–5).

According to Lévi-Strauss's typology, the belief systems of traditional societies would therefore serve the function of regulating the interface between nature and culture and limiting the actions of the latter on the former. Elements of this conception of native thinking are also to be found in his work on systems of classification, notably in *Totemism* and *The Savage Mind*. As was noted in the previous chapter, one of the driving arguments of these two books was that the systems of classification observed in nonliterate societies, rather than being the expression of affective states or some mystical 'participation' with nature, possessed a rigour and coherence of their own, comparable to that of Western science, to the taxonomies of zoology or botany, for example. While these societies, in close and intimate contact with the natural environment, retain a sentimental attachment to nature that we have lost, this does not necessarily exclude a certain objectivity in their representations of the natural world. One strand of Lévi-Strauss's argument is therefore strongly relativistic, resisting the traditional characterization of these representations as non- or pre-scientific. At the same time, there seems to be a positive value attributed to the fact that, while,

[29] *SA2*, 312–22; *AS2*, 365–76.

as Lévi-Strauss shows, different native systems of classification are capable of scaling the heights of abstraction, they are firmly rooted in the concrete reality of the natural world, constituting what he terms a 'logic of the concrete'. The practice of *bricolage*, as he defines it in the first part of *The Savage Mind*, is to take the constitutive elements of the logical systems it constructs from pre-constructed or ready-made objects at hand in the immediate environment. The systems of classification analysed in both *Totemism* and *The Savage Mind* share this quality of embeddedness in the natural world, even as they transcend that world in their logical processing of its phenomena. By contrast, a constant criticism of modern civilization in Lévi-Strauss's work is that it has lost the sense of a connection with the living world and therefore any sense of deference to and respect for it. The specific path of development taken by Western science and technology (what Lévi-Strauss elsewhere calls *la civilisation mécanique*, 'mechanical civilization') has meant the emergence of an ideology consistent with its separation of the natural and the human realm, a narcissistic humanism which values only its own species and sanctions the destruction of the natural environment in the name of progress.[30]

The positive value Lévi-Strauss attaches to native systems of classification extends also to what he characterizes as their *non-instrumentality*. In both *Totemism* and *The Savage Mind*, he is critical of the conventional stereotyping of so-called 'primitive' societies as being forever subject to the regime of necessity. He therefore rejects the functionalist interpretation, which sees the activity of classification as serving merely instrumental ends: one classifies because this or that species of plant or animal is fundamental to this or that aspect of material subsistence – eating, clothing, housing, etc. On the contrary, he points out that much of the classification that takes place in nonliterate societies is not directed to any specifically utilitarian ends. In *The Savage Mind*, for example, a large part of his argument is devoted to demonstrating the essentially speculative tendency of native thinking, its inexhaustible intellectual curiosity, its interest in knowledge for the sake of knowledge. A distinctive trait of 'savage' thinking, according to Lévi-Strauss, is its unprecedented symbolic drive, its capacity for infinite extension (comparable to the magician's belief in a global determinism), and this is contrasted with the instrumental knowledge of 'domesticated' Western science, which is primarily concerned with the limited ends of production, the imperative of yielding a return. In this, native thinkers are compared to the great naturalist and hermetic thinkers of antiquity and the Middle Ages (*SM*, 42; *PS*, 57).

One can see, from the above distinctions between instrumental and non-instrumental knowledge, that there is a convergence here with what Lévi-Strauss

---

[30] See 'Urban Civilization and Mental Health' and 'Witnesses of Our Time' (*SA2*, 283–7; *AS2*, 333–7).

had previously defined, in quasi-economic terms, as the 'surplus' of signification, or the floating signifier. While these societies might be economically and
technologically 'poor' in relation to modern industrial civilization, they are on
the other hand rich in symbolic production.[31] Moreover, Lévi-Strauss would
see these native systems of representation, which articulate the continuity of the
human and the natural, as a kind of protective insulation against the alienating
forms of social and economic development experienced in Western societies.[32]
This leads us to the central question of history.

Many times, Lévi-Strauss has emphasized that the 'stationary' history of
cold societies does not mean a lack of history. All societies are the product of
a long-term historical development, it is simply that some societies choose to
represent this development differently. In the same way that he relativizes the
achievements of Western science and technology, Lévi-Strauss questions the
objectivity and universality of the category of representation modern societies
call 'history'. This emerges most clearly in the famous critique of Sartre in the
final chapter of *The Savage Mind*, entitled 'History and Dialectics'. 'History
and Dialectics' is primarily a response to the first volume of Sartre's *Critique of
Dialectical Reason*, published in 1960. The ambition of the *Critique*, as Sartre
saw it, was to combine existentialist philosophy with a Marxist interpretation of
history. A central distinction made in the book was between analytical reason
and dialectical reason. The first worked within the finite boundaries of a closed
system of reasoning, a little in the manner of a geometrical proof, static and self-
sufficient. The second was reflexive to the extent that it was aware of its social
and historical situation and was therefore always in the process of transcending
this context in order to question its own foundations. Lévi-Strauss's interest
in the *Critique* (he devoted a series of seminars to it in 1960–61)[33] can be
attributed to the fact that in the course of the book Sartre draws on a range
of examples from anthropology, sometimes quoting directly from Lévi-Strauss
himself. What Lévi-Strauss was unable to accept in Sartre's analysis was the assigning of the two orders of reason, analytic and dialectical, to modern scientific
thinking and so-called 'primitive' reasoning, respectively. In the opening pages
of 'History and Dialectics', he questions Sartre's absolute distinction between
the two types of reason and concludes that they are complementary sides of the
same reason, universally applied, rather than being the exclusive attribute of this
or that culture. But the real centre of 'History and Dialectics' is his disagreement
with Sartre on the subject of history. Like others of his generation, Sartre was

---

[31] See chapter 3, note 13.
[32] The term used in the original French is *glacis*, glazing or covering.
[33] Lévi-Strauss had invited Jean Pouillon, a close associate of Sartre who had begun specializing
in anthropology after reading *Tristes tropiques*, to present the *Critique* in the seminars (François
Dosse, *Histoire du structuralisme*, vol. I, p. 23; *History of Structuralism*, vol. I, p. 7).

strongly influenced by Alexandre Kojève's interpretation of Hegelian dialectics in his 1930s lectures, and this coloured his subsequent reading of Marx. His own personal, concrete experience of occupation and resistance during the Second World War sharpened his sense of the immediacy of historical forces and the need for the individual to engage with them.[34] When, following the attacks which prompted his defence of existentialism in *Existentialism is a Humanism*, he moved closer to Marxism, attempting to reconcile the two perspectives, he adopted the quasi-teleological conception of history characteristic of the Marxism of the time, which viewed the development of human history as ultimately a unitary and convergent one. So while in his writing and in his political activity Sartre was an intransigent partisan of Third World emancipation, he saw that emancipation in socialist-progressivist terms, as necessarily involving the eventual integration of traditional societies into the mainstream of world history. The result in the *Critique*, according to Lévi-Strauss, is that Sartre treats the non-Western cultures described in ethnographic studies as residual forms of humanity lacking a historical consciousness, which need to be taken in charge by historical societies, either through their assimilation of the historical sense through the colonial experience, or by their being given historical sense in the mediating discourse of ethnology. Whatever the case, Lévi-Strauss denounces, in visibly angry tones, the narrowness, egocentrism and ethnocentrism of this view of humanity, which suppresses, in one stroke, the essential richness and diversity of human experience (*SM*, 248–9; *PS*, 329). Such blindness, he claims, is symptomatic of a philosopher who is unable or unwilling to think beyond the categories of his own culture. Thus, while Sartre is incomparable in his reconstruction of lived experiences in his own society, past or present – a technique of internal comprehension to be admired and emulated – when he comes to the example of other cultures, he seems unable to recognize that the 'savage' is capable of complex and abstract reasoning, relegating his or her thought processes to the status of a primitive (analytical, non-dialectical) mentality (250–1; 331–2).

The problem, as Lévi-Strauss sees it, is that it is difficult to tell whether Sartre is taking history in the ontological sense, as an absolute, lived fact – which he (Lévi-Strauss) would obviously not refute – or whether he is referring to the history of historians or, possibly, the history of philosophers. His conclusion is that, for Sartre, the category of history functions like a myth. In fact, he suggests that the central problem of the *Critique* can be reduced to one question: under what conditions is the myth of the French Revolution possible? While he accepts that the Revolution is an indispensable point of reference for any individual who wishes to play a role in the present historical process, it does not follow that his

---

[34] 'Entretiens sur moi-même', in *Situations* X (Paris: Gallimard, 1976), pp. 91–226.

or her interpretation of the Revolution is the most objective or true. It is here that Sartre is not dialectical enough, according to Lévi-Strauss, as the 'truth' of the Revolution is a purely situated one:

If we place ourselves outside it – as the man of science is bound to do – what appeared as an experienced truth first becomes confused and finally disappears altogether. The so-called men of the Left still cling to a period of contemporary history which bestowed the blessing of a congruence between practical imperatives and schemes of interpretation. Perhaps this golden age of historical consciousness has already passed; and that this eventuality can at any rate be envisaged proves that what we have here is only a contingent context like the fortuitous 'focusing' of an optical instrument when its object-glass and eyepiece move in relation to each other. We are still 'in focus' so far as the French Revolution is concerned, but so we should have been in relation to the Fronde had we lived earlier. (*SM*, 254; *PS*, 336–7)

The optical and perspectival metaphor, a recurrent figure in Lévi-Strauss's work, underlines the relativity of historical consciousness. His subsequent reference to Cardinal de Retz's account of the Fronde, the political troubles which shook France in the early part of Louis XIV's reign and threatened its system of absolute monarchy, shows the essential overdetermination of the historical event and the difficulty of capturing its meaning as it recedes into the past and as its immediate relevance is lost to us. He suggests that in the next century or two the idea of the French Revolution, to which contemporary individuals are still so very intensely attached, will appear as a myth, or perhaps will not even register at all in the consciousness of our descendants (255–6; 338).

As Lévi-Strauss's distinction between the 'man of science' and 'so-called men of the Left' indicates, his criticism of the reification of history is not limited to Sartre alone. Through Sartre, he is attacking the more general trend in French philosophy to privilege historical knowledge over all other forms of scientific investigation. Behind the scene of his engagement with Sartre in 'History and Dialectics', there is therefore the wider arena of debate concerning the relative claims to objectivity and universality of different forms of knowledge. Once again, it is a question of the place of anthropology within the human sciences and its relationship with other disciplines, here history. Lévi-Strauss reiterates the argument he had made some ten years earlier in 'History and Anthropology' on the complementarity between the two subjects. History devotes itself mainly to diachronic analysis, looking at examples of human society distributed in time; anthropology concentrates on synchronic relations in a range of human societies distributed in space. In practice, both subjects combine elements of the other's predominant (synchronic or diachronic) mode of analysis. In this sense, the two disciplines would seem to be on an equal and reciprocal footing (*SM*, 256; *PS*, 338–9). However, just as he reduces Sartre's conception of history to the status of a myth, Lévi-Strauss goes on to apply a similar kind of relativism to the discipline of history itself. He first questions the consistency of the idea of a historical 'fact'. Each separate episode of a war or revolution is composed of a multiplicity of individual psychological experiences, themselves an expression of unconscious impulses, which in their turn can be reduced to neurological and bio-chemical determinants. It is the historian, or the historical agent, who abstracts the historical 'fact' from this overdetermined continuum. Second, he argues that the historical fact is itself the object of an arbitrary selection. A total history is impossible, and for a history to be at all intelligible, a set of past events must make sense for a given group of individuals at a given moment in time. In this sense, history is necessarily partial and partisan. The French Revolution as written from the Jacobin or aristocratic perspective is not the same Revolution, and one could multiply *ad infinitum* the number of virtual perspectives on this particular historical event, to the point at which one would have to concede that the Revolution, as it is normally understood, did not exist (257–8; 340–2).[35]

In fact, argues Lévi-Strauss, history, like all knowledge, must use a code if it is to have any purchase on its object of analysis, which is an undivided continuum. In the case of our own, academic history, this coding is chronological, though not in the simple, absolute sense of a linear sequence of dates. Rather, history proceeds by assigning significance to different groups or classes of dates, in which each date makes sense only in relation to other dates in the group or class, and where the groups themselves form discontinuous and mutually irreducible sets. Moreover, while the conventional apprehension of history is that of a continuous movement through the ages, with a progressive narrowing of the chronological frame of reference (from the tens or hundreds of millennia of prehistory to the millennia, and finally the centuries, decades, years, weeks, etc. of recorded history), from the point of view of the virtual history of humankind, each period would in principle be susceptible to the same frame of reference used in other periods, with a corresponding shift in the amount of importance attached to this or that feature or event (258–60; 342–5).

The symmetry of Lévi-Strauss's treatment of Sartre's notion of history on the one hand, and the history of historians on the other, is clear. While Sartre's history is compared to myth, the historian's history is compared to a system of classification, in effect granting it the same status as the native systems of classification which have been the principal subject of his book. For Lévi-Strauss, this is not necessarily a problem. It is quite logical that Sartre, as a historical agent, should need to make sense of his own, lived situation, and in the present historical conjuncture the myth of the French Revolution is a suitable point of reference for that experience. Similarly, the historian needs a code to make sense of the chaos that is (real) history. The problem, for Lévi-Strauss, is

---

[35] The same point is made over ten years earlier in 'History and Anthropology' (*SA*1, 16–17; *AS*1, 23).

when the historian or the historical agent behaves as if his or her history is the only form of intelligibility, the only form of truth, a truth applicable to the whole of humanity:

We need only recognize that history is a method with no distinct object corresponding to it to reject the equivalence between the notion of history and the notion of humanity which some have tried to foist upon us with the unavowed aim of making historicity the last refuge of a transcendental humanism: as if men could regain the illusion of liberty on the plane of the 'we' merely by giving up the 'I's' that are too obviously wanting in consistency. (*SM*, 262; *PS*, 347)

Lévi-Strauss is striking here at the heart of Sartre's programme, central to the *Critique of Dialectical Reason*, of converting what had been the ahistorical individualism of his earlier existentialism into a historicized philosophy of collective action. But again, the field of reference of his attack is wider than the individual instance of Sartre, more generally suggesting an unholy alliance of history and philosophy and their propagation of a false humanism. Indeed, the whole of the final chapter of *The Savage Mind* reads like a kind of lesson, a lesson in relativism given by anthropology to philosophy and history, which have not, to use Sartre's own terminology, been sufficiently 'dialectical' in their practice. There is, of course, a degree of irony and provocation in Lévi-Strauss's critique of Sartre (the historical agent) and the historians: his reference to 'so-called men of the Left', his assertion that the Revolution did not exist, his comparison of Sartre's opposition between 'self' and 'other' with the reasoning of a native Melanesian (*SM*, 249; *PS*, 330). But this does not diminish the strategic importance of the scenario set up in 'History and Dialectics': on the one hand the historian and the philosopher, who are unable to transcend a particular, situated conceptual universe; on the other, the anthropologist, the 'man of science', with a more detached and objective perspective on the range and nature of human experience. What is more, this lesson in relativism, dispensed from what Lévi-Strauss claims to be one of the most scientific of the human sciences, comes from what he would have us believe is also the most human of the human sciences. Because Lévi-Strauss is not content simply to turn the tables on history and philosophy, to show the essential relativity of their constructions of the world; he is also concerned to show the inherent superiority of other forms of consciousness, in what amounts to an alternative form of humanism.

Following his analysis of the problems of historical reconstruction, Lévi-Strauss asserts, quite simply, that 'the characteristic feature of the savage mind is its timelessness' (263; 348). This assertion repeats the argument of the previous chapter of *The Savage Mind*, 'Time Regained', where he is pondering the relative absence of totemic systems of representation in the great civilizations of Europe and Asia. The explanation, he thinks, is that 'the latter have elected to explain themselves by history and that this undertaking is incompatible with that of classifying things and beings (natural and social) by means of finite groups' (232; 308). Totemic classification proceeds by postulating a homology between two distinct series of phenomena, animal and plant species and human groups, the second series originally deriving from the first – human culture is seen as having emerged from the (super)natural realm. Both series persist in parallel across time, but are out of time to the extent that they remain absolute realities, unchanged since their point of separation. The original and originating natural realm serves as a constant point of reference for the checking and regulation of changes that might appear in the socio-cultural realm. Lévi-Strauss concludes that 'in theory, if not in practice, history is subordinate to system' (233; 308). In historical societies, on the other hand, the two series, natural and cultural, are merged into one series, and instead of a classification based on finite groups one has an open-ended representation of the world, an infinite series in which each term is derived from the one that precedes it.

If in historical societies there is what might be termed a collapsing of nature and culture, the implication here is that culture takes precedence over nature, i.e., that in modern technological civilization the natural is merely an object of transformation for the cultural. The respect for nature derived from the belief that it is in some sense *super*natural, i.e., that the human and the cultural are literally descended from the animal and the vegetal realms, therefore disappears when the two realms are no longer held as distinct. The virtue of native systems of thought is that, working with the finite repertories provided by the natural world, they construct infinitely complex systems of representation, but while these systems might be used to represent or regulate social relations, they keep the natural world at a distance, as it were, as an object of reverence.[36] The closed infinity of 'savage' thought is therefore opposed to the open infinity of historical consciousness, forever in pursuit of the changing and the contingent.[37]

Again, Lévi-Strauss's characterization of native thought as essentially atemporal or anti-temporal does not mean, literally, that the societies in question

[36] See, for example, *OTM*, 503–4; *OMT*, 418–19, on the respective attitudes of 'civilized' and 'primitive' cultures regarding modes of physical contact with the natural world.

[37] The self-reflexive and self-referential nature of 'savage' thought is depicted in 'History and Dialectics' by the image of a room with mirrors, reminiscent of the metaphor previously used to describe the decoding of myth. To continue the quotation given above: 'The characteristic feature of the savage mind is its timelessness; its object is to grasp the world as both a synchronic and a diachronic totality and the knowledge which it draws therefrom is like that afforded by a room of mirrors fixed on opposite walls, which reflect each other (as well as objects in the intervening space) although without being strictly parallel. A multitude of images forms spontaneously, none exactly like any other, so that no single one furnishes more than a partial knowledge of the decoration and furniture but the group is characterized by invariant properties expressing a truth. The savage mind deepens its knowledge with the help of *imagines mundi*. It builds mental structures which facilitate an understanding of the world in as much as they resemble it. In this sense savage thought can be defined as analogical thought' (*SM*, 263; *PS*, 348).

have no history or exist in some sense outside of history, but rather that they have chosen to represent themselves in this way. In 'Time Regained', he revives the distinction made in the interviews with Charbonnier between hot and cold societies, but here the distinction is extended to the respective modes of representation of history in these two types of society:

It is tedious, as well as useless, in this connection, to amass arguments to prove that all societies are in history and change: that this is so is patent. But in getting embroiled in a superfluous demonstration, there is a risk of overlooking the fact that human societies react to this common condition in very different fashions. Some accept it, with good or ill grace, and its consequences (to themselves and other societies) assume immense proportions through their attention to it [*par la conscience qu'elles en prennent, amplifient ses conséquences dans d'énormes proportions* – literally: by the consciousness they take of it, amplify its consequences to immense proportions]. Others (which we call primitive for this reason) want to deny it, and try, with a dexterity we underestimate, to make the states of their development which they consider 'prior' as permanent as possible. It is not sufficient, in order that they should succeed, that their institutions should exercise a regulating action on the recurrent sequences by limiting the incidence of demographic factors, smoothing down [*amortissant*] antagonisms which manifest themselves within the group or between groups and perpetuating the framework in which individual and collective activities take place. It is also necessary that these non-recurrent chains of events whose effects accumulate to produce economic and social upheavals, should be broken as soon as they form, or that the society should have an effective procedure to prevent their formation. We are acquainted with this procedure, which consists not in denying the historical process but in admitting it as a form without content. There is indeed a before and an after, but their sole significance lies in reflecting each other. (*SM*, 234–5; *PS*, 310–11)

Again, Lévi-Strauss's distinction between hot and cold societies is based on the opposition of two types of feedback, but here, significantly, there is the added dimension and complication of intention or agency. What we referred to earlier as the positive feedback of modern industrial society, its exponential technological development and the different kinds of social differentiation that go with it, is *amplified* by the consciousness this form of civilization has of its own development, with consequences not only for itself, but for the whole of humanity. In parallel fashion, the negative (regulative, delimitative: the sense of the French verb *amortir* is to deaden or to dampen) feedback of cold societies is not restricted to what might be called the 'infrastructural' control mechanisms of kinship structures and political organization (ensuring, as we saw above, demographic stability and political consensus), but extends to these societies' ways of representing those historical forces which always and inevitably threaten to modify established forms of social organization. Like myth which, as we saw in the previous chapter, serves to mediate the lived contradictions of social existence, native systems of classification, as they are depicted in *The Savage Mind*, perform a homeostatic function, to the extent that history appears to them as an empty category.[38]

The rejection of history thus joins the other forms of resistance to modern civilization, discussed above, as a mark of the relative authenticity of cold societies. A central premise of Sartre's notion of authenticity, as discussed above, was that the individual is free to choose, and the extent to which the behaviour of an individual is judged 'authentic' or 'inauthentic' is measured along the scale of his or her preparedness to exercise that freedom. As was remarked, Lévi-Strauss has little time for what he considers to be the illusions of subjectivity, and would treat the idea of freedom with caution and scepticism. However, transposed into the terms of his typology of cultures, there does seem to be some kind of link between what he refers to as cultural authenticity and choice. In fact the whole of the passage of 'Time Regained' devoted to the question of history seems to assume a form of intentionality in the two modes of processing history: the civilizations of Europe and Asia have *chosen* to represent themselves historically, they have taken the side (*le parti*) of history; traditional societies are always 'seeking, by the institutions they give themselves, to annul the possible effects of historical factors on their equilibrium and continuity in a quasi-automatic fashion' (233–4; 309); their obstinate attachment to atemporal schemas of representation is the expression of 'a consciously or unconsciously adopted attitude [*parti*]' (236; 312–13). The qualification of 'quasi-automatic' and the modulation between 'conscious' and 'unconscious' attitudes inevitably raises the question of intentionality, agency and responsibility. To what extent, one could ask, is it possible to say that a society has consciously chosen its own path of development, and to what extent are so-called 'hot' and 'cold' societies, in their divergent paths of development, *responsible* for their respective fates? Lévi-Strauss never directly addresses this question, but whatever the complications inherent in his characterization of the two types of history, it is clear that, when it comes to the question of the *cause* of their divergence, the different strands of his analysis all point to one specific phenomenon: writing.

The lessons of writing

When, in 1950, Lévi-Strauss moved to the Ecole Pratique des Hautes Etudes to take up the chair in the history of religions, the title of the chair, 'Religions of non-civilized peoples', had remained unchanged since the time of Mauss. As Lévi-Strauss admits, the designation was in the 1950s an unacceptable one.

---

[38] See the opposition made earlier in *The Savage Mind* between 'structure' and 'event', where Lévi-Strauss describes the deferred adjustments of ideal configurations (structure) to the perturbing force of demographic change (event) as a kind of cybernetic feedback mechanism (*SM*, 68–9; *PS*, 92).

He therefore decided to change the title of the chair to 'Religions of nonliterate peoples' (*Religions des peuples sans écriture*): while it was impossible to call these people 'uncivilized', that they had no system of writing was a fact.[39]

Lévi-Strauss's renaming of his chair, in view of the blatant ethnocentrism of its previous title, was undoubtedly in its context an appropriate and necessary gesture. However, the new title is not an entirely neutral one: inevitably, it says something about the nature of the object of anthropological study, as Lévi-Strauss conceives it. Thematically, the question of writing is the point of intersection of all of his thinking on the relative nature and value of modern and traditional societies. We have already seen how Lévi-Strauss views the conventionally privative designations of other cultures as concealing what in fact are positive attributes. In nonliterate societies – so-called non-civilized or non-industrial societies – he argues, interpersonal communication is more proximate and more immediate than in modern societies, where our relationships, in many spheres of social life, are mediated through written documents. Our relationship with our own past is a similarly indirect and mediated experience, accessed through the written archive rather than through a living oral tradition (*SA*1, 366; *AS*1, 400–1, quoted above). More generally, the modes of technological development and historical consciousness which Lévi-Strauss takes to be responsible for the destructive expansion of Western civilization are both impossible without the defining technology of writing (*CLS*1, 26–7; *ELS*, 28–9). In societies without writing, on the other hand, the rejection of historical change and the subordination of the cultural to the (super)natural ensure that their relationship with the world is not simply an instrumental one, and that their interventions in the natural world are checked and limited by the sense of its sacredness, its essential priority to the human and the social.

All of these themes and all of these oppositions are brought into sharp and dramatic focus in what at first sight would seem the most unlikely of places, the autobiographical narrative of *Tristes tropiques*, in a chapter called 'A Writing Lesson'.[40] The chapter is part of one of the ethnographic sections of the book, devoted to the South American people named Nambikwara. The Nambikwara, it will be remembered, were the subject of Lévi-Strauss's analysis of political power and leadership, investigated in chapter 2 above. The picture he constructed of these relations was a composite one, based on his contacts with different but related groups of the Nambikwara: Sabané, Tarundé and Wakletoçu. 'A Writing Lesson' describes an episode concerning the chief of the last of these groups, the Wakletoçu. In a first scene, Lévi-Strauss describes how, as a routine part of his field research, he distributed paper and pencils among the group, in order to observe and record their reactions. The conclusion of this little experiment is that the Nambikwara do not know how to write, nor do they

---

[39] See *CLS*2, 54–5; *PL*, 81–2.   [40] *Tristes tropiques*, chapter 28.

draw, apart from certain point or zigzag patterns decorated onto the shells of their gourds. He is therefore surprised when after a few days they begin drawing horizontal, undulating lines on the paper. He assumes that they are attempting to imitate his own writing and drawing as they would have observed it, but notes that they progress no further than this imitation. The chief, on the other hand, appears to be more enterprising, and alone among his people seems to have understood the function of writing. When working with the ethnologist, he scribbles meaningless lines on his pad in imitation of his guest, and pretends that these lines possess a sense, which he then proceeds to read out (*TT*2, 296–7; *TT*1, 349–50).

This apparently harmless scene is the prelude to a second, more ambivalent and more violently charged scene, recounted in the same chapter. The ethnologist has asked the chief to take him to other, related Nambikwara groups so that he can draw up a complete demographic record of the population. When the chief, his group, and the ethnologist's team arrive, the other groups, who have never seen white Europeans before, are visibly hostile. To calm the situation, the chief insists that they proceed immediately with the customary exchange of gifts. It is at this point that he takes out his pad and begins to read – or rather, pretends to read – the list of gifts to be exchanged between the groups. This 'comedy', as Lévi-Strauss describes it, lasts for two hours (294–6; 347–50). The ethnologist is both irritated and troubled by this scene, and it is only later, at night, unable to sleep, that he thinks he is able to explain the reason for his unease:

Writing had, on that occasion, made its appearance among the Nambikwara but not, as one might have imagined, as a result of a long and laborious training. It had been borrowed as a symbol, and for a sociological, rather than an intellectual purpose, and its reality remained unknown. It had not been a question of acquiring knowledge, of remembering or understanding, but rather of increasing the authority and prestige of one individual – or function – at the expense of others. It had not been a question of knowing specific things, or understanding them, or keeping them in mind, but merely of enhancing the prestige and authority of one individual – or one function – at the expense of the rest of the party. A native still living in the Stone Age had guessed that this great means towards understanding, even if he was unable to understand it, could be made to serve other purposes. (*TT*2, 297–8; *TT*1, 352)

There follows a long passage in which Lévi-Strauss speculates on the historical function of writing and its role in social and cultural change. In sequence, these are the main points of his argument (*TT*2, 298–300; *TT*1, 352–5):

- For thousands of years and even today, writing has been the privilege of a powerful elite.
- The considerable transformations in human existence brought about by the use of writing, with its capacity for the almost infinite extension and amplification of human memory, should not blind us to the fact that one of the most

crucially productive periods of human prehistory, upon which all of civilization's subsequent achievements rest (the neolithic), took place in the absence
of any known system of writing.

- The period between the invention of writing and the expansion of modern
  science in the nineteenth century was a period of relative stagnation in which
  the quantity of knowledge fluctuated rather than increased.

- The only constant historical correlate of the appearance of writing is the
  formation of cities and empires with a high degree of caste and class differentiation. The primary function of written communication is therefore to
  enslave and subordinate. The intellectual or aesthetic dimension of writing,
  its use in the disinterested pursuit of knowledge, is secondary to this function.

- The spread of literacy in Western countries was accompanied by the extension
  of state control – for example the introduction of military service – and
  a process of proletarianization. Internationally, the exportation of Western
  knowledge to newly independent states can be an instrument of mystification
  and manipulation.

The fragility, or at best, qualifiability of this series of assertions about writing,
which come as a kind of commentary and moral coda on the 'extraordinary
incident' witnessed by the ethnographer and his companions, is clear. The
philosopher Jacques Derrida, in a now classic reading of Lévi-Strauss, reveals
all of the inconsistencies and contradictions of what is effectively a *theory* of
writing, appended to the parable of the 'Writing Lesson'. As Derrida's analysis
shows, Lévi-Strauss's scene of writing is a more like a scenario, a set-up of
which the Nambikwara chief is the unwitting protagonist, representing the
corrupting effects of an alien technology on a hitherto harmonious and innocent
community.[41] If one widens the frame of analysis beyond this scene to the
more general context of Lévi-Strauss's depiction of the Nambikwara in *Tristes
tropiques*, and especially of their chiefs, the schematism of his theory of writing,
and the extent to which it conforms to what we have learnt so far concerning
the lessons of anthropology, becomes even more apparent.

The six chapters on the Nambikwara, like the monograph Lévi-Strauss had
published several years earlier, present the social life of the Indians in all its aspects, moving from a description of material culture, family life and intersexual
relations to the discussion of intergroup relations and finally concluding with an
analysis of leadership and power. It is this last aspect, the analysis of leadership
and power, that is most directly relevant to the present discussion. While in the
order of narration of *Tristes tropiques* this analysis comes after the parable of

---

[41] 'The Violence of the Letter: From Lévi-Strauss to Rousseau', in *Of Grammatology*, trans. Gayatri
Chakravorty Spivak (Baltimore and London: Johns Hopkins University Press, 1976), pp. 101–40;
'La Violence de la lettre: de Lévi-Strauss à Rousseau', in *De la grammatologie* (Paris: Editions
de Minuit, 1967), pp. 149–202. For a more detailed study of Derrida's reading of Lévi-Strauss
see Christopher Johnson, *Jacques Derrida. The Scene of Writing* (London: Phoenix, 1997).

the writing lesson, it logically precedes the scene in the sense that it is essential to a more complete understanding of what is at stake during this critical episode. Our previous commentary of Lévi-Strauss's theory of authority showed that it was based on the notion of reciprocity between chief and group at a number of levels, political, economic and social, but that at the end of his analysis there remained the residual and imponderable aspect of psychological make-up and psychological motivation. His remarks on the characters of the different Nambikwara chiefs, based on his own, personal relations with them, led him to the conclusion that beyond the social and structural factors that are the condition of leadership, there is the universal psychological fact of temperament and ability which distinguishes such individuals from the rest of the group. What is interesting here is the process of identification and projection which appears to be going on in Lévi-Strauss's description of his ethnographic subjects. It should be remembered that during his period of fieldwork with the Nambikwara the ethnologist is not alone but part of an expedition, a team, including his wife. In this sense, he himself is a kind of 'chief', and as such, appears to enjoy a special relationship with the chiefs of the different Nambikwara groups.

There is first the chief of the group located at Utiarity, the chief of the writing lesson: this is the group which the ethnographer appears to have frequented the most and which is the primary focus in the chapters on the Nambikwara. Second, there are the chiefs of two groups who, though speaking different dialects, have been obliged to join forces: Tarundé and Sabané are the names given in the text. As was remarked, Lévi-Strauss uses elements of each of these individual cases to construct a composite picture of power relations in Nambikwara society, though it is with the first two individuals, the Utiarity chief and the Tarundé chief, that he enjoyed the closest relations (he did not speak the Sabané dialect). In the 1948 monograph on the Nambikwara, these three chiefs receive the designations A1, B1 and C20 respectively.[42] The Utiarity chief (A1) is a useful and willing collaborator in the ethnographer's fieldwork, and is an invaluable informant: 'He was a most useful informant, since he understood the problems, saw the difficulties and showed an interest in the work' (308; 365). This close collaboration has a price, time has a price. As Lévi-Strauss explains in his subsequent anatomy of Nambikwara politics, the exigencies of the chief's function mean that he is continually absorbed in serving the needs of the group. Conscious of this, he rewards his informants liberally, though he notes that the gifts rarely remain in the chief's possession for very long (310; 369). There is thus a further cycle of exchange or reciprocity binding the ethnographer to his informants, normally the chiefs. Information is not a zero quantity, it is also a commodity, a service, and it has its price.

---

[42] *La Vie familiale et sociale des Indiens Nambikwara* (Paris: Société des Américanistes, Gonthier, 1948), pp. 40–1, 50–1, 53, 103.

Not surprisingly, there appears to be a degree of mutual identification between the two men: both are in positions of authority in their respective groups.
However, for the ethnographer the structure of identification is complicated
by a certain resistance or reservation, discernible even before A1's political
appropriation of writing. This attitude emerges most clearly in the portrait
Lévi-Strauss gives of the two chiefs he has worked with most closely, A1 and
B1: 'I was well acquainted with two such chiefs: the one at Utiarity, whose
group was called Wakletoçu, and the Tarundé chief' (308; 365). What stands
out here is the contrast established between the two individuals. Both men are
in their thirties (the ethnographer is approximately the same age), and both are
intelligent leaders, but from the point of view of temperament, they appear to
be diametrically opposed. A1 is a remarkably resourceful individual: he is able
to anticipate and act upon the challenge of new situations, to follow through
his projects with a consistency that is normally lacking in the often changeable
and capricious Nambikwara. At the same time, the ethnographer's evident ad-
miration and respect for such an individual holds a nuance of reservation: 'he
showed himself to be an efficient organizer, capable of assuming sole responsibility for the welfare of his group, whom he led competently, although in a
somewhat calculating way' (308; 365). This qualification is developed in the
portrait given of the Tarundé chief, B1:

The Wakletoçu chief struck me as being a shrewd, very resourceful individual, who was
always planning some political move. The Tarundé Indian was not a man of action, but
rather a contemplative with a charming and poetic turn of mind and great sensitivity. He
was aware of the decadent state into which his people had fallen, and this realization
gave a melancholy tone to his remarks. (*TT*2, 308; *TT*1, 366)

Given the conditions of the Nambikwara social contract as Lévi-Strauss will
go on to describe them, and the rigours they impose on the chief, it is difficult
to understand how B1 can have obtained and retained his position of power.[43]
What is clear is the ethnographer's affinity with the more philosophical Tarundé
chief, whose attitude to the visitor's fieldwork differs markedly from that of his
Wakletoçu colleague. While A1 is an invaluable informant, he is also too absorbed in his social and conjugal duties to be an entirely consistent source.[44]
By contrast, B1's investment in the ethnographic process is total: 'His curiosity

---

[43] The numerically inferior Tarundé are indeed forced to enter into a coalition with the Sabané
group. The chief of this third group, C20, unlike his Tarundé and Wakletoçu counterparts, fulfils
the dual function of chief and shaman. Already at the beginning of the chapter on leadership
and power the Sabané chief, pretexting a supernatural occurrence, has been involved in negotiations with a third party, plausibly with the intention of betraying his present allies. See chapter 2,
p. 66.

[44] To complete the quotation above on A1's participation: 'However, his duties took up a good deal
of his time; for days on end he would be away hunting ... Frequently too, his wives would invite
him to join in amorous play' (404; 366). Is it possible to detect a hint of impatience behind this
statement of fact?

about European customs and about those of other tribes I had been able to study was in no way inferior to my own. Anthropological research carried out with him was never one-sided: he looked upon it as an exchange of information and he was always keen to hear anything I had to tell him' (309; 366). While there is no evidence here that the ethnographer does not reward B1 for his information as he had done with his other subjects, in this case there is an additional dimension to the transaction in that like is exchanged for like – curiosity for curiosity, information for information – a bilateral or reciprocal transaction. The implication is that from the point of view of ethnographic research at least, this represents a more authentic modality of exchange. Again by implication, the unilateral exchange would be the straight economic transaction of money for time, money for information. The opportunity cost of the time A1 devotes to the ethnographer's gathering of data, for example, is the time and labour diverted from his onerous obligations as chief. It is therefore important that the diversion should pay.

The schematism of the binary opposition of temperaments proposed in this passage – active and contemplative, pragmatic and philosophical – would suggest that for Lévi-Strauss the opposition itself extends further than mere empirical individuals, beyond the simple reality of an interpersonal situation experienced by the ethnographer in the field. In his interpretation (or translation) of that reality, and within the context of his discourse on power, he seems in fact to be putting forward two contrasting models of intelligence, two attitudes towards knowledge. The two chiefs are equally intelligent, he says, but in different ways. A1's mode of intelligence is mainly anticipative and proactive; his interest in knowledge is instrumental. As Lévi-Strauss notes in his subsequent analysis of leadership, the imperative of generosity, on which the chief's power depends, requires the intellectual quality of *ingenuity*. 'Ingenuity is the intellectual form of generosity' (311; 369). For his part, B1's attitude to knowledge is more pure than applied; he seems to be interested in information on the ethnographer's culture and those of other peoples from a purely intellectual point of view. If for Nambikwara chiefs the obligation of generosity requires the intellectual quality of ingenuity, then B1 is uncharacteristic in his *curiosity*, his pursuit of knowledge in and for itself. The ethnographer is unable to discern whether this curiosity is in effect motivated by more pragmatic designs, but suspects that it is not: 'Perhaps he hoped to use the information to improve the material equipment and intellectual level of his group. However, his dreamy temperament was hardly conducive to practical achievement' (309; 366). The anecdote that follows is instructive in this respect. The ethnographer wishes to verify an aspect of cultural diffusion, namely the use of panpipes. The chief has never seen the instrument, but asks for a drawing from which he manages to construct a basic but usable copy. This combination of curiosity and ingenuity applied to an article of cultural and artistic, rather than political or economic utility, completes the portrayal of B1 as a model of disinterested knowledge.

Throughout the passage, in fact, Lévi-Strauss's preference or prejudice is clear. The contrast he establishes is not (cannot be) neutral, and inevitably carries with it an element of judgement. While for the ethnographer there is a certain level of self-identification or empathy with both chiefs, his preference is visibly for the Tarundé. Apart from the latter's genuine engagement in the labour of fieldwork, his more contemplative cast of mind is also accompanied by nostalgia for his people's past glory. Lévi-Strauss evidently feels more attuned to this melancholic and retrospective philosophy than to the positive and projective behaviour of the Wakletoçu chief. As has been noted, there is a nuance of suspicion in his evaluation of the resourcefulness of the Wakletoçu chief, and this minimal resistance, this minute reservation is the fissure, the difference that will become an open breach with the extraordinary incident of the writing lesson.

If we return now to the scene of this incident, it is evident that the preference or judgement expressed in the portrait of the two chiefs acquires the force of a *prejudgement* when Lévi-Strauss as narrator comes to reflect on the significance of the episode, so much so that A1's 'political' appropriation of writing simply confirms what the ethnographer had already suspected.[45] In his judgement of the event, he has therefore in a sense already decided on his verdict and the defendant, the Wakletoçu chief, is condemned without repeal. The primary offence is exploitation, an instrumental rather than an intellectual use of writing (knowledge for the sake of knowledge), turned to the sinister manipulation of others.[46] But just as serious in Lévi-Strauss's eyes, it seems, is the crime of *premeditation*. More than his compatriots, the Wakletoçu chief appears to have the gift of foresight, not that of the prophet or seer, but the practical capacity of forward planning and anticipation. From the point of view of Nambikwara politics, this should be a virtue: the political imperative of generosity requires the intellectual quality of ingenuity, and it is difficult to imagine such ingenuity without the capacity of foresight. At the same time, from the point of view of Lévi-Strauss's analysis, this virtue can also become a vice, should the chief overstep the limits the group imposes on him. This is indeed what seems to happen following the scene of the exchange of gifts, the so-called 'comedy' of writing:

[45] Though in the narrative sequence of *Tristes tropiques* the portrait of the chiefs occurs after the episode in question, diegetically the experience on which the portrait is based clearly precedes it. The inversion or confusion of temporal sequence is a consistent feature of *Tristes tropiques*.

[46] This is a questionable verdict. In the context of Lévi-Strauss's analysis of the power structure of Nambikwara society, and in the light of our reconstruction of the chain of events that culminates in the episode of the chief's simulation, it would be difficult to speak precisely of exploitation. For a more extended analysis of the location of responsibility in this scene, see Christopher Johnson, 'The Writing Lesson Revisited', *Modern Language Review* 92.3 (July 1997), 599–612.

But in my Nambikwara village, the insubordinate characters were the most sensible. The villagers who withdrew their allegiance to their chief after he had tried to exploit a feature of civilization (after my visit he was abandoned by most of his people) felt in some obscure way that writing and deceit had penetrated simultaneously into their midst. They went off into a more remote area of the bush to allow themselves a period of respite. Yet I could not help admiring their chief's genius in instantly recognizing that writing could increase his authority, thus grasping the basis of the institution without knowing how to use it. (*TT*2, 300; *TT*1, 355)

Those who secede from the group therefore function as a kind of self-correcting mechanism, a quasi-automatic reflex that checks the chief's transgression of the limit. For this analysis to remain consistent, however, it is necessary that these individuals have only an 'obscure' understanding of the subversive potential of writing, thereby retaining an innocence and lack of premeditation distinguishing them from their more calculating chief. So while the chief has obviously miscalculated the political situation within his group, his error is less miscalculation than the faculty of calculation itself – seeing further than the others.[47] In the moral and theoretical coda to the scene of the writing lesson, there is a positive value attached to the absence of counting, combining and calculation in so-called nonliterate societies. In contrast with the cumulative and exploitative history of literate civilization, such societies would be restricted to 'a fluctuating history which will always lack both a beginning and any lasting awareness of an aim' (298; 353). With his unusual foresight, his gift of anticipation, the Wakletoçu chief is thus implicitly assimilated with the civilization that has directly or indirectly been the cause of his people's misfortunes. As such, he is both absolutely essential to the political economy of Nambikwara society and potentially a threat to it. For the ethnographer, who by vocation has become the voice and advocate of the other and the censor of his own civilization, the justified conclusion to the parable of the writing lesson is the punishment of the chief's hubris, the subsequent trimming of his power.

The problem is, as the above quotation suggests, that the 'respite' the rebellious Nambikwara have bought for themselves in abandoning their chief is, and can only be, a temporary one. The episode of the writing lesson recapitulates, in microcosm, the lessons of anthropology as we have followed them in Lévi-Strauss's other texts: the proximate relations of demographically limited groups; political consensus; the suspicion of instrumentality; the resistance to historical change. But as the narrative of *Tristes tropiques* so eloquently testifies, the societies which exemplify this model, or aspects of it, are rapidly in the process of disappearing. Lévi-Strauss himself considers the effects of the

---

[47] During the writing lesson proper, the Utiarity group's scribbling on paper distributed by the ethnographer and his companions, the chief distinguishes himself from his compatriots: 'The majority did this and no more, but the chief had further ambitions [*le chef voyait plus loin*]' (388; 350).

globalization of Western literate culture to be essentially irreversible. Increasingly, the voice of these societies fades into the background noise of a global monoculture, and the only remaining voice is that of the ambivalent mediator of cultural diversity, the ethnologist.

A new humanism

Shortly after writing *Tristes tropiques*, Lévi-Strauss published a short piece, a few pages in length, under the title 'The Three Humanisms' (1956).[48] The first humanism, he says, is the rediscovery, in the late Middle Ages and Renaissance, of Greco-Roman antiquity, which he sees as a first incarnation of ethnology, to the extent that it opened up another world, an alien world, with the realization that we can only properly understand ourselves by comparison with what is different to us. The apprenticeship of languages, the learning of Latin and Greek was an essential part of this 'technique of estrangement' (*technique de dépaysement*): a linguistic training is necessary to gain access to this past world. Even though these languages are now dead languages, the study of them provides the kind of intellectual discipline comparable to that needed for the practice of ethnology. The second humanism is simply an extension of the scholarship of classical humanism to the other great world civilizations, those of China or India, for example; in France this branch of study goes under the title of nonclassical philology. The third humanism is the discipline of ethnology itself, which extends the study of humanity to cultures ignored by the traditional humanisms. Unlike the classical and nonclassical civilizations, these cultures have, so to speak, no high culture, they have no monuments and no written literature. The task of ethnology is to provide an objective, external perspective on these societies, but also, through the practice of fieldwork, the ethnologist's participation in the everyday existence of a particular group, an internal perspective on their lived experience, their affective and mental life. Compared to its more scholarly predecessors, created for the privileged elites of privileged civilizations, ethnology is a more *democratic* form of humanism, in that it takes account of the most humble and most disregarded examples of human existence (*SA2*, 271–4; *AS2*, 319–22).

If, as Lévi-Strauss reiterates in his early work, ethnology is a relatively new discipline, a new science and a new humanism, then here he reminds us that it is not entirely without precedent, that it has a genealogy. But he also delineates another genealogy for his discipline, a more personal one, it could be said, which attributes the paternity of ethnology to the eighteenth-century thinker Jean-Jacques Rousseau. In the final chapters of *Tristes tropiques*, where Lévi-Strauss is attempting to define the meaning and the possible missions of anthropology, the figure of Rousseau is a central point of reference. Contrary to

[48] *SA2*, 271–4; *AS2*, 319–22.

the popular misrepresentation of Rousseau as advocate of a primitivist utopia, he points out that, unlike some of his contemporaries (Diderot, for example), Rousseau never idealizes a supposed state of nature. He sees Rousseau as the most 'ethnographic' of the eighteenth-century *philosophes*, with an extensive knowledge of other cultures – even if he himself had no first-hand experience of them – and a genuine curiosity for other mentalities. Rousseau is also credited with a properly scientific approach to the information available on exotic societies. Instead of seeing in non-European cultures the direct expression of a primitive and natural state of humanity, he treats them as samples, the elements of a model, an approximate reconstruction of humanity in its pre-civilized state. If Rousseau appears to favour a previous, more humane stage of human existence, this is not a purely natural state of humanity, which is impossible (the social state being an irreducible component of the human), but rather an intermediate stage of development, between the state of nature and the social state, approximate but not equivalent to that of 'primitive' societies in his own century.[49] Lévi-Strauss equates this intermediary stage, this ideal type of social organization, with what modern archaeological science has defined as the neolithic period:

Rousseau thought that the way of life now known as neolithic offered the nearest approach to an experimental representation of the type. One may, or may not, agree with him. I am rather inclined to believe he was right. By neolithic times, man had already made most of the inventions necessary for his safety. We have already seen why writing can be excluded; to say that it is a double-edged weapon is not a sign of primitivism ... In the neolithic period, man knew how to protect himself from cold and hunger; he had achieved leisure in which to think ... In that mythic age, man was no freer than he is today; but only his humanness made him a slave. Since his control over nature remained very limited, he was protected and to some extent released from bondage – by a cushioning of dreams [*le coussin* amortisseur *de ses rêves* – my emphasis]. (*TT*2, 391; *TT*1, 468–9)[50]

Lévi-Strauss's reading of Rousseau is doubtless a tendentious and selective one,[51] but its performative effect is clear. The reference to Rousseau provides

[49] See the conclusion of Rousseau's *A Discourse on Inequality*, trans. Maurice Cranston (London: Penguin, 1984), p. 115; *Discours sur l'origine et les fondements de l'inégalité parmi les hommes. Discours sur les sciences et les arts* (Paris: Flammarion, 1992), pp. 229–31.

[50] Compare this with Alfred Métraux's evocation of the neolithic in an interview given in 1961: 'Without wishing to lapse into a simplistic type of Rousseauism, it seems to me that humanity was perhaps wrong to progress beyond the stage of the neolithic. You'll doubtless ask me: why the neolithic, why not the palaeolithic, why not the Bronze Age or the Iron Age? Well, if I've chosen the neolithic and not, for example, the palaeolithic, it's because in the neolithic period humanity had already acquired more or less all of the necessities of life. Having adopted a sedentary existence, it practised farming and had already domesticated animals. Of course, it hadn't yet developed writing, and an organized state probably didn't exist: humans lived in small communities, but my impression is that they were happier than today.' (Fernande Bing, interview with Alfred Métraux, *L'Homme* 4.2 (May–August 1964), 22. My translation.)

[51] See David Pace, *Claude Lévi-Strauss*, pp. 63–77.

his discipline with a distinguished lineage, the past master validating the present endeavours of anthropology. Rousseau can be seen as the father of modern anthropology in the sense that he anticipates both its scientific programme and its moral mission. However, his role in Lévi-Strauss's construction of anthropology extends beyond this. Just as important, it seems, is his function as a kind of thinking partner, with whom Lévi-Strauss is able to question and contest some of the basic assumptions of traditional humanism. This is most clearly illustrated in a text first published in 1962, 'Jean-Jacques Rousseau, Founder of the Sciences of Man', originally a lecture given in Geneva on the 250th anniversary of Rousseau's birth.[52] Lévi-Strauss begins this homage to Rousseau with a restatement of his epistemological contribution to the human sciences, his anticipation of the programme and methodology of modern anthropology. In a prophetic note in the *Second Discourse*, Rousseau predicts the modern practice of ethnographic fieldwork as he imagines the great minds of his century applied to the observation of hitherto neglected exotic cultures.[53] In the *Essay on the Origins of Language*, he anticipates the very essence of the ethnological perspective when he claims that the proper understanding of human nature requires us to distance ourselves from our own, immediate social experiences (*SA2*, 34–5; *AS2*, 45–7).[54]

However, the centre of the chapter is a scarcely veiled attack on contemporary philosophy, and the kind of humanism Lévi-Strauss believes it has promoted. Contrary to the common interpretation of Rousseau as a philosopher of introspection, Lévi-Strauss argues that for Rousseau, self-analysis is never a closed circuit of reflection, but always involves the necessary passage through the other. A constant of Rousseau's thought, he claims, is the systematic attempt at identification with the other, along with the refusal to assimilate the other with oneself. Rousseau's conception of personal identity is that it is non-identical with itself, constituted through and through by what is outside and foreign to it. In this, he subverts the mainstream tradition of philosophy as represented in the philosophy of Descartes. The cartesian Cogito restricts itself to the intuitions of first-person experience, passing without interruption from the internal impressions of the isolated individual to the external extension of the world, in the process bracketing out the intermediary instance of interpersonal relations, society and culture. While this suspension of the human might be sufficient to found the science of physics, it leaves out the essential dimensions of the biological and the social (*SA2*, 35–8; *AS2*, 47–50).

It is clear from Lévi-Strauss's reading of Rousseau and his staging of Rousseau contra Descartes that he is not simply describing a past scenario,

[52] *SA2*, 33–43; *AS2*, 45–56.
[53] In *Totemism*, Lévi-Strauss describes the *Second Discourse* as 'without doubt the first anthropological treatise in French literature' (*T*, 99; *TA*, 146).
[54] This is the allusion of the title of Lévi-Strauss's third collection of essays, *The View from Afar* (*Le Regard éloigné*).

a closed chapter in the history of philosophy, but addressing the very present and very contemporary question of the difference between philosophy and the human sciences, and the radically different kinds of humanism they represent. The type of humanism which philosophy has practiced in the wake of Descartes is in his view a truncated humanism, harmful to the extent that it promotes the myth of the exclusive dignity of the human, valorizing human nature over all other forms of being and all other forms of life. The unprecedented inhumanity of the twentieth century, characterized by the systematic violence of human against fellow human is, according to Lévi-Strauss, an inevitable consequence of this humanistic egoism:

> We started by cutting off man from nature and establishing him in an absolute reign. We believed ourselves to have thus erased his most unassailable characteristic: that he is first a living being. Remaining blind to this common property, we gave free rein to all excesses. Never better than after the last four centuries of his history could Western man understand that, while assuming the right to impose a radical separation of humanity and animality, while granting to one all that he denied the other, he initiated a vicious circle [*cycle maudit*]. The one boundary, constantly pushed back, would be used to separate men from other men and to claim – to the profit of ever smaller minorities – the privilege of a humanism, corrupted at birth by taking self-interest [*amour-propre*] as its principle and its notion. (*SA2*, 41; *AS2*, 53)

Amour-propre – literally, self-love – is the impulse which in Rousseau's *Second Discourse* is both a cause and consequence of humankind's emergence from its primitive state. An increased self consciousness leads to the comparison of self with others, which leads to the desire to be better than others, to negate and to dominate them. *Amour-propre* is to be distinguished from the more primitive and more basic instinct of *amour de soi*, or self-preservation, an instinct common to all animal life. Rousseau counterbalances this necessarily egoistic impulse with the equally primitive and basic affect of pity, which Lévi-Strauss interprets as the spontaneous identification of the self with the other, whether that other be a relative, a compatriot, a fellow human, or indeed any other sentient being (38; 50). The direction, so to speak, of this kind of identification is from the other to the self (one allows the self to be affected by the other), whereas the kind of identification practised by anthropocentric humanism works in the opposite direction: it is the narcissistic projection of the self onto the world, an attempt to fashion the world in its own image, opening an infernal cycle (*cycle maudit*) of assimilation and exploitation in which the frontier of otherness is perpetually displaced. The 'free identification' of pity, the empathetic apprehension of the other, on the other hand, results in a reconciliation of self with world: 'Then, freed from an antagonism which philosophy alone sought to stimulate, the self and the other recover their unity' (40; 52).

Lévi-Strauss's reading of Rousseau is therefore a kind of re-routing of humanism, as it has developed in Europe since the Renaissance, an attempt to revive what he sees as its forgotten, or repressed, possibilities. Like Rousseau, his reading of history is a catastrophic one, in the sense that he views the historical development of humanity as a series of fatal turning points, in which each apparent progress is matched by a degradation, a subtraction from what is most essentially human. The conventional, heroic narrative of the 'last four centuries' of human history, a narrative sanctioned by humanist philosophy, emphasizes the progressive emancipation of humankind from the bonds of nature, its mastering of both the natural environment and its own evolution. The end result is, according to Lévi-Strauss, a mutilation of nature and, by extension, the mutilation of humankind itself. However, if it is not possible to reverse the course of history, this does not preclude a certain recuperation of the past and an extrapolation of that past to the future. It is as if at each turning point, at each point of bifurcation in the historical process, there are alternative, virtual paths of development, traces of which persist in our present reality. At this level of virtual realities, to repeat the roulette metaphor of *Race and History*, the game is not over. The notion of the recuperability of Western civilization, the possibility of a *return* (the term is Lévi-Strauss's) to a more authentic stage of cultural development, is a constant theme in the final chapters of *Tristes tropiques*:

If men have always been concerned with only one task – how to create a society fit to live in – the forces which inspired our distant ancestors are also present in us. Nothing is settled [*Rien n'est joué*]; everything can still be altered. What was done, but turned out wrong, can be done again. 'The Golden Age, which blind superstition had placed behind [or ahead of] us, is *in us*.' (*TT*2, 393; *TT*1, 471)

The societies studied by ethnologists offer a virtual image of past states and past possibilities which are not totally lost to us, and which can be reactivated (ibid.).[55] The mission of anthropology, as Lévi-Strauss describes it, is 'always to go back to the sources', as it is only at the source, at the beginning, that humanity creates anything of worth – the rest is decadence and decay (408; 489). The final contribution of anthropology – of *structural* anthropology – would be to provide an 'experimental representation', a virtual model of more authentic forms of social organization, which can be applied to the reform of our own society (392; 470).

One can see, in retrospect, the nature and the magnitude of the challenge Lévi-Strauss's anthropology posed to philosophy. As we have witnessed in the course of this chapter, the various criticisms levelled at structuralism – its reductionism, its anti-humanism, its ahistoricism – are all countered, reformulated and turned back against philosophy itself: its lack of scientific awareness, its ethnocentrism and anthropocentrism, its obsession with history. In the exemplary

---

[55] As we saw in chapter 2, the idea of a return to or reactivation of previous social and cultural configurations is an organizing motif of Mauss's *The Gift*. On Mauss's rhetoric of the 'return', see Jacques Derrida, *Donner le temps* (Paris: Editions Galilée, 1991), pp. 88–9; *Given Time*, trans. Peggy Kamuf (Chicago: University of Chicago Press, 1992), pp. 65–6.

figure of Rousseau, Lévi-Strauss is able to combine the different strands of his defence and illustration of anthropology. Not only does Rousseau anticipate the scientific programme of modern anthropology; not only does he look beyond Europe for examples of a universal humanity; he also provides the model of a renovated humanism which recognizes the essential continuity of all existence. Structuralism is therefore a new form of humanism, one which combines the ambition of scientific analysis with the imperative of a cosmic awareness. The risk for philosophy was clear: it was in danger of being outflanked on two fronts, the scientific and the humanistic, of being reduced to just another voice, a marginal voice, in the concert of the human sciences. Lévi-Strauss himself looks back on this period with the following observation:

> C.L.-S. What I find unbearable in this quarrel about the 'subject' is the intolerance of those who remain obedient to a philosophical tradition that goes back to Descartes. Everything begins with the subject, there is nothing but the subject, and so forth. I wanted to see things from another angle, and I don't concede that this right can be disputed.
>
> D.E. At the time, you were challenging traditional philosophy more vigorously.
>
> C.L.-S. Because it claimed to be the only way. One had to fight for one's place in the sun. Let this philosophy agree to being one approach among many, and the conflict evaporates. (*CLS*2, 163; *PL*, 227)[56]

From the vantage point of his conversations with Eribon in the late 1980s, it seems that Lévi-Strauss believes the battle with philosophy to be over, with a decisive victory for the human sciences. However, as the interview with Eribon reminds us, the battle was not won simply through an abstract exchange of ideas. The set of values explored in this chapter might be seen to have a certain universality, to the extent that they express the critical mission of a discipline, anthropology, devoted to a wider (and deeper) understanding of human experience. At the same time, these values cannot be entirely abstracted from the instance of their enunciation, the individual Lévi-Strauss. Indeed, it is arguable that the message of anthropology, the alternative set of values it articulated, would not have acquired the power it did without the personal mediation of Lévi-Strauss. If we are to fully appreciate the impact of Lévi-Strauss's construction of anthropology in the 1950s and 1960s, it is therefore necessary to return, once again, to the autobiographical narrative of *Tristes tropiques*.

---

[56] See also Lévi-Strauss's interview with Raymond Bellour in 1967: 'Philosophers, who have enjoyed a kind of privilege for such a long time because we have recognized their right to talk about everything and at every moment, must now resign themselves to the fact that much research will take place outside of philosophy' (Raymond Bellour, 'Entretien avec Claude Lévi-Strauss', *Les Lettres françaises* 1165 (12 January 1967), 4. Quoted in François Dosse, *Histoire du structuralisme*, vol. II, pp. 276–7; *History of Structuralism*, vol. II, pp. 218–19).

5   Anthropology and autobiography

Comme les mathématiques ou la musique, l'ethnographie est une des rares vocations authentiques. On peut la découvrir en soi, même sans qu'on vous l'ait enseignée.

(Like mathematics or music, anthropology is one of the few genuine vocations. One can discover it in oneself, even though one may have been taught nothing about it.)[1]

Tous les matins, je me rendais à la *New York Public Library*. Ce que je sais d'ethnologie, c'est pendant ces années-là que je l'ai appris.

(Every morning I went to the New York Public Library. What I know of anthropology I learned during those years.)[2]

The publication of *Tristes tropiques* in 1955 is a defining moment in Lévi-Strauss's career, and a significant moment in the intellectual history of postwar France. Quite apart from its impact in anthropology – a number of French ethnologists cite *Tristes tropiques* as the initial inspiration of their choice of vocation – it drew favourable critical responses from across the intellectual spectrum, from Sartre to Blanchot.[3] The book has since become a classic, and is still in print almost fifty years after its publication, both in French and in its numerous translated versions. The book was not originally Lévi-Strauss's idea. The initial impulse came from Jean Malaurie, the veteran explorer and ethnologist who had recently launched a series named *Terre humaine*, in which the first publication had been his own *Les Derniers Rois de Thulé*.[4] Malaurie had read Lévi-Strauss's 1948 thesis on the Nambikwara Indians which, he confessed, he had found very boring, but the photographs accompanying the

---

[1] *TT*2, 55; *TT*1, 57.   [2] *CLS*2, 43; *PL*, 65.

[3] Other significant commentators included Raymond Aron, Georges Bataille and Michel Leiris. See *CLS*2, 58; *PL*, 87. According to Jean Pouillon, Sartre's reception of *Tristes tropiques* was an enthusiastic one. In particular, he appreciated the reflexive dimension of the book, the inclusion of the ethnographer's own perspective as observer of other cultures. Pouillon thinks that Sartre failed to see the full implications of *Tristes tropiques*, and the extent to which the book undermined his own position (François Dosse, *Histoire du structuralisme*, vol. I, p. 23; *History of Structuralism*, vol. I, p. 7).

[4] *Les Derniers Rois de Thulé* (Paris: Plon, 1976); *The Last Kings of Thule*, trans. Adrienne Foulke (London: Jonathan Cape, 1982).

thesis, he felt, revealed a complex and sensitive character. He therefore asked Lévi-Strauss to rewrite his thesis as a kind of 'philosophical travelogue' on the Indians of the Amazonian forests. The result was a text which, according to Malaurie, set the tone for the entire series.[5]

Lévi-Strauss completed *Tristes tropiques* in a relatively short space of time, less than five months, between October 1954 and March 1955. He later admitted to having written the book in a state of irritation and guilt, feeling that it was an unnecessary distraction from his more serious and more important academic work.[6] The book itself is a curious mixture of genres, part autobiography, part ethnological treatise (the chapters on the Nambikwara are in many places direct transpositions, sometimes verbatim, from the 1948 thesis), part philosophical quest, all of this delivered in a style reminiscent of Chateaubriand and Proust.[7] Malaurie's characterization of a 'philosophical travelogue' is broadly correct, to the extent that it is the narrative of the author's travels – ethnographic or otherwise – which provides the organizing focus for his reflections on the past, present and future of human nature and human experience. But the deep structure of the book is that of the internal journey, the spiritual quest, the rite of passage.[8] Typically, this intellectual itinerary could be seen to consist of three parts or stages: the moment of revelation, the realization of the vocation of ethnology; the moment of initiation, the difficult and demanding experience of fieldwork; finally, the return, the moment of social reintegration. Broadly, these three moments correspond with the first two sections of the book (chapters 1–6), the central sections on the four Amazonian cultures – Caduveo, Bororo, Nambikwara, Tupi-Kawahib (chapters 17–36) – and the final section, appropriately entitled 'The Return' (chapters 37–40). *Tristes tropiques* is therefore not an autobiography in the normal sense of the term, despite the first-person narration of the book. There is no detailed account, for example, of childhood experience or of psychologically formative events. In this respect, the book is not a confession, and the reader does not immediately get the sense of the disclosure of a personality, of the 'man behind the work'.[9] If in *Tristes tropiques* the

---

[5] Interview with Jean-Luc Douin and Catherine Portevin, *Télérama* 2394 (2–8 December, 1995), 13.

[6] See *CLS2*, 58; *PL*, 86–7.

[7] In his interviews with Eribon, Lévi-Strauss reveals that the text had been considered as a candidate for the prestigious Prix Goncourt, but that as a piece of nonfiction it unfortunately did not qualify for nomination (*CLS2*, 58; *PL*, 87).

[8] In 'The Cerebral Savage', Clifford Geertz precisely compares the structure of *Tristes tropiques* to that of the Heroic Quest (*The Interpretation of Cultures* (New York: Basic Books, 1973), pp. 345–59).

[9] In his autobiographical book *The Headman and I*, Louis Dumont comments on the essential impersonality of *Tristes tropiques*, where, he says, Lévi-Strauss 'remains outside . . . There is no back and forth movement between experience and consciousness' (*The Headman and I* (Austin: University of Texas Press, 1978), p. 10, quoted in Julia Okely and Helen Callaway (eds.), *Anthropology and Autobiography* (London: Routledge, 1992), p. 11).

'character' of Lévi-Strauss as such is not foregrounded, nevertheless, through the narrative of his professional life there emerges the sense of a *persona* which seems strangely consonant with the discipline he has chosen to practise.

Elective affinities and the neolithic mind

'Chosen' is perhaps not the most appropriate word, because what the reader is given in the opening chapters of *Tristes tropiques* is a protagonist who does not so much choose his vocation as he is chosen by it. The explanation Lévi-Strauss gives of how he came to ethnography is notable for its *impersonality*, described almost entirely in terms of structural and sociological factors. His choice is a negative rather than a positive one, reached through a series of differentiations and exclusions. In 1928 he is preparing his degree in two subjects, law and philosophy. In those times, he says, students in the first year of the *licence* belonged to two distinct 'species' or 'races', on the one hand those preparing for medicine and law, on the other those studying arts and science subjects. The first group are aggressive, extrovert and already confident of their future role and status in society; their political orientation is towards the far right. By contrast, the second group are introverted, usually destined for teaching or research, and live in a kind of extended childhood, on the margins of society; politically, their sympathies are normally to the left (*TT*2, 54–5; *TT*1, 57). According to this sociological explanation of different classes or types of individual, the young Lévi-Strauss studying both law and philosophy would logically have been a member of both groups, though temperamentally he is obviously a member of the second group, that of the socially semi-detached intellectual or scientist. This explains his subsequent gravitation towards philosophy, which he confesses was motivated less by a real passion for the subject than by the repulsion he felt for other subjects – in fact, he is highly critical of philosophy as it was taught in the 1930s.[10] But apart from this intellectual reservation, there are more personal reasons for his final abandonment of philosophy: following the *agrégation*, and at the end of a year spent in secondary education, he finds it impossible to repeat the same programme of teaching. This is because of his peculiar inability, as he describes it, to focus his attention on the same object twice. In view of this seemingly congenital resistance to repetition, and confronted with the prospect of teaching the same thing for the rest of his life, ethnology appears as an attractive escape route, a means of avoiding repetition (52–3; 54–5).

[10] Lévi-Strauss reproaches this philosophy for its 'verbal artifices' and 'mental gymnastics', pro-viding a training which 'exercised the intelligence but had a desiccating effect on the mind'. Such a philosophy is not 'the servant and auxiliary of scientific exploration, but a kind of aesthetic contemplation of consciousness by itself' (*TT*2, 51–2; *TT*1, 52–4). These remarks are echoed in the autobiography of Jacques Soustelle, an Americanist contemporary of Lévi-Strauss (*Les Quatre soleils* (Paris: Plon, 1967), pp. 14–15; *The Four Suns*, trans. E. Ross (London: André Deutsch, 1970), pp. 5–6).

On one level, therefore, Lévi-Strauss provides a lucid analysis of the situational and psychological factors determining his choice of vocation. Ethnology appears as the logical end-point of a process of selection and elimination of binary alternatives at each stage: law–philosophy; philosophy–ethnology. Again, what is striking about this process is the distance and impersonality of its narration. One has the impression that the protagonist is merely the passive site of his experiences and that his 'choices' are more reactions to structural and situational determinants than the result of a genuine vocation. As he admits, the migration from philosophy to ethnology was a common occurrence amongst his contemporaries, and even the temperamental bias which places him in the camp of the left-wing, socially detached intellectual is depicted as the generic trait of a specific social group (56; 58). Lévi-Strauss's ostensibly autobiographical account seems therefore to be constantly working against conventional individuation. In fact, if there is anywhere a residue of the individual voice in this account it is in the bizarre infirmity which cuts short his teaching career; that is, his mental incapacity for repetition.

However, at the same time and on another level, parallel to the explanation of the contextual and conjunctural factors determining his choice of vocation, Lévi-Strauss gives another explanation, a more essentialist explanation, it could be said, which provides retrospective and positive validation to what after all has been a negative choice, an option that remains after all others have been eliminated. Following the relation of his unfortunate experience of secondary teaching, he hazards:

Today I sometimes wonder if anthropology did not attract me [ne m'a pas appelé], without my realizing this, because of a structural affinity between the civilizations it studies and my particular way of thinking. I have no aptitude for prudently cultivating a given field and gathering in the harvest year after year: I have a neolithic kind of intelligence. Like native bush fires, it sometimes sets unexplored areas alight; it may fertilize them and snatch a few crops from them, and then it moves on, leaving scorched earth in its wake. At the time, however, I was incapable of achieving any awareness of this deeper motivation. I knew nothing about anthropology, I had never attended any course. (TT2, 53; TT1, 55)

There are many things that might be said about this surprising passage, but I will restrict myself to the following remarks. First, up to this point we have been referring, with certain qualifications, to Lévi-Strauss's 'choice' of vocation, but according to the etymology of the word, and according to a well-established tradition of autobiography, one does not choose a vocation, the vocation chooses you, or rather *calls* you.[11] It is the voice of this calling that is described here, the voice of ethnography which calls the individual Lévi-Strauss. Second, and

---

[11] Here a more literal translation would be needed to convey the implication of 'calling' in the original French: *je me demande parfois si l'ethnographie ne m'a pas appelé.*

again following a well-defined tradition of autobiography, there is the notion of the unconscious nature of the calling: at the time he was unaware of its underlying necessity, its deeper cause. Finally (and this is the most surprising aspect of the passage), the deep-level determination of this vocation is attributed to a structural affinity, an elective affinity between the individual Lévi-Strauss's mind and the cultures he as an ethnologist studies. This is something more than the sense of sympathy and solidarity an anthropologist might acquire for his or her subjects during the experience of fieldwork, for example. It is rather, as Lévi-Strauss describes it, a kind of transcendent harmony or consonance preceding any concrete contact with the other culture. The content or specification of this affinity is significant: like so-called 'neolithic' cultures, semi-nomadic groups using slash and burn techniques, he is unable to wisely exploit a fixed terrain from year to year. It is as if having demonstrated, along the horizontal, relational axis of context and conjuncture the external (structural) components of his choice of specialization, Lévi-Strauss feels compelled to motivate that choice at a deeper level of determination, along the vertical axis of the elective affinity. What is relative and contingent at the level of context and conjuncture becomes necessary and essential at the level of this peculiar affinity.

Of course, in one sense, Lévi-Strauss's use of the neolithic metaphor is no more than a metaphor. Its dramatizing and essentializing of a vocation could again be seen as a generic feature of autobiographical discourse, a familiar device of self-construction. However, on another level, and taken in the wider context of *Tristes tropiques* and other, contemporary texts, it is something more than a metaphor. The unconscious voice which calls Lévi-Strauss to ethnology is in fact a strangely overdetermined one, and the metaphor of the neolithic is neither innocent nor arbitrary; metonymically, it is part of a conceptual complex extending beyond the peculiar case of the present example. As was discovered in the previous chapter, the category of the neolithic is an important component of Lévi-Strauss's critique of Western, industrial civilization: on the one hand, it represents a technological advance without which the achievements of modern civilization would have been impossible; on the other hand, it is presented as a stage of cultural development sufficient to humanity's needs, beyond which humanity need never have progressed.

So while the neolithic metaphor, as it is used in *Tristes tropiques*, has no real objective status, while it is nothing more than a metaphor, as part of a network of ideas, values and identifications it possesses a strong internal coherence, and also poses some difficult questions as to the exact status of the anthropology Lévi-Strauss constructs in his early texts. On the one hand, anthropology as human *science* implies the relative autonomy of its conceptual constructs from the subject that formulates them. In accordance with the natural-scientific ideal of objective detachment, the concepts and models it produces are deemed to possess a truth and universality independent of their instance of enunciation, so that the author himself is in a sense contingent to their realization. Within this project, the aim of structural anthropology is to arrive at structures so general as to be common to all societies, absolute to the extent that they are universal categories of the human mind. The subject of the human science of structural anthropology is therefore indifferent; the voice that speaks this science should, in principle at least, be the voice of any subject. On the other hand, such abstraction is clearly impossible, and not simply because we are dealing with a *human* science, a science in which the observer is irreducibly part of the object observed. In the case of Lévi-Strauss, the residual element of subjectivity, with which, necessarily, one has to reckon, is not simply this or that aspect of the character and experience of the empirical individual 'Lévi-Strauss'. As has been noted, this individual is a singularly elusive presence in the pages of *Tristes tropiques*. However, parallel to this reduction of 'self' in the conventional (Western) sense of the term, there seems in *Tristes tropiques* to be a construction of a 'totemic' self, one that would ensure the comprehension of exotic thought at a level still deeper than that of the human mind. It is as if for Lévi-Strauss the hypothesis of human mind does not entirely explain the possibility of such comprehension, requiring a specific substantive content (the neolithic affinity) in addition to the notion of structural similarity. In principle, comprehension should be a possibility for any individual of any culture, like Meno's nameless slave recapitulating Pythagoras' theorem; in practice, such anamnesis requires the guidance of a Socrates.

Through the neolithic metaphor, Lévi-Strauss therefore suggests the absolute nature of his calling to ethnology, which like mathematics or music is one of the rare genuine vocations (55; 57). The narrative of this revelation, as one might call it, comes in an early chapter of *Tristes tropiques*, entitled 'The Making of an Ethnologist' (the original French is '*Comment on devient ethnologue*', more literally, how one becomes an ethnologist). As we have seen, the narrative concentrates mostly on the situational and psychological determinants of his choice of career; the essentialist interpretation, the postulate of the elective affinity is an interpolation of the older narrator, Lévi-Strauss, writing over twenty years after the events narrated in the chapter. Again, according to this older narrator, at the time he was unaware of the more profound reasons for the path he took. A similar kind of unawareness is apparent in the next significant stage of his itinerary, the initiation of fieldwork. The chapters of *Tristes tropiques* devoted to this experience are mainly descriptive, sometimes theoretical (such as the passages on Nambikwara politics or Caduveo face painting), and in general bear the mark of their origins in Lévi-Strauss's more academic work. While these chapters describe an important episode in Lévi-Strauss's personal and professional formation, they lack the reflexive dimension of the earlier and later parts of the book. Indeed, it is only in the first chapter of the final section, 'The Apotheosis of Augustus', which marks as it were the point of transition between the second and third moments of Lévi-Strauss's trajectory, between initiation and return, that this reflexive dimension makes a reappearance. This is the moment of crisis.

Cinna's return

The ethnographer has been separated from his travelling companions, and is alone with two Indian groups on the brink of conflict, and equally hostile towards himself. This makes normal ethnographic work, itself already difficult, practically impossible. The author proceeds to describe the hardships endured by the fieldworker: his solitude and isolation, the extreme vigilance and discretion required, the extreme patience that is often frustrated and humiliated by the caprices and brusque changes of mood of his subjects of study. Above all, there is the question of the motivation and meaning of the vocation he has chosen, and the Chopin melody that turns obsessively in his head is a tenacious reminder of this continuing, and unresolved, dialogue with his own culture. Inevitably, his thoughts turn to his more sensible and more conformist contemporaries who are now ascending the ranks in their academic or political careers (375–7; 449–51). His response to this crisis of faith is to write a play on the reverse side of his fieldwork notes, a free adaptation of Corneille's *Cinna*, which is quite transparently an allegory of his own predicament. The play itself is not given in the text of *Tristes tropiques*; in its place, Lévi-Strauss gives a prose summary of its action and dialogue, the content of which is as follows:

Two men, friends during their childhood, find themselves at a crucial moment in their respective careers, both of them faced with what appears to be an insoluble double bind. The first, Cinna, who had decided to abandon civilized existence, discovers a complicated means of rejoining it, but a means which negates the very meaning and value of his former resistance. The second, Augustus, who from birth had been marked out for social distinction and public recognition, similarly comes to understand that the end result of all of his endeavours is their self-negation. The action proper begins with the Senate's decision that the Emperor Augustus should be granted an honour higher than the empire, in the form of an apotheosis that would place him living in the ranks of the gods. Augustus is satisfied with this deification of his person, as he sees in it a natural consolidation of his power, and a welcome insulation from the plot and intrigue of petty politics. His sister Camilla, however, seeing her brother in danger of becoming irrevocably bound to an oppressive social order, urges him to consult Cinna, who has just returned from his travels, in the hope that his old friend will persuade him to decline the Senate's invitation. Meanwhile, Augustus is increasingly troubled by the delegations sent to him from various interested groups or factions: they all appear to view his apotheosis as a kind of expulsion from the world that would leave them to the free play of their respective interests. Left alone, Augustus is visited by an eagle, not the conventional symbol of the divine, but a wild and foul-smelling beast who informs him that his forthcoming deification will consist precisely in no longer experiencing repulsion when in proximity of the natural. This visitation alerts Augustus to the problem of the relation between Nature and Society, and he determines to see Cinna, who has until now preferred the former. For his part, Cinna is disillusioned with his own life of adventure. During his absence he has thought only of Camilla, whom he hoped to win through a radical rejection of the values of his society, whereas society was in fact always already prepared to accord him this honour. In addition, his experience of the exotic, which after his return has assured him a certain social success and notoriety, now seems meaningless to him. Camilla, seeing that Cinna's general loss of interest in the world extends also to herself, that she is for him only a symbol of the last possible link between himself and society, breaks with him. On the other hand Augustus, recognizing Cinna's message to be that of the eagle, is nevertheless too constrained by the various political interests at stake in his apotheosis to revoke his decision. The day preceding the ceremony, Rome is invaded by the forces of Nature. Despite his disillusion with the exotic, the idea that Augustus can reconcile the two forces, Nature and Society, without the sacrifice he himself has endured, is intolerable to Cinna, and he determines to assassinate the Emperor. Before he can carry out his plan, however, Cinna is summoned by Augustus, who is overwhelmed by the recent turn of events. In a moment of illumination, the two men find the solution to their impasse: Cinna will assassinate the Emperor, who will thereby attain his dreamed-for immortality, while Cinna will enjoy the immortality of the regicide, thus rejoining society while continuing to contest it. (*TT*2, 378–82; *TT*1, 453–7, my paraphrase)

'The Apotheosis of Augustus' is an unfinished play, or more precisely, Lévi-Strauss cannot remember exactly how it was to have ended. As he tells us, his inspiration left him as he was writing the piece, never to return, and the final scenes remained unfinished (378, 381; 453, 457). In spite of this failure of memory, he all the same goes on to recount what *seems to him* to have been the final denouement of the play: 'I think it was Camilla who involuntarily provided the denouement' (381; 457). In this conjectured ending, Camilla persuades Augustus that, even more than the eagle, Cinna is the messenger of the gods. Perceiving a possible 'political' solution to the dilemma, Augustus, instead of dismissing his bodyguard as agreed with Cinna, doubles the guard. He subsequently proceeds to his apotheosis, thus achieving divinity in this world, while he pardons Cinna, who consequently loses on all counts (382; 457).

On a primary level, 'The Apotheosis of Augustus' could be read as a kind of talking cure, a therapeutic response to the alienated predicament of the fieldworker, and an attempted working through of that predicament. Like mythical discourse, as Lévi-Strauss defines it, the play is an attempt to overcome 'contradictions', here the contradictions inherent in the ethnographer's self-imposed exile from his own society and his desire for some form of reintegration. However, the play also seems to address vital interests or preoccupations that continue to operate at the time of narration. This is evident in the chapter following the rather pessimistic denouement of the play, entitled 'A Little Glass of Rum'. The narrator begins this chapter with a surprising gesture, given what has gone before: he dismisses the play he has been describing as the product of a disturbed and fatigued mind: 'The only justification for the dramatic fable described in the preceding chapter is that it illustrates the mental disorder to which the traveller is exposed through abnormal living conditions over a prolonged period'. This movement of denegation is, however, immediately followed by a gesture of recuperation: 'But the problem still remains: how can the ethnologist overcome the contradiction resulting from the circumstances of his choice?' (383; 458). So the content of 'The Apotheosis of Augustus', however extravagant the conditions of its conception, is nevertheless paradigmatic of a central problem of the ethnographer's profession, the seemingly intractable problem of cultural preference, the privilege given to a culture different to one's parent culture. The remainder of the chapter is devoted to a careful negotiation of this problem, which continues to be treated in different modalities until the end of the book. The individual instance of self-exile dramatized in 'The Apotheosis of Augustus' is therefore expanded to encompass the global question of the 'ethnographer's choice';[12] it becomes a kind of case history within the general pathology of a profession. Between the negative conclusions of 'The Apotheosis of Augustus' and the final sentences of the book, and through this negotiation of the problem of cultural preference, a certain transvaluation occurs. On the one hand, the alienation of the ethnographer is found not to be a unique one, but rather a modulation of the general contradiction from which modern humanity as a whole necessarily suffers (413; 495). On the other hand, and perhaps more importantly, the paradoxes of the ethnographer's predicament (the bias of his or her cultural preference) are to an extent resolved and recuperated by an appeal to a cultural relativism which, while recognizing the basic equality of all societies (which are neither absolutely good nor absolutely evil), is nevertheless able to discern what in other societies would be the principles of social organization applicable to the reform of our own society (392; 470).[13] This apology for the ethnographer's vocation, which follows and responds to the confession of his alienation in 'The Apotheosis of Augustus', does not however offer a totally satisfactory response to the dilemma portrayed in the play or 'fable', as Lévi-Strauss calls it. In fact, it appears to address only one aspect of the total situation which 'The Apotheosis of Augustus' allegorizes. By focusing, in what are often identifiably existentialist terms, on the philosophical and ethical question of

---

[12] 'L'Ethnographe et son choix' ('The Ethnographer and his Choice') is the title of the final section of an article appearing in *Les Temps Modernes* in 1955, which is a series of extracts from the forthcoming *Tristes tropiques* ('Des Indiens et leur ethnographe', *Les Temps Modernes* 11.116 (August 1955), 1–50). The concluding section of the article is in fact a more or less direct transcription of 'A Little Glass of Rum'. In the context of *Les Temps Modernes* and its readership, the inclusion of this passage adds an appropriately self-reflexive dimension to the more straightforwardly ethnographic material presented in the three preceding sections of the article.

[13] This recalls Lévi-Strauss's reference to degrees of cultural authenticity in *Structural Anthropology* 1 (*SA1*, 367; *AS1*, 402). See chapter 4 above, pp. 120ff.

cultural preference, the criticisms to which this preference necessarily exposes itself, and its possible justifications, Lévi-Strauss certainly provides a powerful defence and illustration of his chosen profession. But the effect of this focus is to collapse into a single dilemma what even in the highly mediated narrative of 'The Apotheosis of Augustus' is presented as a more complex situation. The apology of the ethnographer's 'choice' initiated in 'A Little Glass of Rum' largely leaves aside, or steps over, the problem of the ethnographer's return and the modality of his reintegration, which is arguably the central preoccupation of the play. As if to avoid the aporia of the play's conclusion, which presents a Cinna totally bereft of a mission or role in society, Lévi-Strauss appears at this point to prefer to concentrate on the claims of anthropology to scientific interest, on its potential truth value, rather than the properly sociological dimension of the conditions of its production.

The two elements, the passion of the ethnographer (Cinna) and the truth of which he is the bearer, are of course inseparable: they are two sides of the same reality or, more exactly, two sides of the same sheet, as we learn in the passage introducing the play. 'The Apotheosis of Augustus' is written on the reverse side of the ethnographer's field notes ('on the back of sheets of paper covered with word lists, sketches and genealogical tables', 378; 453). Together, these two elements, the data which will provide the basis of the ethnologist's science, and the comedy of exile he must endure in the pursuit of that science, constitute the total social fact of the ethnographic experience. On the one side, there is the exotic society, the object of ethnographic observation; on the other side, there is the ethnographer's own society as the subject and producer of this knowledge. The two sides are coextensive, they form a continuum. If we return to the passage introducing the play, there appear in fact to be two, interrelated preoccupations programming its writing. Asking himself why he has chosen the path of exile, interrupting his university career while his erstwhile contemporaries complete and consolidate their own, academic or political, the protagonist wonders:

By whom or what had I been impelled to disrupt the normal course of my existence? Was it a trick on my part, a clever diversion, which would allow me to resume my career with additional advantages for which I would be given credit? Or did my decision express a deep-seated incompatibility with my social setting [*groupe social*] so that, whatever happened, I would inevitably live in a state of ever greater estrangement from it? (*TT*2, 376; *TT*1, 450–1)

The second element of this self-interrogation, the question of the ethnographer's possible incompatibility with his social group, does indeed become a theme of the fable that follows: Cinna is an outsider in his own society in that his choice or preference, as Lévi-Strauss puts it, is the exact inverse of that of Augustus, which has led the latter to the heights of power, the empire. As has been seen, it is this second question, the problematic psychology of the cultural dissident, that Lévi-Strauss addresses in the subsequent and concluding chapters of *Tristes tropiques*. However, as concerns the action of 'The Apotheosis of Augustus', the dramatic tension of the piece derives not so much from a psychological exploration of the persona of the outsider as from the antagonisms generated by his attempted reinsertion into his own society. Within the dramatic economy of the play, Cinna's non-conformism is a given, like its polar opposite, the conformism of Augustus, who at the beginning of the play is on the point of becoming the deified representation of the social order. What gives impulse to the play, sets it in motion, is Cinna's return, his hope or expectation that the sacrifice of his self-exile will be recompensed by an enhanced position in the social order, a position at least equal to that of Augustus. This would correspond rather with the first question the protagonist of *Tristes tropiques* puts to himself before he writes the play, quoted above: is the path he has chosen, that of a radical departure from his own society, simply a ruse, a calculated detour from which he will return with enhanced prestige and power? Like Cinna, the ethnographer-protagonist suffers a crisis of faith; he comes to see the vanity and vacuity of the exotic that is so valued by his own society, ultimately encountering only the deserts of his own memory, the residua of his own culture – for Cinna the verses of Aeschylus and Sophocles he recites to himself; for the ethnographer the fragment of Chopin (377, 380; 451, 456). Like Cinna also, the protagonist of *Tristes tropiques*, despite his scepticism or reservations regarding the nature of the knowledge he has acquired, would wish nevertheless to accede, by virtue of that knowledge, to a position equal to, perhaps more brilliant than, those occupied by his more 'conformist' contemporaries.

To qualify the inflection Lévi-Strauss gives to our interpretation of the play in the following chapter – towards the problem of the ethnographer's 'choice', the moral mission and eventual utility of anthropology – it would therefore be necessary to add that 'The Apotheosis of Augustus' is also a play about knowledge and power. The truth of which Cinna is bearer cannot be separated from the plus-value it represents in a certain economy of power. In this, the play seems to reproduce, in the figure of Cinna, what might be called an elementary structure of socialization. The exorbitant and circuitous path Cinna has chosen in order to rejoin his society, and the voluntary self-exile of the ethnographer it allegorizes, are both in fact thematically contained and prefigured in an earlier chapter of *Tristes tropiques*, which deals precisely with the question of the will to power, the quest for power, of the exorbitant individual. In 'The Quest for Power' (part 1, chapter 4), Lévi-Strauss offers a sociological or anthropological explanation of the forces motivating the explorers and adventurers who, often at the price of extreme hardship, return with so many sensationalized, invariably inaccurate and distorted accounts of the exotic cultures they have encountered. He takes the example of certain North American Indian societies as an illustration of the universality of this pattern of behaviour, showing it to be a social phenomenon involving both individual and collectivity. In these societies, the social status of each individual is dependent upon the nature of certain trials the adolescent must undergo upon reaching the age of puberty. These range from solitary fasting or isolation in extreme and hazardous conditions, to physical self-mutilation or the exhausting repetition of gratuitous tasks. Such activities are normally designed to induce a state of delirium in which some magical animal will make its apparition: 'a vision will reveal which one will henceforth be their guardian spirit, so that they can take its name and derive special power from it, which will determine their privileges and rank within their social group' (40; 39). For these individuals, Lévi-Strauss continues, the restricted horizons of their societies offer no play for their talent or imagination, and it is only by risking their being at the extreme margins of the social order that they are able to bring about a revocation of that order in their favour. Rather than being simply a question of individual versus collective consciousness, however, such behaviour would be rigorously socially determined and socially sanctioned:

Among these Indians of the North American plains and plateau, individual beliefs are not at variance with collective doctrine. The dialectic as a whole springs from the customs and philosophy of the group. It is from the group that individuals learn their creed; belief in guardian spirits is a group phenomenon, and it is society as a whole which teaches its members that their only hope, within the framework of the social order, is to make an absurd and desperate attempt to break away from it. (TT2, 40; TT1, 39)

The relation linking the explorer to our own society is no different to that of the American Indian initiate. The *mana* of the explorer, the prestige bestowed upon him or her by society, derives not so much from the quality of the information of which he or she is bearer, but from the measure of his or her lack of measure (*démesure*) in the quest for that information: 'What counts is the attempt in itself, not any possible aim' (41; 40).

The relationship between these young adventurers and their older predecessor ('elderly predecessor of those scourers of the jungle', 41; 41) is an ambivalent one. On the one hand, as the possessor of a positive knowledge or truth, the science of ethnology, the narrator is able to relativize and in a sense demystify the persona of the adventurer, demonstrating by comparative analysis what would be a universal structure of social behaviour, a self-mystifying comedy played out between individual and collectivity. At the same time, again as possessor of a more objective truth, provided by the more rigorous data-gathering procedures of the participant-observer, he delivers a stringent critique of the inauthenticity of the testimonies given by these adventurers, indicating the deleterious effects of our pathological demand for the exotic upon the cultures concerned (41; 40–1). On the other hand, however, the difference between the adventurer, as he or she is portrayed here, and the ethnographer-narrator, would appear to be only a difference of degree. The ethnographer is certainly the bearer of a more authentic and more objective knowledge, but he is still, nevertheless, part of the same social economy in which those he condemns are implicated. He is equally subject to the sociological law that prescribes radical estrangement or departure as a possible means to power and position in the existent social order. The problem is that perhaps by the very virtue of having seen through this comedy, enacted between society and individual, of having exposed the social mechanism that sets the terms of this exchange, he is unable to enter into this economy with the requisite degree of self-mystification or suspension of disbelief. As a result, his own radical departure does not endow him with the *mana* or magic acquired by his civilized or exotic counterparts. His own quest for power is a failure:

Can it be that I, the elderly predecessor of those scourers of the jungle, am the only one to have brought back nothing but a handful of ashes? Is mine the only voice to bear witness to the impossibility of escapism? Like the Indian in the myth, I went as far as the earth allows one to go, and when I arrived at the world's end, I questioned the people, the creatures and things I found there and met with the same disappointment: 'He stood still, weeping bitterly, praying and moaning. And yet no mysterious sound reached his ears, nor was he put to sleep in order to be transported, as he slept, to the temple of the magic animals. For him there could no longer be the slightest doubt: no power, from anyone, had been granted him...'. (*TT*2, 41–2; *TT*1, 41)

The myth to which the narrator refers here, and from which he quotes, remains anonymous, but it is clear that the configuration it describes, the failure of the quest for power of the exorbitant individual, is carried over into the myth or fable of 'The Apotheosis of Augustus'. Cinna, too, is a failed shaman. He is unable to derive from his experience of the exotic the sacred surplus, the *mana* that bestows power. The exotic other, stripped of the romanticizing aura of the traveller's tale, finally amounts to the same: 'the earth resembled this earth and the blades of grass were the same as in this meadow' (380; 456). In an ironic twist, it is not Cinna who is visited by the magical animal (the eagle), but Augustus, who is thus granted a direct and immediate contact with the divine (the natural), without labour, without the trial of separation endured by Cinna.

This then is the situation projected or anticipated by the young ethnographer who writes the play. The figure of Augustus could be assimilated with those contemporaries mentioned in the passage preceding the play, who have suc- ceeded in their respective careers without the necessity of a ritual separation from their society. In this he is also the virtual image of what Cinna would or could have been.[14] Cinna is clearly the ethnographer, who foresees in his

---

[14] In a number of interviews, Lévi-Strauss has mentioned his earlier passion for politics and political activity. While a student, he was secretary of the socialist study group for the five

dramatic hallucination the inevitable denouement of his own return. But this denouement, it should be remembered, is a double denouement. As has been seen, the play, as it appears in *Tristes tropiques*, is subject to the mediation of a second, supplementary instance or voice, that of the older narrator. Significantly, it is he who completes the drama: his memory failing him, he provides what he thinks *would have* been the final denouement. This is no idle observation, for it testifies to what in effect would be the continuing relevance, the vital relevance, of the predicament allegorized in 'The Apotheosis of Augustus'. The drama, both tragic and comic, of Cinna's return, is not only a fictional working-through of the doubts and apprehensions of the ethnographer in the field, which would have been superseded and resolved at the point of narration. It also translates what is the ongoing dialogue of the narrator-anthropologist with his present social or institutional placement.

If one steps for a moment outside of, or aside from *Tristes tropiques*, it can be seen that the text inhabits its own complex and problematic reality. Written in 1954–55, over fifteen years after the events narrated in 'The Apotheosis of Augustus', the circumstances surrounding the text appear to exhibit the same structure of subordination and marginalization described in the play, here transposed onto the plane of the academy. As we learn in his conversations with Eribon, Lévi-Strauss wrote *Tristes tropiques* at a time when he had largely abandoned his ambition of being elected to the Collège de France, having already failed twice in his attempt to give to French anthropology the institutional and intellectual pre-eminence he felt it deserved. In consequence of this failure, he confesses to Eribon, he considered his university career to be practically finished (*CLS2*, 58; *PL*, 86). On the professional plane, therefore, his wager, the risk he has taken in his unconventional choice of discipline, ethnology, has not yielded a reward proportionate to that risk, and the expenditure of self it has implied. Like Cinna, Lévi-Strauss has abandoned the conventional route to social advancement. Had he remained in France and pursued his original specialization (philosophy), he would plausibly now occupy a privileged position in the university hierarchy. This much is intimated in the musings that precede the narration of 'The Apotheosis of Augustus'.[15] In the play itself, moreover, Cinna is given to understand that society was already prepared to concede the

Ecoles Normales Supérieures and also secretary of the French federation of socialist students (*CLS2*, 9; *PL*, 17). During his first year of teaching in Mont-de-Marsan in 1932, he was a socialist candidate in the local elections, until he crashed a friend's car while driving without a licence (*CLS2*, 14; *PL*, 24). The story of the car crash is typical of the role of chance and accident in Lévi-Strauss's autobiography, the external and contingent event literally closing off a potential point of bifurcation in his career. See note 25 below.

[15] 'It was now nearly five years since I had left France and interrupted my university career. Meanwhile, the more prudent of my former colleagues were beginning to climb the academic ladder: those with political leanings, such as I had once had, were already members of parliament and would soon be ministers' (*TT2*, 376; *TT1*, 450).

power he sought through the hyperbole of departure (*TT*2, 380; *TT*1, 455).[16] During his absence, Augustus has been consolidating his power and preparing his apotheosis, which the narrator humorously (or so it appears) compares to the Académie française: ' "It was only what he deserved", in other words, the equivalent of the Académie française...' (379; 454). This momentary puncturing of the allegory, this ironic allusion to what is traditionally the highest sanction of academic or artistic achievement in France, gives the reader a clearer indication of what is at stake in 'The Apotheosis of Augustus': the quest for temporal or political power described in the play is a transparent allegory of the will to intellectual power in the academy.

If in 1955 Lévi-Strauss, by his own estimation, still has not properly arrived in the university, it is also and inseparably because anthropology has not arrived. The first ending of 'The Apotheosis of Augustus', the unfinished version written by the younger ethnographer, projects an accommodation between Augustus and Cinna, in which Cinna's assassination of Augustus will guarantee the latter immortality and himself a definite, if contestatory, role in society (381; 457). This first denouement can be interpreted as the projected (desired) success not only of the individual outsider (the younger ethnographer), but also by extension of the disciplinary faction or clan of which he is a member, the truth of which he is the bearer (ethnology). This version of the drama in fact corresponds closely to the place Lévi-Strauss projects for his discipline in a number of texts contemporary to *Tristes tropiques*, in which the rightful place of anthropology is seen to be at the centre of the human and social sciences – displacing more established disciplines such as philosophy or sociology – while at the same time remaining in an elliptical relationship with the university, providing an alternative voice or message.[17]

The second ending of 'The Apotheosis of Augustus' envisages, for Cinna at least, a far more pessimistic resolution of the play: Augustus doubles his guard, appropriates and accommodates Cinna's truth within a renovated social order, and finally (in a final echo of the Cornelian model) pardons Cinna himself. Cinna therefore loses on all counts; Augustus has in effect stolen his thunder. Whereas the first ending of 'The Apotheosis of Augustus' might express the projected (ideal) place of anthropology in a specific interdisciplinary context, this second conclusion would correspond with the reality of its institutional

---

[16] The key figure in the mediation of this power is Camilla. She is the 'gift', the prize or price of Cinna's adhesion to the existing social order, as it is defined in the person of Augustus. In accordance with the Maussian model, which sees exchange – ritual, commercial or matrimonial – as a necessary device for the regulation and containment of violence, Camilla's marriage to Cinna would through the bond of kinship (she is Augustus' sister) defuse the rivalry between the two men. As the narrator remarks, Camilla symbolizes Cinna's last possible link with society, his last chance to rejoin the social order (381; 456). While Augustus is from the start prepared to give Camilla to Cinna, the latter is intent on gaining her merit by less conventional means.

[17] See chapter 1, pp. 26–8.

placement, which in 1955 is a relatively subordinate one, in danger of being absorbed by a number of more established disciplines. In this context of institutional subordination and lack of advancement, personally experienced by Lévi-Strauss, *Tristes tropiques* could therefore be seen as a final attempt at exorbitant departure, this time not simply of ethnology from the parent disciplines of philosophy or sociology, but a departure from ethnology itself. With its complex mixture of subjectivity and objectivity, ethnography and autobiography, the personal and the professional, *Tristes tropiques* is a defiance of genre and of professional protocol. As Lévi-Strauss reveals in the Eribon interviews, he was himself aware when writing the book that it would provoke displeasure amongst his professional colleagues, and tells how the venerable Rivet, director of the Musée de l'Homme, abruptly severed relations after the book's publication (*CLS2*, 59; *PL*, 87). As we have seen, Lévi-Strauss's own explanation and justification of this renegade text is that he saw his career in the university as being irrevocably blocked; its publication could not therefore prejudice what had already been lost.

With the benefit of hindsight, of course, the radical departure of *Tristes tropiques* is followed by a triumphal return. The negative configuration of Cinna's return is not repeated. Paradoxically, *Tristes tropiques*, a text of doubt and demystification, confers on its author a certain *mana*, and gives to his discipline an aura of authenticity over and above its claims to objectivity and academic respectability.[18] Within five years, anthropology, in the figure of Lévi-Strauss, will have taken its place in the Collège de France; later, in 1974, it will take its place in the Académie française itself. From the relatively marginal position of the anthropologist and his discipline in 1955, however, and as the final conclusion of 'The Apotheosis of Augustus' testifies, the eventuality of such an apotheosis can hardly have been self-evident.

Fieldwork and its discontents

We began our analysis of *Tristes tropiques* with the remark that the deep structure of the book was that of the classic rite of passage, consisting of three stages or moments: the moment of revelation, the moment of initiation, the moment of reintegration. So far, we have been looking at the chapters of *Tristes tropiques* dealing with the first and final moments of the protagonist's quest. These chapters, we argued, were of a more reflexive and self-analytical nature than the straightforwardly descriptive and theoretical chapters detailing the ethnographer's initiation into his craft. On the one hand, this is perfectly natural, given

---

[18] See also Mondher Kilani, 'Fiction et vérité dans l'écriture anthropologique', in François Affergan (ed.), *Construire le savoir anthropologique* (Paris: Presses Universitaires de France, 1999), pp. 94–5.

the more academic register of this particular part of the book, and its origins in some of Lévi-Strauss's early professional publications. On the other hand, however, there is a sense that there is an unspoken dimension to the initiation of fieldwork, as Lévi-Strauss experienced it, and as it is described in *Tristes tropiques*, that something quite fundamental relating to his internalization of that experience has been left unexpressed. There is a hint of this in the remarks preceding the narration of 'The Apotheosis of Augustus', where the author refers, briefly, to the trials and tribulations of the ethnographer in the field, victim of the whims, resistance or elusiveness of his or her ethnographic subjects. So while the experience of fieldwork, as presented in *Tristes tropiques*, is in many ways a liberation, an adventure, a voyage of discovery, it is at the same time a painful and potentially alienating experience. This description echoes remarks in other, more or less contemporary texts on the theme of what might be termed the *passion* of the ethnographer.[19] Typically, these remarks are articulated in the third person; they are presented as items in a generic case history of the profession, rather than the expression of a singular and isolated experience. Doubtless, the hardships and frustrations of which Lévi-Strauss speaks are a common experience of the ethnographer in the field, but it is also the case that he appears to have felt them in a particularly acute manner. Characteristically, his response to this experience is to indicate its *intellectual* value. In 'The Place of Anthropology in the Social Sciences' (1954), it will be remembered, ethnography, the collection of data in the field, was described as the experimental or empirical side of anthropology, distinguishing it from more speculative disciplines such as sociology. However, in the same article he goes on to qualify that fieldwork is not simply the experimental, but also the *experiential* side of the discipline, something which cannot be experienced vicariously, a personal experience all members of the profession must undergo. Here, the emphasis is on the intellectual rather than the affective content of the experience, which allows a reconstitution, from the inside, of the disparate elements of a social system:

Thus we recognize a profound reason, associated with the very nature of the discipline and the distinctive features of its subject, why the anthropologist needs the experience of fieldwork. It represents for him, not the goal of his profession, or a completion of his schooling, or yet a technical apprenticeship – but a crucial stage of his education, prior to which he may possess miscellaneous knowledge [*des connaissances discontinues*] that will never form a whole. After he engages in fieldwork his knowledge will acquire an organic unity and a meaning [*ces connaissances se 'prendront' en un ensemble organique, et acquerront soudain un sens* – my emphasis] it did not previously possess. (*SA*1, 373; *AS*1, 409)

---

[19] See, for example, 'Diogène couché', *Les Temps Modernes* 10.110 (March 1955), 1317–18; 'The Scope of Anthropology', *SA*2, 15; *AS*2, 25.

This description of the epistemological contribution of fieldwork belongs to an identifiable family of statements in Lévi-Strauss's work, though the homology can only be properly tracked if one reconstitutes some of the original French. Statements of this type describe the emergence of the continuous from the discontinuous, in Lévi-Straussian terms, the *precipitation* of structure or the *crystallization* of sense. In the terms of the analogy used here, the ethnographer's knowledge acquires a kind of critical consistency as previously disparate items of experience bond together (*se 'prendront'*) to form a coherent unity. In the present context, the insight provided by fieldwork is something like the spontaneous intuition of Mauss's total social fact – it is a sudden, and integral, illumination. But if one turns to the opposite side of the ethnographic equation, to the object of ethnographic knowledge, the ethnographer's illumination could be said to be formally no different than, for example, the shaman's initiation into the mysteries of his profession. Quesalid, it will be remembered, following a period of ambivalence and scepticism, finally arrives at a point of qualified belief in the effectiveness of his art. Lévi-Strauss's gloss on this conversion is that the shaman's system of explanation allowed the 'coalescence' or 'precipitation' of the different elements of the thereapeutic experience, from the points of view of practitioner, public and patient, so that they formed a coherent whole: 'To the conscious mind, this last phenomenon constitutes an original experience which cannot be grasped from without' (*SA*1, 182; *AS*1, 201).

In the chapter following 'The Sorcerer and his Magic', 'The Effectiveness of Symbols', the therapeutic effectiveness of magical practices was compared with the psychoanalytical cure, though the comparison was obviously intended to be less complimentary to psychoanalysis, with its claims to scientific interest, than to its non-Western counterpart. In 'The Place of Anthropology', interestingly, it is the systems of validation in anthropology and the psychoanalytical profession which are compared. In his discussion of the institutional organization of anthropological studies, Lévi-Strauss distinguishes between the training of teachers (*maîtres*, literally, masters) and research workers (*chercheurs*), those aspiring to membership of the profession. His main observation about the first category is that in addition to the requisite academic qualifications, all teachers must have the experience of fieldwork – there is no longer any place for the traditional armchair anthropologist. The situation is more complicated when one turns to future members of the profession, who are confronted with the 'vicious circle' of being asked to undertake research for which they have no definite pre-qualification. Lévi-Strauss's response to this conundrum is to propose the epistemological justification quoted above: more than a technical qualification, more than an obligatory item of professional apprenticeship, fieldwork opens up a dimension of intellectual insight impossible to achieve in the more abstract and formal framework of academic transmission. He continues:

The position is comparable to that in psychoanalysis. The principle is universally rec-ognized today that the professional psychologist must have a specific and irreplaceable practical background, that of analysis itself; hence all the regulations require that every would-be psychoanalyst be psychoanalyzed himself. For the anthropologist, fieldwork represents the equivalent of this unique experience. As in the case of psychoanalysis, this experience may or may not be successful, and no examination, whether competitive or not, can prove conclusively whether it is. Only experienced members of the profession, whose work shows that they have themselves passed the test, can decide if and when a candidate for the anthropological profession has, as a result of fieldwork, accomplished that inner revolution that will really make him into a new man. (*SA*1, 373; *AS*1, 409–10)

The initiatory quality of fieldwork, as Lévi-Strauss describes it, seems to resolve the problem of the 'vicious circle' of validation with regard to the aspirant, the younger member of the profession. But it is easy to see that the resolution is only a partial one, as it has merely shifted the problem to another level, that of the 'ex-perienced members of the profession', charged with determining whether the initiation has been successful or not. The latter have presumably experienced an illumination similar to that of their younger colleagues, but the problem, simi-lar to that experienced by Freud and the psychoanalytical profession, remains: once the system of validation has been established, who will have validated the masters? Despite his disenchantment with his professional progress to date, discussed above, nevertheless in 1954 Lévi-Strauss is speaking from a position of relative power and authority, from a chair at the Ecole Pratique des Hautes Etudes, one of the most prestigious research institutions in France: he is one of the masters; indeed, he is in the process of becoming *the* master of his dis-cipline. The problem is, it is not clear exactly who has sanctioned the master of masters. His teaching post at the University of São Paulo having given him access to the native populations of the Mato Grosso, Lévi-Strauss's fieldwork in Brazil was initially conducted under the joint aegis of the University and the Musée de l'Homme in Paris. The expeditions to the Caduveo and Bororo in the summer of 1935 resulted in an article on the Bororo and an exhibition at the Musée de l'Homme in the winter of 1936–37. It was on the strength of this exhibition and his publications that Lévi-Strauss received funding for the field-work expeditions of 1938 (Nambikwara, Mundé, Tupi-Kawahib).[20] Though there was some institutional support for both of these ventures, Lévi-Strauss had received no formal training in anthropology prior to his entry into fieldwork research. Yet such training was not lacking in France. In spite of the relatively late development of anthropology, by the early 1930s Marcel Mauss, teaching at the Ecole Pratique des Hautes Etudes and the Musée de L'Homme, had already prepared most of the first generation of French ethnologists for research work in the field.[21] Indeed, Lévi-Strauss was unusual, perhaps unique amongst his

[20] *Magazine Littéraire* 311 (June 1993), 16–17.
[21] See Marcel Fournier, *Marcel Mauss* (Paris: Fayard, 1995), p. 602.

contemporaries, in that he did not experience the direct personal contact of this inspirational and charismatic figure. The individual who would later become the master of French anthropology was therefore entirely self-taught, an auto-didact, one who had learnt his craft on the margins of the normal institutional structures.[22]

To return to the question of validation: if, unlike most of his contemporaries, the patriarchal influence of Mauss does not figure in Lévi-Strauss's autobiography, it was nevertheless Mauss, along with Henri Lévy-Bruhl and Paul Rivet, who finally sanctioned his entry into the profession. At the beginning of the section on the Nambikwara in *Tristes tropiques*, he writes: 'One year after my visit to the Bororo, all the required conditions for turning me into a fully fledged anthropologist had been fulfilled. Lévy-Bruhl, Mauss and Rivet had given me their retrospective blessing [*bénédiction... rétroactivement accordée*]; my collections had been exhibited in a gallery in the Faubourg Saint-Honoré; I had delivered lectures and written articles' (*TT*2, 249; *TT*1, 287). It is tempting to point out that none of these venerable figures meets the conditions of validation detailed by Lévi-Strauss in 'The Place of Anthropology'. They all belong to the previous generation of armchair anthropology – none of them had undertaken any fieldwork. But apart from this inevitable irony, it remains that despite the 'retroactive' sanction of his masters, there is a sense in which Lévi-Strauss continues to be a non-validated, or rather, perhaps, self-validated member of his profession. Something of this eccentricity is detectable in the manner in which he describes the function of fieldwork. On the one hand, the description is intended to be a generic one, applicable to any initiate to the profession. On the other hand, it seems to be as much a projection of his own experience of fieldwork and his conception of its relation to theory. Symptomatic of this is the manner in which he plays down the conventional, academic definition of field-work (for the initiate, it is 'not the goal of his profession, or a completion of his schooling, or yet a technical apprenticeship') and instead emphasizes its revolutionary effect on the *mind* of the initiate: the 'profound reason' for the 'original experience' that is fieldwork, beyond its prosaic function of observation and description, is an intellectual conversion, a kind of a mental reconfiguration of the ethnographer-participant. Later, in 'The Scope of Anthropology', following a description of the difficulties of fieldwork (exile, hunger, illness, sometimes danger, along with the constant contradiction of one's own beliefs and customs), Lévi-Strauss suggests that this most subjective of experiences, what we

---

[22] In 'Diogène couché', which is an extended response to Roger Caillois's criticisms of *Race and History*, lévi-Strauss rectifies some of Caillois's remarks on his professional biography: 'I'll just remind you then of the fact that as concerns ethnography, I'm entirely self-taught; during the whole of my period as a student, I never frequented the Musée de l'Homme or the Institut d'Ethnologie, nor did I attend a single ethnography class' ('Diogène couché', 1218, my translation).

above termed the *passion* of the ethnographer, can nevertheless be the source of objective knowledge. Again, he is referring not to the banal fact of data collection, the simple observation and recording of an exotic reality, but to a more profound transformation of the observing subject:

[Anthropology] is undoubtedly the only science to use the most intimate kind of subjectivity as a means of objective observation. For it is indeed an objective fact that the same mind, which gave itself to experience and let itself be molded by it [*qui s'est abandonné à l'expérience et s'est laissé modeler par elle*], becomes the theater of mental operations which do not abolish the preceding ones, but which yet transform the experiment [*l'expérience*: experience or experiment] into a model. This makes possible other mental operations whose logical coherence is based, in the final analysis, on the sincerity and honesty of whoever can say, like the explorer bird of the fable: 'I was there, such a thing happened to me. You will believe that you were there yourself', and who, indeed, succeeds in communicating this conviction. (*AS2*, 15–16; *SA2*, 25)

The passion of the ethnographer is passive to the extent that he (or she) *abandons* himself (herself) to the experience of the exotic and allows his (her) mind to be, quite literally, *modelled* by the experience. Subjective experience becomes objective model. But what might be termed the *possession* of the subject by an alien reality is not a total one. In his preceding remarks on the difficulties of fieldwork, Lévi-Strauss points out the risk, for the observer-participant, of permanent absorption by the object of his (her) observation. Here, significantly, he qualifies that while the mind becomes the 'theatre' of ethnographic experience, it does not entirely lose its original configuration. Within the space of the 'same mind', there is a coexistence of 'mental operations', of self and other, and a dialectical combination of the two in the resultant model. It is as if the regressive selection of psychological traits which in the *Elementary Structures of Kinship* was seen to be a fundamental feature of social integration, forever binding an individual to his or her particular social universe, were here subject to a kind of reconfiguration, in which previously inaccessible mental worlds are suddenly made available to the subject's immediate intuition. In a later interview, published in the Marxist journal *La Nouvelle Critique* in 1973, this mode of intuition is described as an *unconscious* development of the fieldwork experience. Once again, Lévi-Strauss's remarks on the possible insights of ethnographic research are prefaced by a description of its privations, this time less general and slightly more personal in tone:

Contact with an exotic natural environment, and with entirely new forms of social existence, is like a punch in the face for the foreign visitor, which forces him out of his passivity. The most enduring memory I have of such experiences is the constant physical and mental fatigue. But ethnologists can react in two ways to the experience: some begin to work frenetically, day and night, accumulating notes, observations and documents; others, by contrast, turn in on themselves and let themselves float, as it were; they give themselves over to an unconscious process [*travail inconscient*] which works in all kinds of ways, assimilating observations and eliciting trains of thought which sometimes only become conscious years after the period spent in the field. I don't think one should ever decide in advance what one is looking for and how one is to look for it.[23]

This schematic, binary opposition of the possible responses to fieldwork experience doubtless lacks nuance, but it is easy to see which of the two types Lévi-Strauss sees himself as corresponding to. On the one hand, the opposition seems to be a caution against an overly programmatic approach to fieldwork, as taught in the universities and codified in ethnographic manuals. To abandon oneself to the unconscious transmissions of the fieldwork experience, to allow one's mind to be 'remodelled' by it, to use Lévi-Strauss's previous metaphor, is to open oneself up to an intuitive and associative mode of thinking which the hyperactive empiricist, intent on the infinite accumulation of data, can never achieve. On the other hand, it is clear that what Lévi-Strauss presents as a general opposition of types (empiricist versus intuitive theorist) is more a projection of his own experience of fieldwork than a description of its diverse reality. In fact, in the different statements on fieldwork reviewed so far, it is possible to discern a pattern, a recurrent structure, repeated with the regularity of a symptom. There is first the narrative of the alienation of fieldwork, of the different physical and mental sacrifices the ethnographer must make in the name of his (her) vocation. While many of Lévi-Strauss's professional colleagues might agree with this characterization, it seems that for him the experience was particularly difficult, at times even traumatic, and that this generated an equal and opposite reaction to the experience, a form of denegation or displacement of it. A critical point seems to be the episode narrated in *Tristes tropiques*, which prompts the ethnographer to question his choice of profession and leads him to write 'The Apotheosis of Augustus'. It is important to note that up to this point, the ethnographer has been, not a solitary observer-participant, entirely isolated from his native civilization (as is the preferred norm in, for example, British anthropology), but part of an expedition, a team which includes, among others, Lévi-Strauss's own wife, Dina Dreyfus, who specialized in the study of material culture, and a doctor. The cause of his separation from the main group is a particularly virulent and dangerous eye infection, which spreads from the Indians to their Western visitors – his wife is the first victim and has to be evacuated. This is at Utiarity, and the Indians in question are the Nambikwara. Unable to advance, the ethnographer leaves the main group with the doctor and proceeds to the station at Campos Novos, where several Nambikwara bands had been sighted (*TT*2, 300–1; *TT*1, 355–6). It is here that he encounters the two hostile and recalcitrant groups, and it is here that he experiences his momentary crisis of faith.

---

[23] 'Un ethnologue et la culture', interview with Catherine B. Clément and Antoine Casanova, *La Nouvelle Critique* 61 (February 1973), 31. My translation.

We have already looked at Lévi-Strauss's fictional dramatization of the ethnographer's choice in our commentary of 'The Apotheosis of Augustus', and we have also argued that the remainder of the book represents an attempt to recuperate that choice, to dissipate the mood of uncertainty generated by the play. This is what happens, in microcosm, with Lévi-Strauss's various statements on the nature and function of fieldwork. The narrative of alienation, of the immediate affective response to the hardships of fieldwork, is never left as an absolute statement; it is always followed and completed by an assertion of the redeeming value of insight, even if, as is the case in the passage quoted above, that insight is an unconscious and deferred one. The crisis at Campos Novos is in fact paradigmatic of this structure of recuperation, or redemption, in that the ethnographer's observation of the hostile Nambikwara groups subsequently becomes the basis of a Maussian analysis of the regulatory function of the gift (*TT*2, 301–3; *TT*1, 357–9). If this structure is not immediately apparent in the narrative sequence of *Tristes tropiques*, it is because the two moments are separated and reversed, the theoretical processing of the experience taking place some hundred pages earlier, in the chapters on the Nambikwara.[24]

It could be said then that Lévi-Strauss's treatment of the experience of fieldwork is a dialectical one, in that the experience itself is negated, conserved and sublated in the transition from observation to theory, from the raw to the cooked. As he reveals in the opening sentences of *Tristes tropiques*, it is fifteen years since he left Brazil for the last time, and these fifteen years could be seen as the period of incubation, the latency period in which the disparate items of his experience have been doing their unconscious work, silently falling into place, providing the mental architecture necessary for a proper understanding of that experience. This is the Proustian dimension of structuralism, in which time lost in the field is miraculously regained in the retrospective intuition of coherence. The reality of Lévi-Strauss's intellectual development is of course much more complicated. A significant omission in the pages of *Tristes tropiques* is the lack of any detailed account of his North American experience during the Second World War. His crucial encounter with Jakobson, his contact with most of the major American anthropologists of the time, the months of intensive research spent in the New York Public Library – none of these experiences find their way into the autobiographical parts of *Tristes tropiques*. And yet, the North American experience – in total nearly seven years, from 1941 to 1947 – is probably the most crucial episode in Lévi-Strauss's professional biography. It is here, one suspects, that a second initiation, perhaps *the* initiation, takes place. More than thirty years after the writing of *Tristes tropiques*, and fifty years after Lévi-Strauss's first contact with the Nambikwara, Didier Eribon questions him on the reasons for his relatively limited fieldwork experience:

[24] See chapter 4, note 45.

D.E. This is one of the objections often made against you: you have read a great deal but have done little fieldwork.

C.L.-S. That was a result of circumstances. If I had gotten a visa for Brazil in 1940, I would have gone back to my initial fieldsites and done more work. If the war hadn't broken out, I would probably have gone on another mission. Fate led me to the United States, where due to a lack of means and the international situation I was not in a position to launch any expeditions but where, on the other hand, I was entirely free to work on theoretical issues. In that respect, I can say, the possibilities were limitless.

I also became aware that in the previous twenty or thirty years a considerable quantity of material had been accumulated; but it was in such disarray that one didn't know where to begin or how to utilize it. It seemed urgent to sort out what this mass of documents had brought us. Finally, why not admit it? I realized early on that I was a library man [*homme de cabinet*], not a fieldworker. I don't mean this disparagingly, quite the contrary, fieldwork is a kind of 'women's work' (which is probably why women are so successful at it). Myself, I had neither the interest nor the patience for it.

D.E. However, despite the dangers that we have already mentioned, you seemed to take a great deal of pleasure from it.

C.L.-S. Indeed. But these were my first trips. I'm not sure that, had there been others, I wouldn't have felt a growing exasperation when faced with the disproportion between usable time and time wasted [*le temps utilisable et le temps perdu*]. (*CLS*2, 43–4; *PL*, 66)

As is so often the case in Lévi-Strauss's autobiography, chance, external contingency, seems to play a decisive role in the determination of his trajectory.[25] Again, he is the passive subject of circumstance, here the vagaries of bureaucracy and the intervention of the war. But the misfortune of missed opportunity is more than compensated by the revelation offered by the New York libraries. It is here, confronted with the infinite extension of the archive, that Lévi-Strauss might be said to have undergone a second initiation. In a familiar figure of description, he evokes both the 'accumulation' of ethnographic material – the 'mass' of documents and their disarray – and the necessity of bringing some order to this chaos. This task of organization is experienced as a liberation rather than a burden: it permits the freedom of speculation, the in principle limitless possibilities of theory. The revelation of the archive is therefore also for Lévi-Strauss a self-revelation: his real vocation lies in theoretical work rather than in the uncertain labours of fieldwork. It is all a question of how one spends one's time: in fieldwork, the trade-off between usable time and lost (wasted) time is not, according to Lévi-Strauss, a favourable one, whereas in the closed cabinet of the theorist, one assumes, it is possible to recuperate time, to compensate for the labour of acquisition with the insight of intuition. The dismal and (*pace* Lévi-Strauss) disparaging remark on women seems to be an extension, into the

---

[25] In the narrative of *Tristes tropiques*, the element of chance, or *play*, is evident even in the telephone call on which, he claims, his entire career turned: 'My career was decided [*Ma carrière s'est jouée*] one day in the autumn of 1934, at nine o'clock in the morning, by a telephone call from Célestin Bouglé, who was then head of the Ecole Normale Supérieure' (*TT*2, 47; *TT*1, 47).

realm of gender difference, of his previous distinction between the two types of response to fieldwork: those who engage in a frenetic accumulation of notes and observations and those who abandon themselves to the unconscious effects of their experience, the latent message that will emerge, miraculously reconstructed, in some later illumination. In this bizarre sexual division of labour, women are destined to return to the field, to devote their lives to the collection of data, whereas the work of intellection, which doubtless for Lévi-Strauss requires another form of patience, is reserved for men such as himself.

The apparently contingent and premature termination of Lévi-Strauss's fieldwork career therefore reveals the more profound truth of his mission, a life devoted to speculation and theorization. In this respect, all of his subsequent remarks on the role of fieldwork function as a kind of retrospective rationalization of his individual trajectory, generalized to the whole profession. The coherence fieldwork gives to hitherto 'discontinuous' experience, its 'remodelling' of the ethnographer's mind, his (her?) unconscious assimilation of its lessons, making him (her?) into a 'new man' – all of these descriptions pre-programme the experience of fieldwork, in anticipation of its subsequent transformation into the intuitions of structuralist analysis. In this sense, for Lévi-Strauss fieldwork is an experience – an experiment – that does not need to be repeated. Return to the field, the repetition of observation, is best left to those who are temperamentally more suited to this kind of activity, women or frenetic empiricists. The horror of repetition, already apparent in Lévi-Strauss's experience of secondary teaching, his 'neolithic' intelligence, places him at the opposite polarity to this group. Again, as in his description of two 'races' or 'species' earlier in *Tristes tropiques*, the binary alternative of types – data gatherer and theorist – lends a retrospective coherence to the path he has taken, and justifies his place in the hierarchy of the profession. This is the hierarchy implicit in his previous articulation of the three moments or stages of anthropological research: ethnography, ethnology, anthropology.[26]

The North American experience, as we have been calling it, therefore represents a second conversion for Lévi-Strauss, a conversion from ethnography to ethnology, or rather, anthropology – structural anthropology. It is important to note that the ethnographic information stored in the New York libraries would have meant nothing without the appropriate intellectual tools to process that information, and these are provided by the 'revelation' of another chance encounter, the meeting of Roman Jakobson in 1942. It is between the theoretical revelation of Lévi-Strauss's meeting with Jakobson and his patient assimilation of the ethnographic archive in New York that structuralism is born. As has already been remarked, neither of these references finds its way into the pages of *Tristes tropiques* – at most the references to North America are cultural

[26] See chapter 1, p. 12.

ones, part of the 'travelogue' dimension of the book. At first sight, the omission seems a curious one, given the importance of the experience. It seems strange to spend an entire chapter on his intellectual formation, 'The Making of an Ethnologist', without once mentioning the event which, in the fifteen years since his return from the field, has had the most profound influence on his intellectual development. On the one hand, this omission might be explained by the simple reason of context: the book is not intended for a specialist or academic audience, and Lévi-Strauss restricts himself, strategically, to references that would have meaning and resonance for a reasonably literate public. Thus the reference in 'The Making of an Ethnologist' to the 'three mistresses' who have given him intellectual inspiration – the science of geology, the thought of Marx and Freud – gives a simplified digest of structuralist methodology, while the reference to Marx and Freud shows the author to be suitably conversant with two of the major intellectual reference points of his generation, Marxism and psychoanalysis. Later in the book, the analysis of Nambikwara politics is referenced to Rousseau rather than Mauss, even though it is clearly the latter who is the theoretical inspiration for the passages on reciprocity and power. Again, the name of Rousseau, who in the closing stages of the book is hailed as the founding father of anthropology, would have greater resonance for the wider readership to which *Tristes tropiques* is addressed.

On the other hand, apart from these contextually strategic considerations, there is another, perhaps more aesthetic reason for the omission in *Tristes tropiques* of the North American chapter of Lévi-Strauss's autobiography. This has to do with the overall *integrity* of the book, as it were, as the narrative of a rite of passage. The classical form of this narrative, as described earlier, is threefold: the moment of revelation, the moment of initiation, the moment of reintegration. While the last moment, as we have seen, necessarily involves some kind of transaction between self and society and, in the best scenario, a dialectical resolution of their differences, the first and second moments consist in the singularization of the self and his or her separation from society, a solitary confrontation with the object of their devotion. The neolithic metaphor, examined above, with its postulate of an elective affinity between self and other, implies a direct, one-to-one relationship with that object, as does the experience of fieldwork. Despite the fact that Lévi-Strauss's fieldwork was not a solitary enterprise – as has been noted, he was accompanied by a whole team of individuals – the tenor of the ethnographic chapters of *Tristes tropiques* is that of the protagonist's solitary communion with his object of study. The aesthetic unity of *Tristes tropiques*, then, derives from this meditative continuity, the sense that the book's protagonist is a *witness*, that there exists a direct and unmediated line of communication between himself and the other. All that is required of the reader is the suspension of his or her disbelief, an acceptance of the constructed nature of this narrative. From this perspective, to introduce the extraneous, biographical element of the North American episode would destroy the unity of the book, and would amount to a kind of desacralization of the protagonist's quest. From the point of view of structure, such an interpolation would introduce the possibility of a second revelation and a second initiation, the effect of which, necessarily, would be to contradict or at least relativize the importance of the first. Second, the content of this interpolation – the experience of a community of scholars (his American colleagues in New York), the institutionalized knowledge of the university, the *mediated* assimilation of ethnographic experience (his reading in the New York Public Library) – presents a picture of professional integration that runs contrary to the main narrative of individual adventure. This particular episode of Lévi-Strauss's biography depicts the patient labours of the cabinet scholar as opposed to the immediate intuitions of the initiate, and gives an altogether more prosaic feel to what in *Tristes tropiques* is presented as a spiritual journey, undertaken in isolation and on the margins of conventional academic activity.

And yet the triangulation of the North American experience is essential if we are to fully understand the psychology behind the writing of *Tristes tropiques*. As was noted earlier, the original initiative for the book was not Lévi-Strauss's, and he wrote it with the guilty conscience of one who knew that he should be devoting his time to more serious matters. But time lost in the writing of this book is time regained in terms of work done on the self, the working through of certain psychological complexes which emerge only laterally and symptomatically in his more academic work. If, as we have seen, the microdrama of 'The Apotheosis of Augustus' represents the moment of reintegration, a moment of crisis both past and present, and is an attempt, symbolically, to come to terms with this difficult experience, then on a larger scale the narrative of *Tristes tropiques* seems to dramatize a more abstract point of transition, a conversion in the author's mind and soul from the raw to the cooked, from the complications and the uncertainties of fieldwork to the relative stability of anthropological knowledge. Thus read, the book is a work of mourning and detachment, a farewell to travel and a farewell to fieldwork; in this respect, the North American episode, the period during which this conversion effectively takes place, could be said to constitute one of its missing chapters.

A man without memory

The biographical detail of the time Lévi-Strauss spent in the United States reminds us of one important fact: he learned his craft independently of the academic institution in France. He was both geographically distant from the instances of academic validation back in France and physically isolated within the public space of the library, the natural home of the autodidact: 'Every morning I went to the New York Public Library. What I know of anthropology I learned during those years' (*CLS2*, 43; *PL*, 65). Everything about Lévi-Strauss's biography seems therefore to place him on the margins of French anthropology – his initial lack of training; his area of specialization (he was an Americanist, whereas African anthropology was the predominant specialization in France); the long periods spent outside of France, where the main contact was with Anglo-Saxon anthropology; his autodidacticism. And yet, in a period of less than ten years, from the publication of the *Elementary Stuctures* in 1949 to the appearance of *Structural Anthropology* in 1958, this in principle most marginal of individuals had established himself as the central practitioner of his discipline in France. One would expect an individual apparently so motivated to possess a sense of self commensurate with this achievement, but in fact quite the opposite seems to be the case. On a number of occasions, Lévi-Strauss has confessed that he lacks a normal sense of individual identity or personality. This self-effacement is not, as one might suspect, simply a manoeuvre to protect and preserve a certain, everyday privacy; rather, it seems in Lévi-Strauss's case to be a genuine aspect of personal temperament. In the conversations with Eribon, he does not view this trait as being in any way unusual – rather the reverse, in fact. It is society, he argues, which requires us to develop a sense of individuality, rather than any spontaneous impulse, essential to our existence as human beings (*CLS2*, 168; *PL*, 233). The diminished sense of identity experienced in relation to himself extends to his relationship with his work, where he frequently confesses to a chronic failure of memory *vis-à-vis* the different texts he has written. In the introduction to the 1977 Massey Lectures, published under the title *Myth and Meaning*, for example, he explains:

Although I am going to talk about what I have written, my books and papers and so on, unfortunately I forget what I have written practically as soon as it is finished. There is probably going to be some trouble about that. But nevertheless I think there is also something significant about it, in that I don't have the feeling that I write my books. I have the feeling that my books get written through me and that once they have got across me I feel empty and nothing is left.

You may remember that I have written that myths get thought in man unbeknownst to him. This has been much discussed and even criticized by my English-speaking colleagues, because their feeling is that, from an empirical point of view, it is an utterly meaningless sentence. But for me it describes a lived experience, because it says exactly how I perceive my own relationship to my work. That is, my work gets thought in me unbeknown to me. I never had, and still do not have, the perception of feeling my personal identity. I appear to myself as the place where something is going on, but there is no 'I', no 'me'. Each of us is a kind of crossroads where things happen. The crossroads is purely passive; something happens there. A different thing, equally valid, happens elsewhere. There is no choice, it is just a matter of chance. (*MM*, 3–4)

One might accept, with certain qualifications, Lévi-Strauss's previous remark on the constructed nature of personality – this is part of the anthropologist's stock-in-trade, to question and to relativize categories of thought and modes of behaviour we would normally take for granted. The category of the self is such a category, one which, according to a certain history of human consciousness, has had a profound effect on the development of Western civilization. Here, Lévi-Strauss not only questions this category, he abolishes it. His 'lived experience' of his work is that it is a state of dispossession, that he is, literally, inhabited by something that is not himself, of which he is not the primary author. His theory of myth is therefore given subjective verification in his own, direct experience of writing. Myth is a message distributed over time and space, with no locatable centre of enunciation. Similarly, his own symbolic production is merely a point in a network of cultural signification, a local expression of the whole system. In what seems like an inverted parody of Sartre's existentialism, Lévi-Strauss takes the 'lived experience' of this decentred 'I' to be universalizable. His own singular experience of self is thus applicable to all of us: we are merely the passive sites of events, the interchangeable points of realization of virtual realities. One is reminded of the Lucretian universe, a universe governed by chance (the bifurcation of the *clinamen* occurs at an indeterminate time and place), where everything is, in the final analysis, a property of space and position in space.[27]

In this surprising passage, then, the erasure of self is pushed to a virtual limit, it is presented as a kind of illusion of perspective. In the subject named Lévi-Strauss, the faculty which, above all others, ensures the integrity of the self over time, memory, is atrophied, both in relation to his work and in relation to his own, lived past. In the prologue to his interviews with Eribon, Lévi-Strauss associates this failing with the 'neolithic intelligence' he had attributed to himself in *Tristes tropiques*:

C.L.-S. My memory is a self-destructive thief. I suppress elements of my personal and professional life as I go, and later I can't reconstruct the facts... In *Tristes tropiques* I said that I have a neolithic mind. I'm not the kind of person who can capitalize on or make what I've acquired bear fruit – instead I keep moving along an endlessly shifting boundary. Only the work of the moment counts for me, and it is over very quickly. I don't have the inclination or the need to record my progress.

D.E. It is almost paradoxical to hear you say that only the moment and the event count for you.

---

[27] Significantly, the epigraph to *Tristes tropiques* is taken from *On the Nature of the Universe*, and is quoted in the original Latin: *Nec minus ergo ante haec quam tu cecidere, cadentque* (So no less than you, these generations have passed away before now, and will continue to pass away). Lucretius' remark on the transience of human existence is an extension and modulation of his physics: atoms fall, incline, combine and conglomerate to form the objects of the material world, which in their turn distintegrate and dissolve into the infinite flow of falling atoms. The nature of the universe is continual flux, its general rule is entropy. The transience of the physical world is mirrored in the instability of human affairs, which are even more subject to the law of change. For Lucretius, the recognition of transience leads to an attitude of detachment and resignation, and it is this mood and message which seem to pervade the pages of *Tristes tropiques*.

C.L.-S. Subjectively speaking, that is what counts. But I get by when I work by accumulating notes [*fiches*, index cards] – a bit about everything, ideas captured on the fly, summaries of what I have read, references, quotations ... And when I want to start a project, I pull a packet of notes out of their pigeonhole [*casier*, filing compartment] and deal them out [*je les redistribue*] like a deck of cards [*à la façon d'une réussite*, as in a game of patience]. This kind of operation [*jeu*, game, play], where chance plays a role, helps me to revive my failing memory. (*CLS*2, vii–viii; *PL*, 5–6)

It might seem paradoxical that an individual who has devoted his life to the archive, to the assimilation and processing of information, has little or no memory. More precisely, perhaps, it is not so much a case here of a lack of memory as of a *self-cancelling* memory, a memory with its own, internal corrective mechanism. Like the societies he calls neolithic, and to which he is bound, essentially, by virtue of his restless mind, it is as if the subject Lévi-Strauss had chosen, at some level, consciously or unconsciously, not to remember – he has not the 'inclination' or 'need' to remember. *Pace* Eribon, this denegation of memory is not a paradox (Eribon is thinking here of existentialism's privileging of the immediate, present-tense experience of the individual subject); rather, it establishes yet another layer of association between Lévi-Strauss and his object of study, a homology between their attitudes towards time. It will be remembered that for Lévi-Strauss one of the distinguishing characteristics of nonliterate societies was their resistance to change: the homeostatic function of their social institutions was matched on the ideological level by representations that gave little importance to the category of history. The problem here is that the savage mind that is Lévi-Strauss, who forgets everything, both personal and professional, must work, must *write*. The solution to his deficit of memory is, inevitably, a technological one, not simply the technology of writing (the translation renders the French *fiches* as 'notes', whereas a more accurate equivalent would be 'card' or 'index card'), but the technology of the archive, of the filing system. His professional work therefore relies on the *accumulation* of card indexes, and the initial selection of the information to be processed is left to the forces of chance. The metaphor of the game of patience is an appropriate one, given the importance of the notion of play (*jeu*) in Lévi-Strauss's thought as a whole.[28] To externalize memory in the material format of the filing system is for Lévi-Strauss to hand oneself over to chance in one's recourse (return) to the archive. As in information theory, the quantity of information contained in the message is a measure of the uncertainty of the message. As in the game of patience, the objective is to discern a pattern in the arbitrary distribution of cards.

A problem similar to that encountered in the case of the reference to the neolithic, examined above, also faces us here. As with the neolithic, one is led

[28] See Edouard Delruelle, *Lévi-Strauss et la philosophie* (Brussels: De Boek/Editions Universitaires, 1989), p. 131.

to ask questions about the exact status of Lévi-Strauss's different statements about himself and his work. The simplest question to ask would be how sincere and how serious the author is in the series of homologies he draws between his own experience of the world and the societies he has elected to study. Everything Lévi-Strauss says about his personal and professional life, from his diminished sense of identity to his choice of vocation to the game of patience he plays with the archive, serves to minimize his role as a conscious agent and emphasize the essential link, the elective affinity that binds him to his object of study. It is difficult to escape the impression that there is something *theatrical* about this presentation, or construction, of himself, that it is part of a kind of dramatization of his life in which he, the protagonist, plays out a specific, predetermined role. Lévi-Strauss himself has given substantive definition to this role by suggesting that the 'key' to his personality lies in the fictional character of Don Quichotte.[29] This seems appropriate, if one remembers the essential nostalgia of a text like *Tristes tropiques*, with its persistent search for vestiges of the past in a transient and degraded present. But there is also a *structural* dimension to Lévi-Strauss's construction of his autobiography. In his work on dual organization, it will be remembered, the opposition between two, distinct groups was seen as residing not in their essential difference, but rather in the structural necessity of establishing a difference. The protagonist of his life drama, an individual without identity and a man without memory, seems to be an uncanny enactment of this principle, since at the time of writing *Tristes tropiques*, in 1955, he is the perfect counterpoint of *the* major protagonist of the French intellectual scene, the existential subject as incarnated in the figure of Jean-Paul Sartre. With Sartre, it could be said that the author is always present as conscious subject and as moral agent, that if it is impossible to dissociate 'life' and 'work', it is nevertheless always life (existence) which is the ultimate point of reference. With Lévi-Strauss, by contrast, life and work are consubstantial, to the extent that life only has substance as an extension of work; if we are to believe the testimony of his autobiographical utterances, he is the perfectly non-present subject, the passive site of transmission for his

---

[29] 'As one moves into old age, bits of the past rise to the surface, or, to put it another way, loops are closed . . . If the time is given me, I'll undoubtedly find once again Don Quixote, which was my passion when I was ten (to amuse my guests, my parents would have one of them open the book at random and start to read; I would go on without hesitation, for I knew my abridged edition by heart). Indeed, some people might ask whether I haven't been guided by a kind of quixotism throughout my career.
  – What do you mean by that?
  – Not the dictionary definition: a mania for righting wrongs, becoming the champion of the oppressed, etc. For me quixotism is essentially an obsessive desire to find the past behind the present. If perchance someone someday were to care to understand my personality, I offer him that key.' (*CLS*2, 93–4; *PL*, 134).
  As the mnemonic feats of the younger Lévi-Strauss show, it is not so much the fact that he has no memory – quite the contrary – but that his memory is a peculiarly selective one.

life's work. The question is, could Lévi-Strauss's construction of his persona be a kind of strategy, conscious or unconscious, playing against the predominant philosophical trend of his time, countering the subjectivism of existentialism with the impersonality of structuralism? Whatever the case, and as this chapter has hopefully demonstrated, there are some strange and persistent homologies between theory, self and other in Lévi-Strauss's autobiographical writing. But then, the notion of homology is itself perhaps the key to both his life and his work.

Conclusion   The will to coherence

Tout classement est supérieur au chaos.
(Any classification is superior to chaos.)[1]

'Surviving Lévi-Strauss'. This was the title of the contribution by the French anthropologist Jean Guiart to a special issue of the journal *L'Arc*, dedicated to Lévi-Strauss in 1968.[2] If one were to speak of the legacy of Lévi-Strauss's work, one that is distributed across the spectrum of contemporary thought, then it is necessary to remember that this legacy weighs the most heavily in the discipline and in the country that were its instance of origination. Already, in 1968, Guiart credits Lévi-Strauss with having transformed French anthropology, presiding over its expansion into new geographical areas and giving it a truly international profile. However, Guiart also sees this strength as a potential weakness, to the extent that Lévi-Strauss is the only figure of such stature in French anthropology. His disappearance would leave the discipline in the same state of disarray in which he had found it earlier in the century. Will France have only one Lévi-Strauss? he asks.[3] Almost twenty years later, in a special issue of *L'Homme*, on the state of French anthropology, a similar observation is made by anthropologist Pierre Smith: Lévi-Strauss's contribution 'has not been replaced by anything more satisfactory or more coherent. One can't get around this legacy without giving the impression that French anthropology has given up on the idea of a common programme, one that has never been formulated in a more reasoned and more complete manner'.[4] The preceding chapters have hopefully given the reader an idea of how Lévi-Strauss came to occupy this unique and singular position. First there is the power and the range of his theoretical contribution, of which France had not seen the like since Durkheim. As has been seen, Lévi-Strauss's self-image is that of the synthesist, the individual who brings order and coherence to the mass of data generated by fieldwork research. Whatever the problems and limitations of structural analysis, as he

---

[1] *SM*, 15; *PS*, 24.   [2] 'Survivre à Lévi-Strauss', *L'Arc* (1968), 66–9.   [3] Ibid., 67.
[4] Pierre Smith, 'Le Souci anthropologique', *L'Homme* 26.97–8 (January–June 1986), *L'Anthropologie: Etat des lieux*, 333. My translation.

defined it, its intellectual achievement has not been surpassed. In many ways, the programme he constructs for anthropology in his earlier texts becomes the 'normal science' for the discipline in France, to the extent that he becomes an indispensable point of reference for successive generations of anthropologists, whatever their individual specializations or orientations. But Lévi-Strauss is much more than a theorist, and here again the comparison with Durkheim is an appropriate one. Because in addition to his theoretical production, Lévi-Strauss has a vision for his discipline that raises him above his own individual contribution and that of his contemporaries. From a very early point, in fact, he is also writing texts of a more descriptive nature, providing detailed overviews of his subject and its diverse orientations. This work of description very quickly becomes one of prescription, as he begins in the early 1950s to impose his own stamp on the discipline, his pronouncements on the scope, methods and missions of anthropology increasingly coming to reflect his own programme of research. At this point, as we have seen, the generic separation between 'theoretical', 'descriptive' and 'prescriptive' texts is not so simple or clear cut. Indeed, many of Lévi-Strauss's earlier texts could be described as overdetermined, or multifinal, to the extent that they seem to be performing simultaneously on a number of different levels. In short, it seems that for Lévi-Strauss there is always an agenda, that he is always concerned with asserting something more general about the nature of the discipline he is practising, its field of reference and its claims to scientific and humanistic interest. This is essentially a *corporatist* way of thinking; that is, Lévi-Strauss is not content simply to speak on his own account and from his own, local perspective, but is also prepared to speak collectively, in the name of French anthropology, in defence of what he believes to be its special contribution to contemporary knowledge. This capacity for synthesis, for overview, for reflexive statement on what one's discipline is about and also what it *should* be about, could be seen as an essential trait of the *maître à penser*, who is not simply a producer of ideas and of theories, but equally and inseparably, an influential commentator on his or her discipline. More than any of his contemporaries, Lévi-Strauss seemed ready and willing to assume this role.

The convergence of individual case history and the history of a discipline can be observed to striking effect in the inaugural lecture given at the Collège de France in 1960. From the personal point of view, the lecture is in many respects the crowning point of Lévi-Strauss's professional career. He has arrived at the most prestigious of research institutions in France, and is free to research, speculate and write on whatever subject he chooses.[5] From the point of view of anthropology, his election to the Collège de France gives to this relatively marginal discipline a degree of visibility and recognition that had hitherto been

5 See *CLS2*, 75; *PL*, 109.

denied it. Through the figure of Lévi-Strauss, therefore, French anthropology acquires a voice whose force is greater than its actual, institutional mass. The price to pay for this promotion, of course, is that the anthropology Lévi-Strauss presents in his inaugural lecture is an anthropology entirely in his own image. In 'The Scope of Anthropology', which could be seen as being the point of synthesis of the formative period of his career, he is able to ask: 'What, then, is social anthropology?', and his response – that it is a semiology – immediately defines the discipline as a structural anthropology in the image of his own programme of research in the preceding ten years (*SA2*, 9; *AS2*, 18). Significantly, reference to his contemporaries, French or otherwise, is virtually non-existent.[6] Instead, Lévi-Strauss prefers to dialogue with his predecessors, the founding fathers of the discipline, Frazer, Boas, Malinowski, and especially his French masters, Durkheim and Mauss; indeed, the most contemporary of his references is the recently deceased Radcliffe-Brown. This lack of reference to his immediate peers is symptomatic of the singularity of his contribution, the extent to which he stands alone – or considers himself to stand alone – in the landscape of modern anthropology.

In a sense, such singularity is inevitable, essential even, because from the start, it was apparent that Lévi-Strauss was more than an anthropologist. On the one hand, he becomes a master of his trade, vastly erudite, combining the scholarly apprenticeship of his North American experience with the theoretical capital of his native French tradition. On the other hand, it is as if the acquisition of the tools of his trade were simply an enabling condition, the preliminary to a work of speculation that transcends the limits of any one, specific discipline. This could be seen as a generic feature of great thinkers, that they break down the conventional divisions between disciplines, offering insights that would be impossible within the normal terms of reference of their parent discipline. The kind of interdisciplinarity Lévi-Strauss proposes and practises in his earlier, programmatic texts is not simply that of superficial, *ad hoc* borrowings from other disciplines, but a systematic assimilation of their respective methodologies. It is thus quite logical that the relative lack of reference to his academic peers in 'The Scope of Anthropology', for example, is accompanied by reference to the theoretical inspiration of thinkers external to anthropology: Saussure, Jakobson, Trubetzkoy.

While it is useful to remember, then, that the first destination of Lévi-Strauss's work was and remains anthropology, it is not necessarily its final destination. Lévi-Strauss himself has repeated that structuralism, as it developed in France in the late 1950s and early 1960s, should be distinguished from what he was attempting to accomplish in anthropology – quite simply, to introduce a measure

---

[6] There is a passing reference to Jean Guiart's work on Melanesia and Polynesia (*SA2*, 13; *AS2*, 22).

of rigour in an area of study where there had been none. To an extent, he is right. The 'father' of French structuralism, as he is often called, has every right to deny paternity of an intellectual movement which very rapidly became an intellectual fad, with all of the distortions and simplifications that accompany such popularization. Lévi-Strauss has therefore not been particularly anxious to police his inheritance – it is impossible to police such an inheritance. For the most part, he has limited himself to correcting what he perceives as misinformed attacks on his own, local practice of structural analysis. This retreat to his specialism, when confronted with the effects of his influence, is understandable and logical. At the same time, there was much in his initial formulation of a structural anthropology that predestined its conversion into the intellectual movement called structuralism. As we have seen, from the beginning Lévi-Strauss was concerned to define not only the internal configuration of his own specialism, anthropology, but also its interface with a range of other disciplines and its place in the wider arena of the human sciences – a place he considers to be a central one. If linguistics is alone among the human sciences to have approached the coherence and rigour of the exact sciences, then anthropology – structural anthropology – is a kind of mediator between the two domains, and is destined to play a leading role in the renovation of the human sciences. The reconfiguration proposed by Lévi-Strauss had implications for neighbouring disciplines such as history and sociology, as the recurrent debates on the human sciences in the 1950s and 1960s testify. But the discipline arguably the most affected by this reconfiguration was philosophy. It could be said that philosophy had the most to lose from the extension of the field of the human sciences. Traditionally the master discipline, the privileged point of reference of intellectual discourse in France, philosophy now found itself in an ambivalent position. In one sense, it was part of the human sciences, it had a stake in any knowledge pertaining to the human, any knowledge that might deepen our understanding of what it means to be human. On the other hand, philosophy could not aspire to the same kind of scientific foundations Lévi-Strauss was claiming for the human sciences, and in this sense its voice could no longer be a central one.

Philosophy figures strongly in the personal biography of Lévi-Strauss – his initial training was in the subject. His subsequent defection to anthropology was in reaction to what he felt to be the rhetorical abstractions of philosophy, and his fear of a life spent repeating its lessons in the classroom. Anthropology offered a kind of knowledge that was at once more concrete and more authentic; as a relatively young discipline, it was the perfect terrain for a work of speculation free of the constraints which disciplines with a longer history and a longer tradition normally impose on their practitioners. But as we have seen, Lévi-Strauss returns to philosophy in his anthropological work. From the *Elementary Structures* onwards, the philosophical content of this work was evident. His formulation of the theory of reciprocity, his conception of the symbolic nature of social institutions, his theory of the human mind – all of these ideas indicate the inherently philosophical orientation of Lévi-Strauss's thought. They pose questions that transcend the field of anthropology proper, or rather, perhaps, extend the field of anthropology into areas that are normally the province of philosophical speculation, and they are the reason for the fascination his work held for a wider constituency of thinkers during the high period of structuralism.

One reading of the event of structuralism is therefore that it was an unintended consequence, a side-effect of Lévi-Strauss's promotion of anthropology and the human sciences and the implicitly philosophical dimension of his work. However, there is a more active and more aggressive side to his early formulations concerning the place and role of anthropology in relation to philosophy. We have seen that as early as 1955, in *Tristes tropiques*, there was a direct and withering critique of existentialism. In later texts, anthropology is presented as providing an alternative to the ethnocentric and anthropocentric humanism characteristic of the Western philosophical tradition. In his retrospective comments on this period, Lévi-Strauss has stated simply that it was necessary to fight one's disciplinary corner, given the intellectual hegemony of philosophy in France at the time. Nevertheless, it seems that it was he who fired the first shots in this veritable conflict of disciplines. Throughout the 1950s, his construction of French anthropology is designed not only to preserve the integrity of the discipline, but to project it into the centre of intellectual debate in France. In this context, the strategic importance of *Tristes tropiques* cannot be overestimated. This was not armchair ideology, conducted from the comfort of the study or the Left Bank café, but a philosophy on the move, the testimony of a restless consciousness attempting to make sense of a chaotic and fast-changing world. The protagonist of *Tristes tropiques* was the perfect personification of the new humanism, a humanism extended, as Lévi-Strauss later defined it, 'to the measure of humanity' (*SA2*, 32; *AS2*, 44).

To say that the phenomenon of structuralism was simply a side-effect of Lévi-Strauss's work in anthropology would therefore be a gross oversimplification. Just as it is impossible to imagine existentialism without a Sartre, it is doubtful that structuralism could have existed in the form that it did without the animating presence of Lévi-Strauss. Everything in his formulation of anthropology and the human sciences indicates that his intended audience is a wider one than simply the specialized constituency of his own discipline. Despite his repeated disclaimers regarding the philosophical content of his work, it is a work that is philosophical through and through, from the epistemological ambitions of his notion of the human mind to his formulation of the ethical and critical missions of the new humanism. It can be said, without exaggeration, that this work transformed the intellectual landscape in France, its points of reference and its terms of exchange. The effect of structuralism was not simply in the imitation of the methods of structural analysis, carried over into other areas of study, but in a whole new way of thinking about knowledge and about the mediation of knowledge. In this respect, Lévi-Strauss is representative of a shift in the perception of the nature and role of the intellectual, as defined in France. On the one hand, as a contemporary of Sartre, he is one of the last of the *maîtres penseurs*; his work has a philosophical ambition that many would argue has now disappeared from French intellectual discourse. On the other hand, it is precisely in Lévi-Strauss's work that the liquidation of the traditional figure of the intellectual is announced and anticipated. A leitmotif of Lévi-Strauss's thought is the distributed nature of contemporary knowledge – it is impossible for the individual to embrace the entirety of what can be thought in the modern world. The idea of the human sciences itself reflects this more modest approach to the system of knowledge. Increasingly, such knowledge is a specialized knowledge, but increasingly, also, it is a shared and communicated knowledge. The interdisciplinary exchange characteristic of the human sciences is dependent on collective and collaborative models of research taken from the natural sciences, all of which tends to relativize the position of the individual and independent thinker. The paradox, of course, is that while announcing this new topography of knowledge, Lévi-Strauss remains an example of the old school of intellectual production, in that the corpus of work he leaves to us represents a highly individualized system of thought.

If we turn now to this corpus, the ensemble of texts – articles, monographs, books, overviews, interviews – that constitute Lévi-Strauss's 'work', then a number of questions arise concerning the status of its contribution to contemporary thought. Whilst the historical contribution to anthropology and to structuralism is more or less undisputed, one encounters problems when trying to assess the overall construction of this work, how it all holds together. In fact, the problem is not, as one would expect with any seminal thinker, that this work does not hold together equally well in all of its parts, that there are areas of greater or lesser coherence and cohesion, but that, on the contrary, there is an *excess* of cohesion in Lévi-Strauss's work, that it all holds together rather too well. The term that perhaps best describes the nature of this cohesion is *closure*.

There is first what might be termed the heuristic closure of Lévi-Strauss's thought. This has to do with the *style* of his exposition, as we have followed it in a number of his foundational texts, which relies on a combination of demonstration and speculation. Its structure is normally a ternary one, a three-step process consisting of first the delineation of a 'problem' (frequently involving the evocation of a state of disorder and chaos); second, the proposition of a solution to the problem (model or hypothesis); finally, the integration of the solution by expressing it in the conditional form of 'If X then Y'. Particularly important is the transition between the second and the third step of the process, the second step consisting of an act of speculation, and the third acting as the point of consolidation or validation of the hypothesis.[7] In itself, this procedure seems unexceptionable, and could be taken to be a necessary part of any process of demonstration aspiring to any degree of rigour. However, in Lévi-Strauss's work the hypotheses he advances are closed and self-validating to the extent that they are not subject to any form of external criticism. Instead, they seem to function as a kind of rhetorical stepping stone, permitting him to proceed to the next stage of his demonstration, in what is essentially a one-way process. There is rarely, if ever, any reflexive questioning or revision of the fundamentals of the theory. The result is that the body of Lévi-Strauss's thought has grown through a process of accretion, through the accumulation of a number of implicitly accepted positions (e.g., the deep-level determination of the principle of reciprocity, the combinatorial and oppositional nature of human cognition, the essentially homeostatic function of social institutions and representations in 'exotic' societies, etc.), and has, through its own forward momentum, become increasingly independent of any external instance of validation.[8]

The second species of closure in Lévi-Strauss could be called methodological closure, and it is closely linked to the form of heuristic closure just discussed. This would be the tendency, when confronted with any given complex (social, symbolic, etc.), to replicate what are essentially the same modes of analysis. This tendency has been noted a number of times during the present study, in a number of different texts. It consists in a relatively limited range of responses, or default positions, which may be summarized as follows:

• The treatment of the complex as an ensemble of traits or elements subject to specific rules of combination. The reduction of these rules of combination to a series of binary oppositions. Areas of application: social (kinship) relations; culture and civilization (art, technology, totemic systems, myth); and scientific knowledge (the configuration of and relationships between disciplines). This model of analysis is taken from linguistics (phonology) but also from information theory.

[7] In the example of the Oedipus myth, examined in chapter 3, the point of consolidation is the point at which Lévi-Strauss summarizes the main elements of the proposed structural method of analysis and then writes: 'If the above three points are granted, at least as a working hypothesis, two consequences will follow' (SA1, 210; AS1, 232).

[8] According to Alain Delrieu, 'Lévi-Strauss begins his anthropological work by starting from a small number of postulates and intuitions which form as many hypotheses stated in an almost assertoric mode, with no preliminary attempt to establish these hypotheses in a systematically critical manner' (Lévi-Strauss lecteur de Freud. Le droit, l'inceste, le père et l'échange des femmes, 2nd edition (Paris: Anthropos, 1999), p. 1, my translation). Lucien Scubla comments: 'Indeed, from 1955 to the present day ... Lévi-Strauss has gone his own solitary way, without really taking into account the reactions of the anthropologists or mathematicians who at one time or another might have taken an interest in his work' (Lucien Scubla, Lire Lévi-Strauss. Le Déploiement d'une intuition (Paris: Odile Jacob, 1998), p. 20, my translation).

- The conceptualization of the relationship between discrete complex systems as relations of transformation. Areas of application: social and cultural systems; mythical systems. Origin of model of conceptualization: mathematics, biology, information theory.

- In the description of the historical development of a complex system, the notion of choice (conscious or unconscious) from a repertory of virtual paths of development. This kind of selection could be seen as regressive to the extent that it would entail the exclusion of other paths of development. Parallel to the category of choice is the notion of chance or play (*jeu*) in the development of the system. Areas of application: psycho-social development of children; historical evolution of cultures; the personal case history of Lévi-Strauss. Origin of model of description: phonology, information theory, biology.

- In the description of the genesis of a system, the notion of the passage from the discontinuous to the continuous, the 'precipitation', 'crystallization' or 'coalescence' of previously disparate elements. Areas of application: 'nebular' description of anthropology and the human sciences; formation of coherent systems of representation (the progressive restriction of the child's mental world; the conversion of the shaman Quesalid; the intellectual illumination of fieldwork). Origin of model of conceptualization: physics, chemistry.

- The resolution of conflictual or hierarchical relationships into relations of complementarity or reciprocity. Linked to this, the more general notions of mediation, regulation and homeostasis (negative feedback). Areas of application: social and interpersonal relations; the relations between cultures (e.g., the idea of a 'coalition' of cultures); the relations between disciplines. Origin of model of analysis: Durkheim's theory of social cohesion; Mauss's theory of reciprocity; cybernetics.

Lévi-Strauss has defined the *bricolage* of exotic cultures as a kind of DIY science, the construction of logical systems from the preconstructed objects or representations to hand in a given environment or tradition, and the construction of his own theoretical system can be said to amount to precisely this – a form of *bricolage*. The different models of description, analysis or conceptualization reviewed above are in each case a combination of different approaches taken from contemporary science – only the theory of reciprocity (itself updated via modern theories of control and communication) is native to the field of sociological theory proper. The problem here is not so much with Lévi-Strauss's theoretical eclecticism as with a certain lack of discrimination in his application of these different models. In other words, while one might be prepared to follow, with qualifications, Lévi-Strauss's application of one particular model in one particular area, it becomes more difficult to accept its application in another, or indeed a number of other, qualitatively different domains. What does it mean, for example, when the model of binary oppositions used to analyse the operations of mythic or totemic thought is also applied to a description of the relationship between different disciplines within the human sciences? Or when the notion of regressive selection is applied both to the psychological development of the child and the historical development of civilizations? This kind of cross-categorical application of different models of analysis causes the reader to question, retrospectively, the consistency of their application in their original or predominant area of application. From the point of view of the system of Lévi-Strauss's thought, this replication of methodologies would be part of his constant desire to unify the different parts of his system, to ensure its overall theoretical coherence. If the 'problem' of anthropology is, as Lévi-Strauss claims, a problem of communication (information theory is a constant point of reference for the different models of analysis reviewed above), then the number of solutions to the problem is, by definition, limited.

The third and final form of closure in Lévi-Strauss's work is what might be termed autobiographical closure, and it is perhaps the most problematic of the different modes of closure treated so far. This is because, while we might question the pertinence of the kind of heuristic and methodological closure described above, it is nevertheless still part of a recognizably scientific procedure which distinguishes between object of analysis, subject of analysis and method of analysis. Within the practice of 'science', as it has come to be called, it is normally assumed that while the relationship between object and method of analysis is open to infinite revision and refinement, the subject of analysis is indifferent, that in principle the construction of scientific knowledge is something that is reproducible by *any* subject. From his early commentary on Mauss, Lévi-Strauss insists that in the social and human sciences the observer is necessarily part of the reality observed, and that any verification of our attempts at objective analysis can finally only be a subjective one. However, this does not mean that all knowledge about the human and the social is ultimately subjective and situated, but rather that between the opposite polarities of external observer and native verification, there is a shared mental continuum. The different mental universes of self and other are not incommensurable, but simply transforms of one another. This common mental ground opens the possibility of a universal intelligibility, the 'any subject' of scientific knowledge.[9] As Lévi-Strauss

---

[9] A similar point is made by Mauro W. Barbosa Almeida: 'Structuralism describes invariance in objects or alternatively, invariance among observers. It is from this point of view relativist but not in the sense of the cultural relativism that asserts the uniqueness of cultural differences. Rather, the relativism of structuralism is analogous to that which physicists have in mind when they speak of a relativity of a theory. This is very far from the idea that everything is relative (meaning that each observer applies his own unique "laws"). On the contrary, the identification

argues in the conclusion of *Totemism*: 'Every human mind is a locus of virtual experience where what goes on in the minds of men, however remote they may be, can be investigated' (*T*, 103; *TA*, 151). While one might perhaps not share his optimism concerning the virtual identity of the human mind, Lévi-Strauss's treatment of the question of subjectivity in the human sciences is therefore firmly rooted in the practices and procedures of the natural sciences.

The problem is that Lévi-Strauss is not the indifferent subject of scientific discourse, that the theory of structuralism is not entirely detachable from the empirical individual named 'Lévi-Strauss'. This has to do not simply with the inevitability of subjective implication, a commonplace in the social and human sciences, but rather with the unusual degree of coherence which appears to exist, at all levels, in Lévi-Strauss's work. The lack of discrimination noted above with regard to the application of different models of analysis also applies in the case of Lévi-Strauss to the relationship between 'life' and 'work'. One important aspect of our analysis of Lévi-Strauss's autobiographical self-construction was his obsession with homology, homology of the kind that might exist, for example, between himself and the object of his chosen vocation, the exotic culture. If the neolithic metaphor, as we examined it in the last chapter, is objectively impossible, it is subjectively necessary in that it provides a deep level motivation for the temperamental bias that leads him to this particular vocation. Another level of cross-categorical homology can be found in the notion of 'surplus' signification, first formulated in the *Introduction to Mauss*. This was used to explain the symbolic remainder, as it were, the 'supplementary ration' of signification over and above a particular society's rational or utilitarian representations of the world. In this category, it will be remembered, Lévi-Strauss placed collective representations such as artistic creation and myth, in effect delineating what would be the main areas of application of structural analysis in the following two decades of research. The context of the initial formulation of the symbolic nature of society in the *Introduction to Mauss* was the question of the pathological nature (or not) of the altered states of consciousness observed in shamanism and cases of possession, and the response to that question was that such cases were not in themselves pathological, when considered in relation to the total symbolic systems of the societies in which they occurred. While they fell outside of the dominant symbolic systems of these societies, they were nevertheless integral to those systems, complementary in their marginality. The case history of Quesalid, the story of his gradual accommodation with the practices of shamanism and the belief systems of his society, would be a concrete example of such integration.

of the relevant transformation group will express what is invariant, at the same time allowing for the diversity found in the world ... Diversity becomes compatible with unity.' ('Symmetry and Entropy. Mathematical Metaphors in the Work of Lévi-Strauss', *Current Anthropology* 31.4 (August–October 1990), 372).

In terms of the overall development of his thought, we saw Lévi-Strauss's early interest in shamanism as one of the first points of access to his second area of specialization, the anthropology of religions. Through his negotiation of the 'problem' of shamanism, he establishes a number of premises that will remain central to the structuralism of his subsequent work: the symbolic nature of social life; the effectiveness of the symbolic; the relative autonomy of the symbolic. But like everything in Lévi-Strauss, this early interest is not a simple one, it is overdetermined. In a strange form of chiasmus, the figure of the shaman, as (s)he is represented in Lévi-Strauss's early texts, seems to be a point-by-point transform of the figure of the anthropologist, situated on the opposite side of the ethnographic equation. In the same way that the shaman operates between or outside the conventional symbolic systems of his or her society – 'off system', as Lévi-Strauss puts it – the anthropologist is an outsider to the extent that he or she has rejected the symbolic closure of his or her own culture in favour of the alternative universes of other cultures. Potentially, this way lies madness, if the alternative message or medicine provided by the shaman-anthropologist is not recognized by society – the sorcerer who is unable to compete with the 'system' of medical explanation developed by Quesalid indeed goes mad (*SA*1, 178; *AS*1, 196). In the autobiographical and quasi-autobiographical pages of *Tristes tropiques*, there is evidence of a similar brush with madness. The author's quest for power, for social recognition, seems, in 1955 as much as in 1938, to have resulted in a relative impasse, and he is faced with the possibility of the ultimate futility of his radical choice of career. The drama of social integration, or reintegration, narrated in 'The Apotheosis of Augustus', is an attempt to come to terms with this disturbing predicament; in a strongly Freudian sense, it represents a working through of the series of double binds which the anthropologist has, consciously or unconsciously, created for himself. As we saw, the denouement of this drama, written on the reverse side of the protagonist's ethnographic notes, was an uncertain one. But somewhere – autobiographically, between the first, traumatic initiation of fieldwork and the second initiation of North America, and structurally, in *Tristes tropiques*, between the crisis of 'The Apotheosis of Augustus' and the book's conclusion – there is reconciliation. Like the shaman Quesalid, the autobiographical Lévi-Strauss reaches an accommodation with his society, his marginality is recuperated in a vocation that requires exceptionality. As he confesses in *Tristes tropiques*, anthropology 'allows me to reconcile my character with my life' (*TT*2, 58–9; *TT*1, 62). Again, like Quesalid, the psychological correlate of this reintegration is the creation (crystallization) of a 'system' with its own, internal coherence, which makes sense of the object of his vocation. The strange thing about the system of structuralism, as we have been following it in this book, is that it becomes in many ways inseparable from its biographical instance of creation. Lévi-Strauss has said that mythology, the study of myth, must take the same form as its object of study, that it must be mythomorphic (*RC*, 6; *CC*, 14). A similar evaluation could be made of his work as a whole, that it is *idiomorphic*; that is, in all of its parts and at all of its levels, this work bears the singular signature of its creator. It is as if the floating signifier, initially part of the theoretical infrastructure of structuralism, were itself the condition of possibility of structuralism, to the extent that the structural analysis of myth, as it develops in Lévi-Strauss's later work, becomes increasingly self-referential, or idiolectical, a closed universe of his own making.

The aesthetic closure of Lévi-Strauss's work – of his life *and* work – is the result of a remarkable will to coherence, comparable to what he elsewhere describes as the totalizing impulse of the 'savage mind'. As such, its legacy to the human sciences is an ambivalent one, a legacy to which one can respond in two ways. On the one hand, one can pick and choose from this corpus of concepts, models, methodologies and values, a little in the manner of the *bricoleur* described in the *Savage Mind*, taking or leaving this or that item of thought or principle, according to the interest or necessity of the moment. This is how many readers of Lévi-Strauss, from anthropology to critical theory, have approached his work, and perhaps this is finally how one should proceed with a thinker such as Lévi-Strauss. On the other hand, one might attempt to reconstruct, from the inside, some of the constants and continuities of the corpus, the different sequences of reasoning and complexes of values that constitute the intellectual fabric of that corpus. Hopefully, such an approach would give a greater degree of insight into not simply *what* Lévi-Strauss thinks, but *how* he thinks, the particular cognitive reflexes that define the parameters of his intellectual universe. This is the line of enquiry that has been attempted in the present study, and it is, necessarily, one that requires a certain suspension of disbelief.

Bibliography

This is not an exhaustive bibliography of the works of Lévi-Strauss or of the critical literature on his work. For more extensive bibliographies, the reader is referred to Pace (1983) and Hénaff (1991). For a useful conspectus of the critical literature on Lévi-Strauss until 1976, see F.H. and C.C. Lapointe (1977)

WORKS BY LÉVI-STRAUSS

BOOKS

Les Structures élémentaires de la parenté, 1949; 2nd edition, Paris and La Haye: Mouton & Co/Maison des Sciences de l'Homme, 1967; *The Elementary Structures of Kinship*, trans. James Harle Bell, John Richard von Sturmer and Rodney Needham, Boston, Mass.: Beacon Press, 1969

Tristes tropiques, Paris: Plon, 1955; *Tristes tropiques*, trans. John and Doreen Weightman, New York: Penguin Books USA, 1992

Anthropologie structurale, Paris: Plon, 1958; *Structural Anthropology*, trans. Claire Jacobson and Brooke Grundfest Schoepf, Harmondsworth: Penguin Books, 1977

La Pensée sauvage, Paris: Plon, 1962; *The Savage Mind*, Oxford University Press, 1996

Le totémisme aujourd'hui, Paris: Presses Universitaires de France, 1962; *Totemism*, trans. Rodney Needham, London: Merlin Press, 1964

Mythologiques; Introduction to a Science of Mythology, trans. John and Doreen Weightman, 4 vols., 1964–71:

> *Le Cru et le cuit*, Paris: Plon, 1964; *The Raw and the Cooked*, New York/Evanston: Harper and Row, 1969
>
> *Du Miel aux cendres*, Paris: Plon, 1966; *From Honey to Ashes*, London: Jonathan Cape, 1973
>
> *L'Origine des manières de table*, Paris: Plon, 1968; *The Origin of Table Manners*, London: Jonathan Cape, 1978
>
> *L'Homme nu*, Paris: Plon, 1971; *The Naked Man*, London: Jonathan Cape, 1981

Anthropologie structurale deux, Paris: Plon, 1973; *Structural Anthropology 2*, trans. Monique Layton, Harmondsworth: Penguin Books, 1978

Myth and Meaning, London: Routledge, 1978

Paroles données, Paris: Plon, 1979; *Anthropology and Myth: Lectures 1951–1982*, trans. Roy Willis, Oxford: Basil Blackwell, 1987

Le Regard éloigné, Paris: Plon, 1983; *The View from Afar*, trans. Joachim Neugroschel and Phoebe Hass, London: Penguin, 1987

ARTICLES AND SHORTER WORKS

'Guerre et commerce chez les Indiens de l'Amérique du Sud', *Renaissance* 1.1–2 (January–March 1943), 122–39

'The Bororo Moiety System, Cerae, Tugaregue', *American Anthropologist* 46 (1944), 266–8

'French Sociology', in Georges Gurvitch and Wilbert E. Moore (eds.), *Sociology in the Twentieth Century*, New York: The Philosophical Library, 1945, pp. 503–37; *La Sociologie au XXe siècle*, Paris: Presses Universitaires de France, 1947, pp. 513–45

'La théorie du pouvoir dans une société primitive', in *Les Doctrines politiques modernes*, New York: Brentano, 1947, pp. 41–63

La Vie familiale et sociale des Indiens Nambikwara, Paris: Société des Américanistes, Gonthier, 1948

'La Politique étrangère d'une Sociéte Primitive', *Politique Etrangère* 2 (May 1949), 139–52

Introduction à l'œuvre de Marcel Mauss, in *Sociologie et anthropologie*, Paris: Presses Universitaires de France, 1950, pp. ix–lii; *Introduction to the work of Marcel Mauss*, trans. Felicity Baker, London: Routledge, 1978

'Le Père Noël supplicié', *Les Temps Modernes* 7.77 (March 1952), 1572–90

'Panorama de l'ethnologie (1950–1952)', *Diogène* 2 (April 1953), 96–123; 'Panorama of Ethnology (1950–1952)', *Diogenes* 2 (Spring 1953), 69–93

'Diogène couché', *Les Temps Modernes* 10.110 (March 1955), 1187–1220

'Des Indiens et leur ethnographe', *Les Temps Modernes* 11.116 (August 1955), 1–50

'Sur les rapports entre la mythologie et le rituel', *Bulletin de la Société Française de Philosophie* 50.3 (July–September 1956), 99–125

'The Social and Psychological Aspects of Chieftainship in a Primitive Tribe: The Nambikwara of Northwestern Mato Grosso', in Ronald Cohen and John Middleton (eds.), *Comparative Political Systems. Studies in the Politics of Pre-Industrial Societies*, New York: The Natural History Press, 1967, pp. 45–62

'Anthropologie, histoire, idéologie', discussion with Marc Augé and Maurice Godelier, *L'Homme* 15.3–4 (July–December, 1975), 177–88

Preface to Roman Jakobson, *Six Leçons sur le son et le sens*, Paris: Editions de Minuit, 1976, pp. 7–18; trans. John Mepham, *Six Lectures on Sound and Meaning*, Sussex: Harvester Press, 1978, pp. xi–xxvi

'Retours en arrière', *Les Temps Modernes* 53.598 (March–April 1998), 66–77

INTERVIEWS

Augé, Marc, 'Ten Questions Put to Claude Lévi-Strauss', *Current Anthropology* 31.1 (February 1990), 85–90

Bellour, Raymond, 'Entretien avec Claude Lévi-Strauss', in *Les Lettres françaises* 1165 (12 January 1967), 1–7

Bellour, Raymond, 'Entretien avec Claude Lévi-Strauss', in Raymond Bellour and Catherine Clément (eds.), *Claude Lévi-Strauss. Textes de et sur Claude Lévi-Strauss*, Paris: Idées-Gallimard, 1979, pp. 157–209

Charbonnier, Georges, *Entretiens avec Claude Lévi-Strauss*, Paris: Plon, 1961; *Conversations with Claude Lévi-Strauss*, trans. John and Dorren Weightman, London: Jonathan Cape, 1969

Clément, Catherine B. and Antoine Casanova, 'Un ethnologue et la culture', *La Nouvelle Critique* 61 (February 1973), 27–36

Eribon, Didier, *De près et de loin* (Paris: Plon, 1988); *Conversations with Claude Lévi-Strauss*, trans. Paula Wissing, University of Chicago Press, 1991

Marchand, Jean José, *Archives du XXe siècle*, six interviews based on questions by Hubert Damish, filmed at Montigny-sur-Aube, 25, 26, 27 July 1972. SFP/Centre National de Cinématographie, 2000

SECONDARY SOURCES

Affergan, François, *La Pluralité des mondes. Vers une autre anthropologie*, Paris: Albin Michel, 1997
   Critiques anthropologiques, Paris: Presses de la Fondation Nationale, 1998

Affergan, François (ed.), *Construire le savoir anthropologique*, Paris: Presses Universitaires de France, 1999

Almeida, Mauro W. Barbosa, 'Symmetry and Entropy. Mathematical Metaphors in the Work of Lévi-Strauss', *Current Anthropology* 31.4 (August–October 1990), 367–85

Althabe, Gérard, 'Vers une ethnologie du présent', in Gérard Althabe, Daniel Fabre and Gérard Lenclud (eds.), *Vers une ethnologie du présent*, Paris: Editions de la Maison des sciences de l'homme, 1992, pp. 247–57

Balandier, Georges, 'Tendances dans l'ethnologie française', *Cahiers internationaux de sociologie* 27 (July–December 1959), 11–22
   Afrique ambigüe, Paris: Plon, 1957
   'Sociologie, ethnologie et ethnographie', in Georges Gurvitch (ed.), *Traité de sociologie*, vol. I, Paris: Presses Universitaires de France, 1962, pp. 99–113
   Conjugaisons, Paris: Fayard, 1997

Barthes, Roland, 'Les Sciences humaines et l'œuvre de Lévi-Strauss', *Annales: économies, sociétés, civilisations* 19 (November–December 1964), 1085–6

Beauvoir, Simone de, *Le Deuxième sexe I*, Paris: Gallimard-Folio Essais, 1976; *The Second Sex*, trans. H.M. Parshley, London: Vintage, 1997

Bellour, Raymond and Catherine Clément (eds.), *Claude Lévi-Strauss. Textes de et sur Claude Lévi-Strauss*, Paris: Idées-Gallimard, 1979

Bender, Donald, 'The Development of French Anthropology', in *Journal of the History of the Behavioural Sciences* 1:2 (1965), 139–51

Benedict, Ruth, *Patterns of Culture*, Boston: Houghton Mifflin, 1989

Bernard, Carmen and Jean-Pierre Digard, 'De Téhéran à Tehuantepec. L'ethnologie au crible des aires culturelles', *L'Anthropologie: Etat des lieux*, special issue of *L'Homme* 26.97–8 (January–June 1986), 63–80

Bing, Fernande, 'Entretiens avec Alfred Métraux', *L'Homme* 4.2 (May–August 1964), 20–32

Blanchot, Maurice, 'L'Homme au point zéro', *La Nouvelle Revue française*, 4.40 (April 1956), 683–94

Bonte, Pierre and Michel Izard (eds.), *Dictionnaire de l'ethnologie et de l'anthropologie*, Paris: Presses Universitaires de France, 1991

Boon, James A., *From Symbolism to Structuralism: Lévi-Strauss and Literary Tradition*, Oxford: Basil Blackwell, 1972
   Other Tribes, Other Scribes. Symbolic Anthropology in the Comparative Study of Cultures, Histories, Religions and Texts, Cambridge University Press, 1982

Bourdieu, Pierre, *Homo academicus*, Paris: Editions de Minuit, 1984; *Homo academicus*, trans. Peter Collier, Cambridge: Polity Press, 1988
    'Sociology and Philosophy in France since 1945: Death and Resurrection of a Philosophy without a Subject', *Social Research* 34.1 (Spring 1967), 162–212
    'Structuralism and Theory of Social Knowledge', *Social Research* 35.4 (Winter 1968), 681–705
Bouveresse, Renée, *La philosophie et les sciences de l'homme*, Paris: Ellipses, 1998
Braudel, Fernand, *Ecrits sur l'histoire*, Paris: Champs Flammarion, 1969; *On History*, trans. Sarah Matthews, London: Weidenfeld and Nicolson, 1980
Brumble III, H. David, *American Indian Autobiography*, Berkeley: University of California Press, 1988
Caillé, Alain, 'D'un ethnocentrisme paradoxal (L'analyse structurale des mythes de C. Lévi-Strauss)', in A. Caillé, *Splendeur et misères des sciences sociales. Esquisses d'une mythologie*, Geneva/Paris: Droz, 1986, pp. 263–302
Campbell, Jeremy, *Grammatical Man. Information, Entropy, Language and Life*, Harmondsworth: Penguin, 1982
Champagne, Roland A., *Claude Lévi-Strauss*, Boston, Mass.: Twayne Publishers, 1987
Charle, Christophe, 'Le Collège de France', in Pierre Nora (ed.), *Les Lieux de mémoire*, vol. II, no. 3, *La Nation*, Paris: Gallimard, 1986, pp. 399–424
Clark, Terry Nichols, *Prophets and Patrons: The French University and the Emergence of the Social Sciences*, Cambridge, Mass.: Harvard University Press, 1973
Clarke, Simon, *The Foundations of Structuralism. A Critique of Lévi-Strauss and the Structuralist Movement*, Sussex: Harvester Press, 1981
Clément, Catherine, *Claude Lévi Strauss ou la Structure et le Malheur*, Paris: Livre de Poche/Biblio-Essais, 1985
Clifford, James, 'On Ethnographic Surrealism', *Comparative Studies in Society and History* 23.4 (1981), 539–64
Clifford, James, George Marcus (eds.), *Writing Culture. The Poetics and Politics of Ethnography*, Berkeley: University of California Press, 1986
Conley, Tom, 'The Sunset of Myth: Lévi-Strauss in the Americas', in George Stambolian (ed.), *Twentieth Century French Fiction: Essays for Germaine Brée*, New Brunswick, N.J.: Rutgers University Press, 1975, pp. 223–40
Courtès, Joseph, *Lévi-Strauss et les contraintes de la pensée mythique*, Paris: Mame, 1973
Davies, Howard, *Sartre and 'Les Temps Modernes'*, Cambridge University Press, 1987
Delacampagne, Christian, Bernard Traimond, 'La polémique Sartre–Lévi-Strauss revisitée', *Les Temps Modernes* 53.596 (November–December 1997), 10–31
Delrieu, Alain, *Lévi-Strauss lecteur de Freud. Le droit, l'inceste, le père et l'échange des femmes*, 2nd edition, Paris: Anthropos, 1999
Delruelle, Edouard, *Claude Lévi-Strauss et la philosophie*, Brussels: De Boeck/Editions Universitaires, 1989
Demoule, Jean-Paul, 'Le Néolithique, une révolution?', *Le Débat* 20 (May 1982), 54–75
Derrida, Jacques, 'La Structure, le signe et le jeu dans le discours des sciences humaines', in *L'écriture et la différence*, Paris: Editions du Seuil, 1967, pp. 409–28; 'Structure, Sign and Play in the Discourse of the Human Sciences', in *Writing and Difference*, trans. Alan Bass, London: Routledge, 1978, pp. 278–93
    'La Violence de la lettre: de Lévi-Strauss à Rousseau', in *De la grammatologie*, Paris: Editions de Minuit, 1967, pp. 149–202; 'The Violence of the Letter: From

Lévi-Strauss to Rousseau', in *Of Grammatology*, trans. Gayatri Chakravorty Spivak, Baltimore/London: Johns Hopkins University Press, 1976, pp. 101–40

Donner le temps, Paris: Editions Galilée, 1991; *Given Time*, trans. Peggy Kamuf, University of Chicago Press, 1992

Descombes, Vincent, *Le même et l'autre. Quarante-cinq ans de philosophie française (1933–1978)*, Paris: Editions de Minuit, 1979; *Modern French Philosophy*, trans. L. Scott-Fox and J.M. Harding, Cambridge University Press, 1980

Les Institutions du sens, Paris: Editions du Minuit, 1996

Diamond, Stanley, *In Search of the Primitive*, New Brunswick/London: Transaction Books, 1974

Digard, Jean-Pierre, 'L'Ethnologie française au Moyen-Orient', *La Recherche* 7.68 (June 1976), 584–8

Dion, Emmanuel, *Invitation à la théorie de l'information*, Paris: Points-Seuil, 1997

Dosse, François, *Histoire du structuralisme, I: Le champ du signe, 1945–1966; II: Le chant du cygne, 1967 à nos jours*, 2 vols., Paris: La Découverte, 1991, 1992; *History of Structuralism*, 2 vols., trans. Deborah Glassman, Minneapolis: University of Minnesota Press, 1997

L'Empire du sens. L'humanisation des sciences humaines, Paris: La Découverte, 1995; *Empire of Meaning: The Humanization of the Social Sciences*, trans. Hassan Melehy, Minneapolis: University of Minnesota Press, 1999

Douin, Jean-Luc and Catherine Portevin, 'Jean Malaurie, l'aventurier des mondes perdus', interview, *Télérama* 2394 (2–8 December, 1995), 10–16

Dubuisson, Daniel, *Mythologies du XXᵉ siècle: Dumézil, Lévi-Strauss, Eliade*, Presses Universitaires de Lille, 1994

Dumont, Louis, *The Headman and I*, Austin: University of Texas Press, 1978

Dupuy, Jean-Pierre, *Aux origines des sciences cognitives*, Paris: La Découverte, 1994; *The Mechanization of the Mind. On the Origins of Cognitive Science*, trans. M.B. DeBevoise, Princeton and Oxford: Princeton University Press, 2000

Durkheim, Emile, *De la division du travail social*, Paris: Presses Universitaires de France, 1986 [1893]; *The Division of Labour in Society*, trans. W.D. Halls, Basingstoke: Macmillan, 1984

Les Formes élémentaires de la vie religieuse, Paris: Presses Universitaires de France, 1985 [1912]; *The Elementary Forms of Religious Life*, trans. Karen E. Fields, New York/London: Free Press, 1995

Evans-Pritchard, *Social Anthropology*, London: Cohen and West, 1951

Fabian, Johannes, *Time and the Other. How Anthropology Makes its Object*, New York: Columbia University Press, 1983

Fournier, Marcel, *Marcel Mauss*, Paris: Fayard, 1995

Freud, Sigmund, *Totem and Taboo*, Harmondsworth: Pelican Freud Library 19, pp. 43–224

Furet, François, 'Les intellectuels français et le structuralisme', in *L'Atelier de l'histoire*, Paris: Champs-Flammarion, 1982, pp. 37–52; 'French Intellectuals: From Marxism to Structuralism', in *In the Workshop of History*, trans. Jonathan Mandelbaum, University of Chicago Press, 1984, pp. 27–39

Gardner, Howard, *The Quest for Mind: Piaget, Lévi-Strauss, and the Structuralist Movement*, 2nd edition, University of Chicago Press, 1981

Geertz, Clifford, 'The Cerebral Savage: On the Work of Claude Lévi-Strauss', in *The Interpretation of Cultures*, New York: Basic Books, 1973, pp. 345–59

'The World in a Text: How to Read *Tristes tropiques*', in *Works and Lives. The Anthropologist as Author*, Cambridge: Polity Press, 1988, pp. 25–48

Girard, René, *Des Choses cachées depuis la fondation du monde*, Paris: Grasset, 1978; *Things Hidden Since the Foundation of the World*, trans. Stephen Bann and Michael Metteer, London: The Athlone Press, 1987

Goodson, A.C., 'Oedipus Anthropologicus', *Modern Language Notes* 94.4 (May 1979), 688–701

Griaule, Marcel, *Dieu d'eau. Entretiens avec Ogotemmêli*, Paris: Fayard, 1966; *Conversations with Ogotemmeli*, London: Oxford University Press, 1972

Guiart, Jean, 'Réflexions sur la méthode en ethnologie', *Cahiers internationaux de sociologie* 45 (July–December 1968), 81–98

'Survivre à Lévi-Strauss', *L'Arc* (1968), 66–9

Gurvitch, Georges (ed.) *La Vocation actuelle de la sociologie*, 2 vols., Paris: Presses Universitaires de France, 1950

(ed.) *Traité de sociologie*, 2 vols., Paris: Presses Universitaires de France, 1962, 1963

Hannerz, Ulf, 'The Shaping of National Anthropologies', *Ethnos* 47.1–2 (1982), 5–35

Hayes, Eugene Nelson and Tanya Hayes (eds.), *Claude Lévi-Strauss: The Anthropologist as Hero*, Cambridge/London: MIT Press, 1968

Heimonet, Jean-Michel, *Politiques de l'écriture, Bataille/Derrida: Le sens du sacré dans la pensée française du surréalisme à nos jours*, Chapel Hill: University of North Carolina Press, Studies in the Romance Languages and Literature, 1987

Hénaff, Marcel, *Claude Lévi-Strauss*, Paris: Belfond, 1991; *Claude Lévi-Strauss and the Making of Structural Anthropology*, trans. Mary Baker, Minneapolis/London: University of Minnesota Press, 1998

Heusch, Luc de, 'Les Voies de l'anthropologie structurale: l'œuvre de Lévi-Strauss et l'évolution de l'ethnologie française', *Zaïre* 8 (August 1958), 787–818

Hollier, Denis, *Panorama des sciences humaines*, Paris: Gallimard, 1973

Hughes, H. Stuart, *The Obstructed Path. French Social Thought in the Years of Desperation*, New York/Evanston: Harper and Row, 1968

Isaacs, Susan, *Social Development in Young Children. A Study of Beginnings*, London: Routledge, 1933

Jacobs, Carol: 'Architectures of Oblivion: Lévi-Strauss's *Tristes tropiques*', in *Telling Time: Lévi-Strauss, Ford, Lessing, Benjamin, De Man, Wordsworth, Rilke*, Baltimore/London: Johns Hopkins University Press, 1993

Jakobson, Roman, *Selected Writings*, vols. I and II, The Hague: Mouton, 1971

James, Wendy and N.J. Allen (eds.), *Marcel Mauss. A Centenary Tribute*, New York/Oxford: Berghahn, 1998

Jamin, Jean, 'Un Sacré collège, ou les apprentis sorciers de la sociologie', *Cahiers internationaux de sociologie* 68 (1980), 5–32

Jenkins, Alan, *The Social Theory of Claude Lévi-Strauss*, London: Macmillan, 1979

Jenkins, Richard, *Rethinking Ethnicity: Arguments and Explorations*, London: Sage, 1997

Jennings, Jeremy, 'Structuralism', in Simon Glendinning (ed.), *The Edinburgh Encyclopedia of Continental Philosophy*, Edinburgh University Press, 1999, pp. 505–14

Johnson, Christopher, 'Lévi-Strauss and the Place of Anthropology', *Paragraph* 13.3 (November 1990), 229–50

'Elective Affinities, Other Cultures', *Paragraph* 16.1 (March 1993), 67–77

'Cinna's Apotheosis: *Tristes tropiques* and the Structure of Redemption', *French Studies* 48.3 (July 1994), 299–309

'Authority', *Paragraph* 17.3 (November 1994), 200–6

'Lévi-Strauss et la logique du sacré', in Christopher Thompson (ed.), *L'Autre et le sacré: surréalisme, cinéma, ethnologie*, Paris: L'Harmattan, 1995, pp. 249–59

'La Leçon de philosophie: de Derrida à Lévi-Strauss', in Michel Lisse (ed.), *Passions de la littérature – Avec Jacques Derrida*, Paris: Galilée, 1996, pp. 125–39

'Mauss's Gift: The Persistence of a Paradigm', *Modern and Contemporary France* 4.3 (July 1996), 307–17

'The Writing Lesson Revisited', *Modern Language Review* 92.3 (July 1997), 599–612

'The Voice of Lévi-Strauss: Anthropology and the *Sciences humaines*', in Seán Hand and Irving Velody (eds.), *Who Speaks? The Voice in the Human Sciences*, special issue of *History of the Human Sciences* 10.3 (August 1997), 122–33

'Introduction', 'From Mauss to Lévi-Strauss', *Sociology and Anthropology*, special issue of *Modern and Contemporary France* 5.4 (November 1997), 405–8; 421–32

Jacques Derrida. The Scene of Writing, London: Phoenix, 1997

'Structuralism, Biology and the Linguistic Model', in J. Wolfreys, J. Brannigan and R. Robbins (eds.), *The French Connections of Jacques Derrida*, Albany: State University of New York Press, 1999, pp. 135–48

'Ambient Technologies, Uncanny Signs', in *Technologies of the Sign*, special number of *Oxford Literary Review* 21 (November 1999), 117–34

Karady, Victor, 'Durkheim, les sciences sociales et l'Université: bilan d'un semi-échec', *Revue française de sociologie* 17.2 (April–June 1976), 267–312

'Stratégies de réussite et modes de faire-valoir de la sociologie chez les durkheimiens', *Revue française de sociologie* 20.1 (January–March 1979), 49–82

'Prehistory of French Sociology' in Charles C. Lemert (ed.), *French Sociology. Rupture and Renewal since 1968*, New York: Columbia University Press, 1981, pp. 33–47

'Le problème de la légitimité dans l'organisation historique de l'ethnologie française', *Revue française de sociologie* 23.1 (January–March 1982), 17–35

Karsenti, Bruno, *Marcel Mauss: le fait social total*, Paris: Presses Universitaires de France, 1994

L'Homme total. Sociologie, anthropologie et philosophie chez Marcel Mauss, Paris: Presses Universitaires de France, 1997

Kilani, Mondher, 'Fiction et vérité dans l'écriture anthropologique', in François Affergan (ed.), *Construire le savoir anthropologique*, Paris: Presses Universitaires de France, 1999, pp. 83–104

Kristeva, Julia, *Les Samouraïs*, Paris: Fayard, 1990; *The Samurai: A Novel*, trans. Barbara Bray, New York: Columbia University Press, 1992

Kuper, Adam, *Anthropology and Anthropologists. The Modern British School*, 2nd edition, London: Routledge, 1983

The Invention of Primitive Society. Transformations of an Illusion, London/New York: Routledge, 1988

Kuper, Adam and Jessica Kuper (eds.), *The Social Science Encyclopedia*, London: Routledge, 1989

Laburthe-Tolra, Philippe, *Critiques de la raison ethnologique*, Paris: Presses Universitaires de France, 1998

Lapointe, François H. and Claire C. Lapointe, *Claude Lévi-Strauss and His Critics: An International Bibliography of Criticism (1950–1976)*, Garland Reference Library of the Humanities, vol. LXXII, New York: Garland, 1977

Leach, Edmund, *Lévi-Strauss*, Glasgow: Fontana, 1974

Leiris, Michel, *Race and Culture*, Paris: UNESCO, 1951

Cinq études d'ethnologie, Paris: Gallimard Tel, 1969

Lenclud, Gérard, 'Le Grand partage ou la tentation ethnologique', in Gérard Althabe, Daniel Fabre and Gérard Lenclud (eds.), *Vers une ethnologie du présent*, Paris: Editions de la Maison des sciences de l'homme, 1992, pp. 9–37

Lévy-Bruhl, Lucien, *La Mentalité primitive*, Paris: Alcan, 1922; *Primitive Mentality*, trans. Lilian A. Clare, Boston: Beacon Press, 1966

Lewis, I.M., *Ecstatic Religion. A Study of Shamanism and Spirit Possession*, 2nd edition, London/New York: Routledge, 1989

Religion in Context. Cults and Charisma, 2nd edition, Cambridge University Press, 1996

Lowie, Robert, *Primitive Society*, London: Routledge, 1921

Lucretius, *On the Nature of the Universe*, trans. R.E. Latham, Harmondsworth: Penguin, 1982

Lukes, Steven, *Emile Durkheim. Life and Works*, Harmondsworth: Penguin, 1973

Magazine Littéraire 58 (November 1971), *Claude Lévi-Strauss*

Magazine Littéraire 223 (October 1985), *Claude Lévi-Strauss*

Magazine Littéraire 311 (June 1993), *Claude Lévi-Strauss: Esthétique et structuralisme*

Malaurie, Jean, *Les Derniers Rois de Thulé*, Paris: Plon, 1976; *The Last Kings of Thule*, trans. Adrienne Foulke, London: Jonathan Cape, 1982

Malinowski, Bronislaw, *Argonauts of the Western Pacific*, Prospect Heights, Il.: Waveland Press, 1984

Manganaro, Marc (ed.), *Modernist Anthropology. From Fieldwork to Text*, Princeton University Press, 1990

Marcus, George E. and Michael M.J. Fischer, *Anthropology as Cultural Critique*, University of Chicago Press, 1986

Mauss, Marcel, *Sociologie et anthropologie*, Paris: Presses Universitaires de France, 1950

Œuvres, 3 vols., Paris: Editions de Minuit, 1968, 1969, 1974

A General Theory of Magic, trans. Robert Brain, London: Routledge, 1972

Sociology and Psychology, trans. Ben Brewster, London, Boston and Henley: Routledge, 1979

Seasonal Variations of the Eskimo, trans. J.J. Fox, London: Routledge, 1979

The Gift. The Form and Reason for Exchange in Archaic Societies, trans. W.D. Halls, London: Routledge, 1990

Mehlman, Jeffrey, 'Punctuation in *Tristes tropiques*', in *A Structural Study of Autobiography: Proust, Leiris, Sartre, Lévi-Strauss*, Ithaca/London: Cornell University Press, 1974

'Lévi-Strauss and the Birth of Structuralism', in *Émigré New York. French Intellectuals in Wartime Manhattan, 1940–44*, Baltimore/London: Johns Hopkins University Press, 2000, pp. 181–96

Mercier, Paul, *Histoire de l'anthropologie*, Paris: Presses Universitaires de France, 1966

Merleau-Ponty, Maurice, 'De Mauss à Lévi-Strauss', in *Signes*, Paris: Gallimard, 1960, pp. 143–57

Merquior, José G., *L'Esthétique de Lévi-Strauss*, Paris: Presses Universitaires de France, 1975

Okely, Judith and Helen Callaway (eds.), *Anthropology and Autobiography*, London: Routledge, 1992

Pace, David, *Claude Lévi-Strauss. The Bearer of Ashes*, London: Routledge, 1983

Panoff, Michel, *Les Frères ennemis. Caillois et Lévi-Strauss*, Paris: Payot, 1993

Piaget, Jean, *Le structuralisme*, Paris: Presses Universitaires de France, 1968; *Structuralism*, trans. Chaninah Maschler, London: Routledge, 1971

Pividal, Raphaël, 'Signification et position de l'œuvre de Lévi-Strauss', *Annales* 19.6 (November–December 1964), 1087–99

'Peut-on acclimater la pensée sauvage?', *Annales* 20.3 (May–June, 1965), 558–63

Racine, Luc, 'Les Formes élémentaires de la réciprocité', *L'Homme* 24.99 (July–September 1986), 97–118

Radcliffe-Brown, A.R., *Method in Social Anthropology, Selected Writings*, M.N. Srinivas (ed.), University of Chicago Press, 1958

Structure and Function in Primitive Society, M.N. Srinivas (ed.), New York: Free Press, 1965

Revel, Jacques and Nathan Wachtel, *Une Ecole pour les sciences sociales. De la VIe section à l'Ecole des Hautes Etudes en Sciences Sociales*, Paris: Editions du Cerf, 1996

Rey, Alain (ed.), *Le Grand Robert. Dictionnaire alphabétique et analogique de la langue française*, 2nd edition, Paris: Robert, 1985

(ed.), *Dictionnaire historique de la langue française*, 2 vols., thirteenth edition, Paris: Robert, 2000

Roger, Philippe (ed.), *Claude Lévi-Strauss*, special issue of *Critique* 50.620–1 (January–February 1999)

Rossi, Ino (ed.), *The Unconscious in Culture. The Structuralism of Claude Lévi-Strauss in Perspective*, New York: Dutton and Co., 1974

Roth, Gary, 'Claude Lévi-Strauss in Retrospect', *Dialectical Anthropology* 18 (1993), 31–52

'Kinship, Structuralism and the Savage Mind: Lévi-Strauss', in Simon Glendinning (ed.), *The Edinburgh Encyclopedia of Continental Philosophy*, Edinburgh University Press, 1999, pp. 528–36

Rousseau, Jean-Jacques, *Discours sur l'origine et les fondements de l'inégalité parmi les hommes. Discours sur les sciences et les arts*, Paris: Flammarion, 1992; *A Discourse on Inequality*, trans. Maurice Cranston, London: Penguin, 1984

Sahlins, Marshall, *Stone Age Economics*, London: Routledge, 1988

Saint-Sernin, Bertrand, *La Raison au XXe siècle*, Paris: Seuil, 1995

Sartre, Jean-Paul, *L'existentialisme est un humanisme*, Paris: Gallimard/Folio-Essais, 1996; *Existentialism and Humanism*, trans. Philip Mairet, London: Methuen, 1973

Critique de la raison dialectique I: Théorie des ensembles, Arlette Elkaïm-Sartre (ed.), Paris: Gallimard, 1985; *Critique of Dialectical Reason I: Theory of Practical Ensembles*, Jonathan Rée (ed.), trans. Alan Sheridan-Smith, London: NLB, 1976

'Jean-Paul Sartre répond', in *Sartre aujourd'hui*, *L'Arc* 30 (1966) 87–96

Situations philosophiques, Paris: Gallimard Tel, 1990

'Entretiens sur moi-même', in *Situations* X, Paris: Gallimard, 1976, pp. 91–226

Saussure, Ferdinand de, *Cours de linguistique générale*, Charles Bally and Albert Sechehaye (eds.), Paris: Payot, 1986; *Course in General Linguistics*, trans. Roy Harris, London: Duckworth, 1983

Schulte-Tenckhoft, Isabelle, *Potlatch, conquête et invention*, Paris: Editions d'en bas, 1986

Scubla, Lucien, *Lire Lévi-Strauss. Le Déploiement d'une intuition*, Paris: Odile Jacob, 1998

Shalvey, Thomas, *Claude Lévi-Strauss: Social Psychotherapy and the Collective Unconscious*, Sussex: Harvester Press, 1979

Shannon, Claude E. and Warren Weaver, *The Mathematical Theory of Communication*, Urbana: University of Illinois Press, 1959

Sheringham, Michael, *French Autobiography: Devices and Desires*, Oxford: Clarendon Press, 1993

Siebers, Tobin, 'Ethics in the Age of Rousseau: From Lévi-Strauss to Derrida', *Modern Language Notes* 100.4 (September 1985), 758–79

Silverman, Hugh J., 'Sartre and the Structuralists', *International Philosophical Quarterly* 18.3 (September 1978), 341–58

Simonis, Yvan, *Claude Lévi-Strauss ou 'la passion de l'inceste'*, Paris: Champs-Flammarion, 1980

Smith, Pierre, 'Le Souci anthropologique', *L'Homme* 26.97–8 (January–June 1986), *L'Anthropologie: Etat des lieux*

Smith, Roger, *Fontana History of the Human Sciences*, London: Fontana Press, 1997

Soustelle, Jacques, *Les Quatre soleils*, Paris: Plon, 1967; *The Four Suns*, trans. E. Ross, London: André Deutsch, 1970

Sperber, Dan, 'Lévi-Strauss', in John Sturrock (ed.) *Structuralism and Since: From Lévi-Strauss to Derrida*, Oxford University Press, 1979, pp. 19–51
   Le Savoir des anthropologues, Paris: Hermann, 1982; *On Anthropological Knowledge. Three essays*, Cambridge University Press, 1985

Stocking, George W., Jr, *Race, Culture and Evolution: Essays in the History of Anthropology*, New York: The Free Press/Macmillan, 1971
   History of Anthropology III: *Objects and Others. Essays on Museums and Material Culture*, Madison: University of Wisconsin Press, 1985

Stocking, George W., Jr (ed.), *A Franz Boas Reader. The Shaping of American Anthropology, 1883–1911*, University of Chicago Press, 1974

Sturrock John, *Structuralism*, 2nd edition, London: Fontana, 1993
   The Language of Autobiography. Studies in the First Person Singular, Cambridge University Press, 1993

Taguieff, Pierre-André, 'Du racisme au mot "race": comment les éliminer? Sur les premiers débats et les premières Déclarations de l'Unesco (1949–1951) concernant la "race" et le racisme', *Mots: Les langages du politique* 33 (December 1992), 215–39
   Les Fins de l'antiracisme. Paris: Michalon, 1995

Tarot, Camille, *De Durkheim à Mauss. L'invention du symbolique*, Paris: La Découverte/M.A.U.S.S., 1999

Taylor, Mark Kline, *Beyond Explanation. Religious Dimensions in Cultural Anthropology*, Macon, Ga.: Mercer University Press, 1986

Terray, Emmanuel, 'Face au racisme', *Magazine Littéraire* 223 (October 1985), 54–5

Thompson, D'Arcy Wentworth, *On Growth and Form*, Cambridge University Press, 1948

Tilley, Christopher, 'Claude Lévi-Strauss: Structuralism and Beyond', in Christopher Tilley (ed.), *Reading Material Culture*, Oxford: Blackwell, 1990, pp. 3–81

Todorov, Tzvetan, *Nous et les autres. La réflexion française sur la diversité humaine*, Paris: Seuil, 1989; *On Human Diversity: Nationalism, Racism, and Exoticism in French Thought*, trans. Catherine Porter, Cambridge, Mass.: Harvard University Press, 1993

Toffin, Gérard, 'Le Degré zéro de l'ethnologie', *L'Homme* 30.113 (January–March 1990), 138–150

Trubetzkoy, N.S., *Principles of Phonology*, trans. Christiane A.M. Baltaxe, Berkeley/Los Angeles: University of California Press, 1969

Wiener, Norbert, *Cybernetics or Control and Communication in the Animal and the Machine*, 2nd edition, Cambridge, Mass.: MIT Press, 1961

   The Human Use of Human Beings. Cybernetics and Society, London: Eyre and Spottiswoode, 1950

Wilden, Anthony, *System and Structure. Essays in Communication and Exchange*, 2nd edition, London: Tavistock Publications, 1980

Index